CHINA AND MALAYSIA IN A GLOBALIZING WORLD

Bilateral Relations, Regional Imperatives
and Domestic Challenges

CHINA AND MALAYSIA IN A GLOBALIZING WORLD

Bilateral Relations, Regional Imperatives and Domestic Challenges

Editors

Émile Kok-Kheng Yeoh
Hou Kok Chung

 Institute of China Studies
University of Malaya

Institute of China Studies
University of Malaya
50603 Kuala Lumpur
Malaysia
Tel: 603-79565663   Fax: 603-79565114

Perpustakaan Negara Malaysia   Cataloguing-in-Publication Data

China and Malaysia in a globalizing world : bilateral relations,
    regional imperatives and domestic challenges / editors Emile Kok-
    Kheng Yeoh, Hou Kok Chung.
    Includes Index
    ISBN 983-3748-49-X
    1. China--Foreign economic relations--Malaysia. 2. Malaysia--Foreign
    economic relations--China. 3. China--Foreign relations--Malaysia.
    4. Malaysia--Foreign relations--China. I. Kok, Emile Kheng Yeoh.
    II. Hou, Kok Chung, 1963-.
    337.510595

Printed by Herald Printers Sdn. Bhd. (19965-V)

Contents

Economic Relations

Domestic Challenges

List of Tables

List of Figures

Editors and Contributors

K.S. **Balakrishnan**, Senior Lecturer, Department of International & Strategic Studies, Faculty of Arts and Social Sciences, University of Malaya, Malaysia. *Email: ksbalakrishnan@um.edu.my*

Dr **Chia** Oai Peng, Associate Professor, Department of Chinese Studies, Faculty of Arts and Social Sciences, University of Malaya, Malaysia. *Email: chiaop@um.edu.my*

Dr **Ho** Khai Leong, Associate Professor, School of Humanities and Social Sciences, Nanyang Technological University, Singapore. *Email: KLHO@ntu.edu.sg*

Dr **Hou** Kok Chung, Associate Professor and Director, Institute of China Studies, University of Malaya, Malaysia. *Email: houkc@um.edu.my*

Dr Samuel C.Y. **Ku**, Professor, Institute of Interdisciplinary Studies for Social Sciences, National Sun Yat-sen University, Taiwan. *Email: cyku@mail.nsysu.edu.tw*

Dr **Li** Yi, Associate Professor, Research School of Southeast Asian Studies and Institute of Malaysian Studies, Xiamen University, China. *Email: liyi1212@hotmail.com*

Dr **Li** Yiping, Associate Professor, Research School of Southeast Asian Studies and Institute of Malaysian Studies, Xiamen University, China. *Email: ypli@xmu.edu.cn*

Dr **Lin** Mei, Associate Professor and Vice Director, Research School of Southeast Asian Studies, Xiamen University, China. *Email: mlin@jingxian.xmu.edu.cn*

Dr **Shen** Hongfang, Professor, Research School of Southeast Asian Studies and Centre for Southeast Asian Studies, Xiamen University, China. *Email: hfshen@xmu.edu.my*

Dr **Sun** Zhenyu, Professor and Director, Ningxia University Ethnology Institute, Ningxia University, China. *Email: sun_zhy@nxu.edu.cn*

Dr Leo **Suryadinata**, Professor and Director, Chinese Heritage Centre, Singapore; formerly Professor of Political Science, National University of Singapore, and Senior Research Fellow, Institute of Southeast Asian Studies, Singapore. *Email: chcleos@ntu.edu.sg*

Dr Émile Kok-Kheng **Yeoh**, Senior Lecturer, Institute of China Studies, University of Malaya, Malaysia. *Email: emileyeo@correo.nu*

Dr **Zhao** Hong, Associate Professor, Research School of Southeast Asian Studies and Institute of Malaysian Studies, Xiamen University, China. *Email: zhaohong2001@hotmail.com*

Dr **Zhuang** Guotu, Professor, Dean of the Research School of Southeast Asian Studies and Director of the Institute of Malaysian Studies, Xiamen University, China. *Email: gtzhuang@xmu.edu.cn*

Prolegomena

China and Malaysia: Bilateral Relations, Global Linkages and Domestic Nexus

Émile Kok-Kheng **Yeoh**

China is a country in transformation. The end of the civil war in 1949 saw the advent of the ideologically driven Maoist era. The adoption of the Soviet model of an autarkic command economy and continuing politically induced social upheaval deprived China the time and opportunity to acquire the knowledge, capital and technological know-how required for socioeconomic development. The result was stagnation in China's share of world GDP from 1952 to 1978 – particularly striking given the country's vast resources and the relatively low-income base that she was starting from. Exactly thirty years ago in 1976, two events shook China – one literally. One of the modern world's largest earthquakes, in terms of the loss of life, devastated the industrial city of Tangshan in the northeast province of Hebei on 28th July 1976. Six weeks later, on 9th September, Mao Zedong (Mao Tse-tung) died[1], and with him, so did the decade-long Cultural Revolution and his languid socialist collectivist autarky[2]. When Deng Xiaoping launched his "Reform and Open" (*gaige kaifang* 改革开放) policy in 1978, around 250 million people in China were living below the international poverty line. Deng's reforms truly transformed China. Napoleon once suggested that China be allowed to sleep, "for when she awakes, she will shake the world." China has indeed shaken the world – not with her armies, but with her factories.[3] Today the world's most populous nation of 1.3 billion people is also the fourth largest economy in terms of GDP,[4] and a global investor with operations established in more than 160 countries.[5] Her relentless economic push – her rise as a great trading nation with an annual economic growth of 9 per cent or higher (9.9 per cent in the 1980s, 10.3 per cent in the 1990s, 9.1 per cent in 2003, and 10.3 per cent in the first quarter of 2006) and export growth of almost 30 per cent (6 per cent in the 1980s, 12 per cent in the 1990s, and 29 per cent in 2003) – is providing tremendous opportunities for overseas investors, reflected in the strong foreign direct investment (FDI) inflows (US$1.5 billion in the 1980s, US$29 billion in the 1990s, and US$57 billion in 2003). Adding to those records are the low external debt (8 per cent of GDP in the 1980s, 16 per cent in the 1990s, and 13 per cent in 2003), remarkable fiscal discipline (deficit being just 3 per cent of GDP in 2003), and an impressive poverty reduction of over 400 million since 1978. While China's share of world GDP actually dropped from 5.8 per cent in 1952 to 5 per cent in 1978, from 1978, in a quarter of a century, it staged a spectacular rise from 5 per cent to 14 per cent. It is a received opinion that China's emergence as a regional and global power is the most pivotal transformation underway in East Asia. The way China handles her economic transition and the manner other countries, especially the existing economic powers like the United States and Japan, deal with China's rapidly growing power and influence are critical issues that are exerting deep impact on global and regional politico-economic order. China's enhanced economic standing in Asia has given her new political influence in the region as her trade with the neighbouring states, in particular the member countries of the Association of Southeast Asian Nations (ASEAN) to her south, has been expanding rapidly in recent years.

China and Southeast Asia

On the part of China, modern, academic interest in her southern neighbours can be traced back to the time of the Japanese expansion into China and Southeast Asia, as explained by Professor Zhuang Guotu, dean of the Research School of Southeast Asian Studies and director of the Institute of Malaysian Studies at the Xiamen University, in the second part of the prolegomena. While Southeast Asian studies in China have been making progress in the last 20 years, Zhuang notes that researchers face a variety of problems due to language barriers, the lack of first-hand experience, inadequate international academic exchanges, and political sensitivities. However, rapid changes in the objective circumstances are making progress in academic interaction between China and her neighbours, and in fact the world at large, inevitable.

To the outside world, China has often remained an enigma. Her rise as a major economic and political player in the world today has given rise to increasing urgency on the part of her southern neighbours to fully grasp the implication of the rapidly changing socioeconomic and geopolitical landscape, both regionally and globally, caused by the expanding influence of their huge, overshadowing neighbour that has a long historical relationship with the region.

It is to contribute towards a better mutual understanding between China and Malaysia and ASEAN at large that a conference entitled "China and Malaysia in the Era of Globalization: Country, Regional and International Perspectives", jointly organized by the Institute of China Studies, University of Malaya, Malaysia, and the Institute of Malaysian Studies, Xiamen University, China, was held in March 2006 at The Mines, a Malaysian resort in the vicinity of the capital city of Kuala Lumpur. This book consists of thirteen of the papers presented at the conference, including the above-mentioned paper by Zhuang, all duly revised by the authors.

China and Malaysia: Bilateral Relations

Three decades ago in 1974, amidst the height of the Cold-War rivalries, the Malaysian Premier Abdul Razak travelled to Beijing and signed a joint communiqué that formalized the establishment of Sino-Malaysian relations. The example set by Razak's visit in normalizing relations with China was soon followed by other ASEAN member states. Such initiative from ASEAN stemmed from the realization that the objective situation had changed. The China that in the collective memory of the region was the giant neighbour bending on exerting suzerainty over the region for centuries, an impression being reinforced in modern times by the country's support of the communist insurgencies across the region, was no longer the menace that she used to be. As China moved away from radical Marxist-Leninist tenets bending on exporting revolution to embrace a neo-authoritarian developmental State formula to focus on her own reform process, her southern neighbours had come to accommodate the notion that the best way to engage China was to treat her as a friend, not adversary. This has been helped by the fact that the former hostilities that had plagued their mutual relationship have been replaced by Beijing's assertion that her growing influence in Asia – her "peaceful rise" (*heping jueqi* 和平崛起) – is a threat to no one but a benefit for all.

Chapter Three to Chapter Seven of this book look at the political relations and foreign policy issues between China and Malaysia as well as Southeast Asia at large. Samuel Ku, in Chapter Three, examines China's changing politico-economic relations with Malaysia and Southeast Asia, from the confrontational relationship of the 1950s-70s to the implementation of three key policy initiatives, viz. the open-door policy that began in 1979, the "good neighbour" policy of 1990 and the "go global" strategy of 2002. Ku points out that further breakthrough – after Razak's 1974 Beijing trip – in Sino-Malaysian relations came in the year 1989 when the Communist Party of

Malaya, led by Chin Peng (*Chen Ping* 陈平), laid down their arms, and China, in the same year, formally severed her ties with the overseas Chinese. Ku sees such change in China's politico-economic relations with Malaysia as not being unique but part of the overall changing relations of the Asian giant with her neighbours in Southeast Asia.

Ku's chapter is followed by two papers that examine Sino-Malaysian relations from two different perspectives – one by Li Yiping that traces the development of Sino-Malaysian relations in the post-Cold War era, which, from China's perspective, represents a successful example for China to develop her relationship with the surrounding countries, and the other by K.S. Balakrishnan that sees improvement in Malaysia's political relations with China as driven by the former's pragmatic constructive engagement policy in the context of a globalizing world. Li provides China's perspective on the evolvement of the her foreign relations with the surrounding countries (*zhoubian guanxi* 周边关系), highlighting the framework formalized in the 1990s: "*zhoubian shi shouyao, daguo shi guanjian, fazhanzhong guojia shi jichu, duobian shi wutai* 周边是首要, 大国是关键, 发展中国家是基础, 多边是舞台 " ("relations with the surrounding countries are primary; those with the great powers are the key; those with the developing countries are the foundation; multilateral relations are arenas"), a policy imperative that he believes has led to the continued development of healthy bilateral relations between China and Malaysia, ranging from closer economic ties to the exercise of prudence in the dispute over the Nansha 南沙 (China's designation for the Spratly Islands). Balakrishnan's chapter, on the other hand, traces in great detail through consecutive Malaysian administrations to explore the origin, evolvement and development of the country's pragmatic constructive engagement policy towards China. His paper provides a highly critical assessment of the realities and highlights the potential setbacks of such a policy, in the spheres of trade and investment, tourism, education, military threat and East Asia's democratization, ranging from dumping to the nude squat scandal, from the Mischief Reef[6] incident to Beijing's support for the military junta of Burma[7].

From Sino-Malaysian relations the next two chapters move on to China's relations with the wider region of Southeast Asia. Ho Khai Leong, in Chapter Six, examines the foreign policies of three Southeast Asian states, viz. Indonesia, Malaysia and Singapore, towards China. While the rise of China has not been viewed by her regional neighbours without trepidation, Ho opines that China is now being perceived by these states much more positively than before, with past problems between them and their giant neighbour somewhat fading from the forefront due to the pragmatic turn of events. One of these problems – the issue of nationality and citizenship of the ethnic Chinese in the Southeast Asian countries – is the focus of Chapter Seven by Leo Suryadinata. While having receded into the background with the progress of diplomatic relations and politico-economic partnership, this issue of Chinese dual citizenship status, which according to Suryadinata had been temporarily put aside but never completely resolved, may re-emerge given the talk in the past few years in China of reviving the status. Delving into the modern history of the region, Suryadinata unveils the root of one of the most thorny issues that has not stopped plaguing China's relations with her Southeast Asian neighbours, and how the recent rise in China's international status and the emergence of the "new Chinese migrants" (*xinyimin* 新移民) are influencing the nature and development of the issue.

China, ASEAN and the World: Economic Linkages

From the economic perspective, taking China into the World Trade Organization (WTO) that is estimated to bring a US$800 billion increase in foreign direct investment up to 2010, the new generation of Chinese leadership has shown its commitment to greater openness and the integration of the country with the rest of the increasingly globalizing world. In this region, China is seen to play a crucial role in the process of East Asian economic integration. Following the establishment of formal China-ASEAN relations in 1996 (China became a participant of the ASEAN Regional Forum (ARF) in 1994 and a dialogue partner of ASEAN in 1996), China proposed in 2001 to set up a free trade area (FTA) and to focus priority cooperation in the areas of agriculture, information technology, human resource development, mutual investments and Mekong river basin cooperation. The ASEAN-China FTA, projected to be the world's largest FTA covering 1.7 billion consumers with a combined GDP of US$2 trillion and to be completed within ten years from the setting of its framework agreement in November 2002, could well be the core of a broader East Asian economic zone in years to come, according to the World Bank. Besides that, China signed the Declaration on the Conduct (DOC) of Parties in the South China Sea in November 2002, followed by her accession to the Treaty of Amity and Cooperation in Southeast Asia in 2003 and the signing of the Joint Declaration on the Strategic Partnership for Peace and Prosperity in the same year, leading to a more intensive and substantive China-ASEAN interaction. China and ASEAN also signed agreements in agriculture, non-traditional security issues and information and communications technology, and China is committed to assist ASEAN in narrowing the development gaps through the Initiative for ASEAN Integration (IAI). As ASEAN's 4th largest trading partner, China is finding her partnership with ASEAN continuing to expand and deepen. In dealing with China, the member states of ASEAN have long moved from confrontation to accommodation on issues that were alienating in the past, as "China threat" has gradually given way to "China opportunity" that opens up a whole brave new world of greatly increased trade and investment especially given the huge potential of the Chinese market.

Chia Oai Peng, in Chapter Eight, presents an in-depth analysis of China's growing economic relationship with ASEAN, amidst a host of changing political, social and cultural nexus that are increasingly linking these two vibrant entities, against an overall background of China's "peaceful rise, harmonious society, and scientific development perspective" declared in 2003 that she believes to portray the country's determination to achieve stability, development and growth on the domestic front, and her pledge of common prosperity and universal peace and harmony in the global community.

Concurrent with the manifest importance of China to ASEAN, Malaysia, as this emerging global powerhouse's largest trading partner among ASEAN members, has found her economic wellbeing and other national interests being increasingly tied up with the modernization efforts of the Asian giant. The rapid expansion of Sino-Malaysian bilateral trade is a case in point: already amounting to US$14.1 billion in 2003, it is projected to be over US$50 billion by 2010. Moreover, China was Malaysia's fourth largest export market in 2003, and Malaysia was China's seventh. The fifteenth largest foreign investor in China consists of companies from Malaysia. Chia's chapter is followed by a paper by Li Yi on Sino-Malaysian bilateral trade. Using the Grubel-Lloyd model of intra-industry trade in her chapter to assess the current status and prospects, Li finds that Sino-Malaysian intra-industry trade has been growing in significance, indicating more advanced intra-industry specialization linking closely the countries concerned. Healthy bilateral political relations have been contributing much to rapidly forging comprehensive economic ties, she observes, and inward FDI and the rapid rise in GDP per capita are seen to play important roles in the growth of intra-industry trade between the two countries.

From Sino-Malaysian relations the next two chapters move on to China and ASEAN's economic relations with two countries in South and Southeast Asia, with Shen Hongfang looking at the impact of China's WTO entry on the Philippine economy mainly within the framework of Sino-Philippine bilateral trade and investment, and Zhao Hong examining the rapid development of economic relations between India and ASEAN in the context of regionalism and globalization, and the impact of such relations on India's foreign development strategies, on China's economic relations with ASEAN, and on the development trend of regional economic cooperation in East Asia. Shen, focusing on the challenges and opportunities for the Philippine economy brought forth by the WTO's acceptance of China's membership, observes that China's WTO membership is having positive impact on the Philippine economy in terms of increased trade surplus on the Philippine side, cross investment and other forms of economic cooperation within the framework of Sino-Philippine bilateral economic relations. Zhao, in his paper on India's economic relations with ASEAN, attributes the enhancement of such relations in the post-Cold War era to a mix of factors including the slow progress of the South Asian Association for Regional Cooperation (SAARC) towards economic integration, the upsurge of regionalism in East Asia, the rise of ASEAN's international influence, American relations with India and the emergence of China as a competitor of India. All these have compelled India, which for political reasons and different understandings on regional cooperation during the Cold War period found her economic relations with ASEAN impeded and constrained, to take the initiative in developing and strengthening her economic links with ASEAN. The rapid development of India-ASEAN economic relations has not only brought changes to India's foreign policies, notes Zhao, but has also created challenges to China's economic relations with ASEAN, as well as deeply impacted on the development trend of regional economic cooperation in East Asia.

China and Malaysia: Domestic Socioeconomic Nexus

The last segment of the book shifts our focus from the external to the domestic front. It begins with a chapter by Lin Mei on Indonesian labour migration to Malaysia, focusing on the features of and reasons for such migration and its impact on bilateral relations. While the disparities of the labour market and the economy, well-established migration networks and improved transportation and information flows between the two countries are causing the flow and determining the pattern of labour migration from Indonesia to Malaysia, says Lin, the existence of illegal migrant workers is undoubtedly causing conflicts and tensions in the relationship between the two countries. Lin's chapter is followed by a paper by Sun Zhenyu examining the issue of religious education in China's Muslim communities, more specifically the Akhung Cultural Training Plan in the Ningxia Hui Zizhiqu[8], in the context of China's modernization. The significance and relevance of the training plan, according to Sun, can be traced back to the progressive leadership of the Khufiyya – one of the four main groups of *menhuan* 门宦,

the Sufi order of the Hui people (the other three being the Kubrawiyya, the Jahriyya and the Qadariyya) and the personal relationship of Hong Hairu 洪海儒 (Hong Shoulin 洪寿林), founder of the Hongmen *menhuan* 洪门门宦, with the ruling Chinese Communist Party. Like the Jahriyya, the Khufiyya is a branch of the Naqshbandiyya, the largest Sufi brotherhood in Central Asia. The Hongmen *menhuan* is one of the three main Khufiyya *menhuan* evolved in Ningxia – the other two being Xianmen 鲜门 and Tonggui 通贵 – since the end of the Qing dynasty.[9]

Sun's chapter directs our attention to an important feature of the Chinese nation – the great diversity of the people in a country that is deceptively homogeneous, and the existence of substantial socioeconomic disparities between the different regions of the country. This brings us to the book's closing chapter by Émile Kok-Kheng Yeoh that analyzes the domestic political and socioeconomic nexus involved in the transformation of modern China that is impacting the world and East Asia as the country is fast ascending to the status of a new global as well as regional economic, political and military power.

The global significance of the rise of China cannot be detached from the country's internal realpolitik related to her daunting domestic contradictions, systemic disruptions and resiliency, and the limits of modus vivendi. Since 1949, although the Chinese central government has consistently sought to exercise strong control over the country, it has at times done so by decentralist rather than centralist policies. Although China is not a federal country, her public finance system does carry features of fiscal federalism. The Dengist policies since economic reform began, for example, have had a strongly decentralist element, with continuing devolvement of control to the provincial governments, sometimes to such an extent that some observers have commented: "the centre pretends to rule and the provinces pretend to be ruled"[10]. This is also a period that has witnessed the revival of old regionalisms, as well as the creation of new regionalisms brought about by increased local autonomy, rapid economic growth and increasingly globalizing trade and business linkages. While the oft-cited "China deconstructs" scenario seems at present far-fetched, the challenges posed by central-peripheral conflicts, ethnic resource contest and ethnoterritorial aspirations are real, in particular as they are being exacerbated by the country's "retreat from equality" and growing interregional economic disparity. In the light of these daunting exigencies, Chapter Fourteen thus provides a fitting finale to this book by exploring the political economy of regional development in China, focusing on the intricate link between the country's ethnic diversity and the role of the State in the economy, as the Asian giant warily enters a new stage of economic reform.

Notes

1. Traditional Chinese mystical beliefs see great natural calamities as omens of tumultuous dynastic changes. Probably one of the deadliest wraths of nature in modern times – the official death toll stood at around 242,000, one third of some unofficial estimates – the Tangshan earthquake on 28th July, in an ominous turn of events during the "Curse of 1976", was preceded by the death of Zhou Enlai (Chou En-lai) on 8th January and that of Zhu De (Chu Teh) on 6th July, and followed by Mao's passing on 9th September that brought his ten-year Great Proletarian Cultural Revolution to a close. The so-called Gang of Four, led by Mao's widow Jiang Qing (Chiang Ch'ing), were arrested on 6th October in what amounted to a palace coup, paving the way for the return of the twice-purged pragmatist and reformist Deng Xiaoping (Teng Hsiao-p'ing) to the government and party in the following year, who was to deal the *coup de grâce* to Mao's failed autarkic collectivist utopia.

2. A cognate of the ideal, *juche* 主體, survives in Kim Il Sung's, and now Kim Jong Il's, Orwellian state of North Korea, today still China's close ally in East Asia.

3. "An Awakening Dragon Shakes up the World" (Editorial), in *China Goes Global*, Financial Times' Asia Insight series, 2005, p. 14.

4. "China has squeaked past Britain by the tiniest of margins to become the world's fourth-largest economy, according to the World Bank's latest calculations. The World Bank said that by its official measure China produced US$2.263825 trillion in output in 2005, just US$94 million, or 0.004 per cent, more than Britain. China comfortably overtook Britain last year based on each country's gross domestic product converted into US dollars at current exchange rates.... The United States, Japan and Germany remain the world's first-, second- and third-largest economies respectively, according to the bank, which posted its 2005 rankings on its website over the weekend." (*China Daily*, 4th July 2006, *http://www.chinadaily.com.cn/china/2006-07/04/content_632199.htm*)

5. Schmidt, Johannes Dragsbæk (2006), "China's 'Soft Power' Re-emergence in Southeast Asia", Copenhagen Discussion Papers, June, Copenhagen: Asia Research Centre, Copenhagen Business School, p. 3.

6. The Mischief Reef (of the Spratlys), known to the Filipinos as the Panganiban Reef, is 150 miles west of the Filipino island of Palawan, and 620 miles southeast of China.

7. See Chapter 14, note 30.

8. Ningxia Hui Zizhiqu is one of the five ethnic minority zizhiqu ("autonomous regions") of China. The other four are Guangxi (Zhuang), Inner Mongolia (Mongol), Xinjiang (Uygur) and Tibet (Tibetan).

9. Mian, Weilin 勉维霖 (1981), *Ningxia Yisilan Jiaopai Gaiyao* 宁夏伊斯兰教派概要 (An Outline of the Islamic Sects in Ningxia), Yinchuan: Ningxia Renmin Chubanshe 宁夏人民出版社.

10. See Chapter 14, note 32.

2

Southeast Asian Research in China: A Historical Review

Zhuang Guotu

Although Southeast Asia is a close neighbour of China, China did not develop any academic study of its southern neighbour until the 1920s. In the 1930-1940s some Chinese scholars in Chongqing and Singapore raised the first wave of Southeast Asian studies stimulated by Japanese expansion into China and Southeast Asia. After 1949 academic studies of international affairs became restricted in Mainland China except studies of overseas Chinese affairs and those directly related to diplomacy until 1978 when China opened itself to the outside world. Since 1978 studies of Southeast Asia in Mainland China are getting more recognition from the government at the central and local levels and the society in general, due to greater interaction with Southeast Asia.

This paper gives a general description of how the Chinese are aware of Southeast Asia in the two thousand years and the course of development of the Southeast Asian studies in the last hundred years, as well as examines the contemporary situation for Chinese scholars and related institutes in this research field.

How the Chinese Came to be Aware of Southeast Asia

As early as 100 BC the geographical knowledge of Southeast Asia was evident in Chinese literature. When Chinese merchants went on "barbarian" vessels heading south down to the "South Sea" and foreign merchants from Southeast Asia came to China, the ports and neighbouring coastal regions where the sailing route passes along the peninsulas and islands of Southeast Asia came to the knowledge of the Chinese.[1] Meanwhile, the so-called tribute envoys from Southeast Asia by land and by sea also brought the information of Southeast Asia to the Chinese.[2] The first Chinese envoys sent to Southeast

Asia seem to happen in 244 AD, and they visited Funan (Cambodia) and left records about their travel in the Chinese literature.[3] During the 3rd-7th centuries Buddhist monks, who traveled between China and Southeast Asia by sea, also brought to China knowledge of Southeast Asia by their travel records. As monks were knowledgeable in this period their works have become the most valuable literatures about Southeast Asia in this period.[4] Although the Chinese courts generally have neither international perspective nor interest in affairs beyond their south border, Chinese officials had the duty to edit information of foreign countries as a part of the court history as a matter of course. As communications and economic and cultural exchange between China and Southeast Asia remained uninterrupted, and the Chinese considered editing history to be one of the most important court duties, information of Southeast Asia has been accumulated at least from the Han Dynasty (100 BC) onwards. However, except for those of monks all the records related to Southeast Asia before the 13th century were bits and pieces, with many of them repeating their ancestors' records accumulated in the official history edited by courts. Therefore, they need to be reconstructed by scholars.

After the 13th century Chinese knowledge of Southeast Asia seems to have experienced a jump. The main reason seems that more Chinese went abroad stimulated by increasing overseas trade, who brought more information about Southeast Asia. The economic boom and technological progress in the Song period (10th-13th centuries) brought about shipbuilding on a great scale and a technological revolution in navigation marked by the use of the compass. For the history of Chinese overseas, it is significant that Chinese vessels instead of "barbarian vessels" became the main sailing vessels for Chinese merchants to come and go between China and foreign countries, which resulted in the possibility that China was able to carry out large-scale overseas trade and the Chinese emigrants were able to go abroad on a large scale. Responding to the increasing trade with Southeast Asia, including tribute trade, more information about Southeast Asia became necessary for the overseas merchants and the local governments in coastal areas of China. Since the 12th century, books specially written to offer South Sea information appeared in this period.[5] Information about some 38 countries or regions in Southeast Asia emerged in the Chinese literature in the 13th century. Responding to the prosperity of Chinese trade with Southeast Asia and the coastal region of the Indian Ocean, more people navigated southwards and traveled to Southeast Asia. More detailed information was collected, and more than 90 areas, including some 56 regions located in Southeast Asia, were mentioned in the Chinese documents written by travel merchants in

Southeast Asia or those who were dispatched as envoys to Southeast Asia in the 14th-15th centuries.[6]

The most valuable Chinese book on Southeast Asian affairs before the 18th century is the *Dongxiyang Kao* (Notes on the Sea Routes of the Eastern and Western Oceans) published in 1616. This book offers trade information and guide concentrating on Southeast Asia, although Japan was also included since Japan was one of the destination of Chinese overseas merchants. A total of 22 countries and their 21 dependencies in Southeast Asia have been mentioned and the situation of early Dutch and Portuguese expansion into Southeast Asia was also described in this book.[7]

Besides these Chinese works that focus or partly focus on the information of Southeast Asia, which amounted to some 50 books before the 18th century,[8] there is also a lot of information about Southeast Asia spread around the literatures of official history (*zhengshi* 正史), chronicle (*shilu* 实录), encyclopedia (*leishu* 类书), local gazetteers (*fangzhi* 方志) and even novels (*biji xiaoshuo* 笔记小说). All these materials are still not totally discovered and used.

Since the Europeans colonized Southeast Asia and the overseas Chinese settled down in large numbers in Southeast Asia, Chinese sources of Southeast Asia included not only those edited and published in China, but also those written and edited by the overseas Chinese. For example, *Kaiba Lidai Shiji* (the Chronicle of Batavia Chinese in 1619-1810), which offers rare information about the Indonesian Chinese, was edited by the Chinese organizations in Batavia.[9]

Several years ago, abundant Chinese archives about Batavia Chinese *Huaren Gongguan Dang'an* 华人公馆档案 dating from 18th-19th century were found in Batavia and shipped for storage in Leiden University in Holland by Professor Leonard Blusse. At the moment the Research School of Southeast Asian Studies, Xiamen University, is cooperating with Professor Blusse to edit, annotate and publish these archives, and so far 5 volumes of the planned 20 volumes in total have been annotated and published in 2001-2005 by the Xiamen University Press.

Although the Chinese have known Southeast Asia for about two thousand years China seems to pay more attention to its northern border than its southern border from where nomadic tribes have threatened Chinese courts for thousands of years. While studies of the northern border affairs continued one after another for generations and centuries, there were still no real studies on Southeast Asia except for the accumulation of information about Southeast Asia brought to China by Chinese and "barbarian" envoys, Chinese merchants and travelers. Even when the Opium War broke out in 1840 and the English invaded southern China from Southeast Asia, the Chinese people and court did not realize the importance of Southeast Asia's strategic position. In the mind of the Chinese courts for thousands of years Southeast Asia had contact only with the southeastern coastal region of China, a region of no great importance for the central government. Chinese court was satisfied with just keeping the Europeans in Southeast Asia far away from Peking (Beijing 北京) since the Opium War.

It is not until the late Ch'ing (Qing 清) period when the Europeans appeared very close to Peking, that some local governors and scholars began to acquaint themselves with their enemies from Southeast Asia. Moreover, information about rich Chinese in Southeast Asia had been reported firstly to the local governments in Fujian and Canton and later, to the central court, and China could look for the support of overseas Chinese in defense against European expansion into coastal China. The Fujian and Canton governors even suggested the court to mobilize the Chinese in Southeast Asia to donate for the building of navy in order to defend against the invasion of Europeans by sea.[10] Therefore, some open-minded local officials and scholars became increasingly interested in Southeast Asia and the overseas Chinese. Some scholars and low-ranking officials went or were dispatched to Southeast Asia to collect information on the Europeans and also the Chinese communities for different purposes.[11] Even though the first diplomatic ambassador sent out was as late as in 1876, all the Chinese diplomatic officials had the responsibility to submit reports on the foreign countries they passed and stayed in. The diplomatic officials like consuls posted to Southeast Asia and its suzerain territory provided more information than the local governors in southeastern China. All their reports proved to be more analytical and in detail than preceding works that just offered what the authors saw and heard. These Chinese envoys can perhaps be canonized as the pioneers of Southeast Asian studies in China. However, most of them are traditional scholars without knowledge of modern politics, economics or geography. They also lost their interest in Southeast Asian affairs when they went back to China and offered a report or some articles about Southeast Asia.[12] Therefore, no specialist in this field appeared among them.

Germination of Southeast Asian Studies in China (1920s-1940s)

In the 1920s academic studies on Southeast Asia appeared in China. It seems that the Southeast Asian studies were stimulated by the research on the Southeast Asian Chinese. It is Mr He Haiming 何海鳴 who taught courses on the history of overseas Chinese expansion in the Department of Consuls in the Civilian University of Peking (Beijing Pingmin Daxue Lingshi Xi 北京平民大学领事系). Another contribution of his was the founding of a journal titled *Qiaowu Xunkan* 侨务旬刊 (Journal of Overseas Chinese Affairs) in Peking with a sub-headquarter in Shanghai, and several branches in Kuala Lumpur, Kalimantan and Chicago. Research articles on Southeast Asia were published in this journal[13] which existed up to 1924. However, Mr He's studies and the journal of *Qiaowu Xunkan* targeted at the overseas Chinese spread through the whole world and not only Southeast Asia.

The academic studies of Southeast Asia in China could be marked with the establishment of the Department of Nanyang Cultural and Educational Affairs in Jinan University (Jinan Daxue Nanyang Wenhua Jiaoyu Shiye Bu 暨南大学南洋文化教育事业部) in Shanghai in 1927, though the main target of this department was to promote overseas Chinese education and studies. The direct goals of this institute were to publish a journal on Southeast Asian studies, to encourage overseas Chinese to be educated in China, and to mobilize scholars to carry out Southeast Asian studies. Some researchers and staff in this institute became the explorers and first specialists in Southeast Asian studies, such as Liu Shimu 刘士木, Yao Nan 姚楠, Li Changfu 李长傅, Su Qianying 苏乾英, etc. This institute published two journals of *Nanyang Yanjiu* 南洋研究 (Southeast Asian Studies) and *Nanyang Qingbao* 南洋情报 (Information of Southeast Asia).[14] Most of the scholars interested in Southeast Asian studies, including those in Southeast Asia such as Xu Yunqiao 许云樵 and Zhang Liqian 张礼千 were contributors of the journal of *Nanyang Yanjiu*. In Peking some historians, such as Zhang Xingrang 张星烺, Feng Chengjun 冯承钧 and Xiang Da 向达, also made contribution to the historical geography of Southeast Asia stimulated by the studies of European scholars such as G. Maspero, P. Pelliot, J. J. L. Duyvendak and others.

The overseas Chinese scholars in Southeast Asia began to show their advantage in the Chinese Southeast Asian studies in the 1930s. In this period, the status of overseas Chinese was not so distinguished as settlers or sojourners in Southeast Asia with Chinese scholars traveling between China and Southeast Asia frequently and the overseas Chinese were considered also as Chinese subjects. Two books on Southeast Asian Studies with more than 600 pages each marked the overseas Chinese becoming more important for Chinese Southeast Asian studies.[15] The joint studies of Chinese scholars in China and the overseas Chinese scholars in Singapore could be marked by the establishment of the South Sea Society (of China) (Zhongguo Nanyang Xuehui 中国南洋学会) in Singapore on 17 March 1940. When the Japanese invaded Southeast Asia, this society moved to Chongqing. After the war it moved back to Singapore in 1946. The first founders of this society are Yao Nan 姚楠, Liu Shimu 刘士木 , Li Changfu 李长傅, Yu Dafu 郁达夫 from China and Guan Chupu 关楚璞, Zhang Liqian 张礼千, Xu Yunqiao 许云樵, who had settled down in Singapore. This society has a *Journal of South Sea Studies* (*Nanyang Xuebao* 南洋学报), which still exists to the present day.

During the 1920s to 1949 some scholars, besides those mentioned above, insisted in Southeast Asian studies in Zhongshan University, Xiamen University, Qinghua University and Lingnan University. Among them stands Professor Ling Huixiang in Xiamen University. He devoted himself to the study of ethnicity and archaeology of Southeast Asia.

Interruption and Restoration of Southeast Asian Studies in Mainland China (1949-)

The academic studies of international affairs, including Southeast Asian studies, were not encouraged by the government after 1949. Due to the isolation of China from the outside world because of the U.S. blockade around the borders of Mainland China, China had tensions with all the Southeast Asian countries, except Indonesia in the 1950s. There was no academic institute for international studies until 1956. However some scholars in Zhongshan University, Xiamen University, Peking University and so on, still insisted on Southeast Asian studies, being motivated purely by their interest. Among them stands Professor Chen Xujing 陈序经[16] who devoted himself since 1949 to the ancient history of Southeast Asian studies, based on the first-hand Chinese documents and new Western publications which he obtained through his friends in Hong Kong. Before the early 1960s Professor Chen finished eight books on the ancient histories of South Vietnam, Burma, Siam, Cambodia and Malaya. These books were unpublished but printed in Hong Kong in the middle of the 1950s and early 1960s, and circulated to a very limited number of scholars. In 1992, these eight books were combined into two volumes and published in Taiwan, titled *Chen Xujing Dongnanya Gushi Yanjiu Heji* 陈序经东南亚古史研究合集 (Joint Volume of Studies on Ancient History of Southeast Asia by Chen Xujing).

In 1956 the first academic institute for studies on international affairs called Nanyang Research Institute (Nanyang Yanjiusuo 南洋研究所) was jointly established by the Central Committee of Overseas Chinese Affairs (Zhongyang Qiaowu Weiyuanhui 中央侨务委员会) and Xiamen University in the Xiamen University campus. Due to the overseas Chinese in Southeast Asia becoming a problem for Mainland China's international relations, and the Chinese government changing its policies towards overseas Chinese from encouraging them to devote their loyalty to China to encouraging them to settle down in Southeast Asia and integrate into the local society, this institute took on the responsibility of focusing its research on the overseas Chinese in Southeast Asia. In just a few years more than 30 scholars were recruited to the institute from different places in China, many of them were returned overseas Chinese. The biggest difficulty for this new institute was how to make information about international context of Southeast Asian studies known to the Chinese scholars and officials. In 1957, this institute published its first journal *Nanyang Ziliao Yicong* 南洋资料译丛 (Journal of the Translation of Southeast Asian References), and many books and articles in English, Japanese, Russian and French were translated and published in this journal. In 1957-1966 this journal became almost the only source where Chinese scholars could get information about international Southeast Asian studies. Up to 1966 this institute had 62 staff, with specialists in all the Southeast Asian languages.

In 1960 another institute on Southeast Asian studies Dongnanya Yanjiusuo 东南亚研究所 was established in Guangzhou, as part of the Guangzhou Branch of the Chinese Academy (Zhongguo Kexueyuan Guangzhou Fenyuan 中国科学院广州分院). In 1964 this institute was changed to belong to Jinan University. In 1959 a research centre for Southeast Asian history Dongnanya Lishi Yanjiushi 东南亚历史研究室 was established in Zhongshan University.

In 1962 after Mao Zedong called for scholars to pay attention to international affairs, many institutes of international affairs were established in universities in China, but all of them were closed down during the Cultural Revolution and restored only after 1978.

In 1972 the institute in Xiamen was restored in response to the improvement of China's international situation after Sino-U.S. diplomatic relations were established and China's need for international studies, particularly information about Southeast Asia. In 1978 the two institutes in Guangzhou were restored, and the research centre for Southeast Asian history in Zhongshan University was promoted into an institute with the name of "Institute for Studies of Southeast Asian History" (Dongnanya Lishi Yanjiusuo 东南亚历史研究所) and later "Institute for Southeast Asian Studies" (Dongnanya Yanjiusuo 东南亚研究所) in 1988.

General Situation of Southeast Asian Studies in Mainland China Today

During 1949-1978 Southeast Asian studies in China faced an embarrassing situation. Although China does not lack experts in Southeast Asian languages since so many overseas Chinese came back to China since 1949 and many researchers in Southeast Asian studies were returned overseas Chinese, few scholars had the chance to work or travel in the country about which they studied, since China had closed its door and was strict about civilians going abroad. The lack of foreign currency means that the Chinese Institute could not afford to purchase foreign publications. Therefore, scholars engaging in Southeast Asian studies focused more on the history of Southeast Asia and the overseas Chinese in Southeast Asia than on contemporary studies. Such situation has more or less lasted to the present day.

After 1978 many institutions for studies of international affairs have been established in response to China's policy of opening to the outside world and the thirst for understanding the outside world. International affairs were given much more attention than before, which resulted not only in an increasing number of institutes on Southeast Asian studies being established in the southern provinces of China but also the institutes of international affairs in Beijing and Shanghai having greater interest in Southeast Asian affairs.

Nowadays the major institutes and researchers on Southeast Asian studies in China can be divided into in three types, according to their institutional location: universities, the Chinese Social Academy and government departments.

Due to the historical background and teaching needs more institutes and researchers are still concentrated in the universities. There are three institutes of Southeast Asian Studies in Xiamen University, Zhongshan University and Jinan University. Each of these institutes has 20-45 staff positions. All these three institutes have their own journals and give degrees related to Southeast Asian studies. In Yunnan University (Institute of Asian Studies), Peking University (Institute of Asian-African Studies, Institute of Oriental Culture), Nankai University (Centre for APEC Studies) and Fudan University (Institute of World Economy), Southeast Asian studies also constitute a major research.

The second team for Southeast Asian studies in China is in sections of the Chinese Social Academy. Two institutes of Southeast Asian studies are in the Social Academy of Guangxi Province and the Social Academy of Yunnan Province. Each of them has its own journal. In the Chinese Social Academy (Institute of World Economy and Politics, Institute of Asian Pacific Studies) in Beijing and the Social Academy of Shanghai (Institute of European and Asian Studies), Southeast Asian studies are getting more important.

The third team for Southeast Asian studies in China belongs to government departments. Outstanding among them is the Institute of Modern International Relations in Beijing. The Institute of International Trade in

Beijing and the Institute of International Issues in Shanghai also give attention to Southeast Asian studies.

Besides the institutes of international studies, the other institutes close to Southeast Asian studies are institutes of overseas Chinese studies as most overseas Chinese reside in Southeast Asia. There are 5 institutes for overseas Chinese studies in Mainland China.

The five institutes of Southeast Asian studies in south China focus separately on different fields. Yunnan's institute focuses on Thailand and Myanmar, with main interest on the issue of ethnicity – particular emphasis being on cross-border nationalities. Guangxi's institute focuses on Vietnam, Laos and Cambodia; Zhongshan University's focuses on the history of Southeast Asia; Xiamen University's focuses on ASEAN economy and ethnic Chinese in Southeast Asia; and the focus of Jinan University's institute is similar to that of Xiamen's.

In 1978 the Chinese Society of Southeast Asian Studies (Zhongguo Dongnanya Yanjiuhui 中国东南亚研究会) was established with its general-secretary section located in Xiamen University, with more than 400 members including most of the researchers and those interested in Southeast Asian issues. It publishes a newsletter twice a year.

Some Comments on Southeast Asian Studies in Mainland China

In the last 20 years Southeast Asian studies in China have made progress in the following fields:

1. Collection and editing of Chinese materials related to Southeast Asian history. As mentioned before, for almost two thousand years materials related to Southeast Asia have accumulated in the Chinese literature. Although Western scholars from the late 19th century began to use such materials, there are still a lot of materials scattered in the tremendous amount of Chinese literature. Several collections of special subjects in the Chinese literature have been edited, such as *A Compilation of References on the Philippines in Chinese Ancient Literatures*; *A Compilation of References on Cambodia in Chinese Ancient Literatures*; *A Compilation of References on the Sino-Vietnam Relations in Chinese Ancient Literatures*; *A Compilation of References on Burma in Chinese Ancient Literatures*; *A Compilation of references on Southeast Asia in the Ch'ing Dynasty Chronicle*; *A Compilation of references on South China Sea Inlands in Chinese Ancient Literatures*. Some historical works on Southeast Asia have been annotated or re-annotated, such as *Zhufa Zhi*,

Daoyi Zhilüe, Xiyang Chaogong Dianlu, Haiwai Jishi, Lingwai Daida and so on.

2. Translation. More than 30 famous books such as those of Hall, Coediers, Wang Gungwu, Purcell, Skinnar and Leo Suryadinata, have been translated. The economic statistics of Southeast Asia have also been translated annually.

3. Series of books on the history and economy of the Chinese in Southeast Asia have been published. Each includes 5-8 books.

4. Studies based on Chinese materials on South China Sea Islands, the Chinese in Southeast Asia and the history of Southeast Asia have made some academic progress.

5. Courses in Southeast Asian studies for postgraduate students in universities. Before 1978, there was no regular training of students in Southeast Asian studies, those who engaged in this research field were trained by being the research assistants of experts. After 1978 the institutes of Southeast Asian studies in Xiamen University, Zhongshan University and Jinan University successively carried out programs for postgraduate students on Southeast Asian studies. Now some 30 postgraduate students have received their master's degree and about 10 students have obtained Ph.D. in Southeast Asian studies annually.

Problems

1. Languages of Southeast Asia. In the main institutes of Southeast Asian studies, much less than enough scholars have mastered the languages of Southeast Asia, compared with the situation in the 1960s when there were many returned overseas Chinese from Southeast Asia who became researchers. This resulted in a shortage of first-hand materials for studies.

2. Working experience in Southeast Asia. The majority of researchers have not spent enough time in Southeast Asia or not been visiting often the countries they are studying. Little fieldwork can be done in Southeast Asia and much depends on the use of second-hand materials.

3. Less participation in international academic exchanges. Due to the financial situation and restriction on going abroad, the majority of researchers have less chance of participating in relevant conferences and getting necessary information on international academic progress.

4. Although several hundred articles and 5-10 books related to Southeast Asian studies have been published in China every year, all of them are written in Chinese and not known to foreign scholars. Moreover, limited with research funds, first-hand materials and the comprehension of

academic information, most of the research results are not of world standard but popularized to give a prevailing knowledge to people and references to the government.

5.   Research topic and publishing restrictions. Southeast Asian studies have been considered as a sensitive political issue. Normally, scholars in China are asked to follow the government's policies and attitudes and not to raise different opinions from those of the government in order not to make any trouble for relations with Southeast Asia. Meanwhile, many materials and information are kept restricted from the public, It means that many materials, particularly government documents and those controlled by the government, are not so available and the research results, in case that it is not appreciated by the authorities, cannot be easily published.

Although researchers mainly engaged in Southeast Asian studies in Mainland China increased to around one hundred in number with some 12 institutes involved in this research field as a major focus aspect or one of the main aspects, they are still not a world power in international academic studies of Southeast Asia. Limited by the shortage of research funds, language mastery, working experience in Southeast Asia and participation in international exchanges, Chinese scholars in the Mainland can offered few academic production of a high level except those related to Chinese materials. However, the situation of Southeast Asian studies is improving with the recognition of the society and the government, an increase in investment, a rise of international exchanges and the regular training of young scholars in response to the rapid development of Sino-Southeast Asian relations. The future years will be a golden time for Chinese studies on Southeast Asia. It is hoped that Southeast Asian studies in Mainland China will develop international standing in the academic world in the near future.

Notes

1.   Before the 18th century the Chinese concept "South Sea (*Nanhai* 南海) or South and West Ocean (*Dongxiyang* 东西洋)" included the South China Sea and the Indian Ocean.

2.   The earliest envoys from Southeast Asia came to the Chinese court in 131 AD, according to Chinese official literature *Hou Hanshu* 后汉书 (*Xinanyi Zhuan* 西南夷传 , p. 2837). They were sent separately by the kings in Java and in Burma.

3.   This record [*Wu Shi Waiguo Zhuan* 吴时外国传 (Foreign Countries in Wu Period) by Zhu Ying 朱应 and Kang Tai 康泰] has been lost and only the title

of the book and part of the content were collected in other Chinese literatures in later period, like *Shuijing Zhu* 水经注 ("Notes on Geography", written in about AD 500).

4. Two of the most important monk Chinese literatures related to Southeast Asia are *Fo Guo Ji* 佛国记 and *Nanhai Jigui Neifa Zhuan* 南海寄归内法传 which have been translated and annotated into English by H.A. Giles as *Fo Kuo Chi: The Travels of Fa-hsian*, 1923, and by J. Takakusu as *Nanhai Chi Kuei Nei Fa Chuan: A Record of the Buddhist Religion as Practised in India and the Malay Archipelago*, 1986.

5. The most famous books are *Lingwai Daida* 岭外代答 written in the late 12th century (1178) and *Zhufan Zhi* 诸蕃志 in the early 13th century (1225), and the latter have been translated and annotated by Frederick Hirth and W.W. Rockhill and published in the title *Chu Fan Chih, Chau Ju-kua, on the Chinese and Arab Trade* in 1911.

6. For the travel works the representative book is *Daoyi Zhilüe* 岛夷志略, and more than 90 regions in Southeast Asia and India Ocean were described. For the works of the Chinese envoys sent to Southeast Asia, the representative works are *Zhenla Fengtu Ji* 真腊风土记 in around 1300; *Yingya Shenglan* 瀛涯胜览 in the early 15th century (1425-1432). All these three books have been translated and annotated: Rockhill, *Tao I Chih Lioh: Notes on the Relation and Trade of Chinese with the Eastern Archipelago and the Coast of the Indian Ocean during the Fourteenth Century*, in *T'ong Pao* (1915), Vol. 16, pp. 61-159; P. Pelliot, *Chen La Feng Tu Chi: Memoires sur les coutumes du Cambodge*, in *BEFEO* (1902), Vol. 2; J.V.G. Mills, *Ying Yai Sheng Lan: the Ocean's Shore*, Cambridge, 1970.

7. In 1992-1993 a joint team of Leiden and Xiamen scholars worked on the translation and annotation of this book, but it was given up when half of the work was finished for various reasons.

8. About introduction of Southeast Asian information in Chinese literatures, see: Gu Hai, *Dongnanya Gudaishi Zhongwen Wenxian Tiyao* 东南亚古代史中文文献提要 (Abstract of Chinese Literatures Related to Ancient Southeast Asia), Xiamen University Press, 1990.

9. This Chinese chronicle in Batavia was translated into Dutch in a crude way [W.H. Medhurst, *Chronologische geschiedenis van Batavia*, Tijdschrift voor Neerland's Indie, 3-? (1840), pp. I-145].

10. See the memorials to the throne by the General-Governor Zhang Zhidong, *Zhang Wenxiang Gong Quanji* (Collections of Literatures of Zhang Zhidong), Memorials, v. 13, pp. 12-13.

11. For example, Zheng Guanying 郑观应, the advisor of General-Governor Li Hongzhang 李鸿章, was sent to Vietnam to collect information about the French in Vietnam (he also had the task of mobilizing overseas Chinese to take action against French invasions in North Vietnam); Governor Zhang Zhidong 张之洞 sent his subordinates to travel in Southeast Asia to understand the

situation of the Chinese there and the necessity of establishing Chinese consulates; famous scholar Ma Jianzhong 马建忠 went to Singapore to obtain knowledge of the modern nation and its wealth in order to promote reforms in China.

12. Many articles and diaries of them are included in *The Collection of Works: From East to West, Chinese Travelers before 1911* (*Zouxiang Shijie Congshu* 走向世界丛书) published in 1985-1987.

13. 141 volumes of this journal and two books about Southeast Asian Chinese had been published during the existence of this journal in 1921-1924.

14. In 1928-1944 the journal of *Nanyang Yanjiu* published 61 volumes; *Nanyang Qingbao* was closed very early on.

15. These are *Nanyang Nianjian* 南洋年鉴 (Chronicle of Southeast Asia) published in 1930, and *Xingzhou Shinian* 星洲十年 (Ten Years of Singapore) in 1931.

16. Chen obtained his degree of Ph.D. from the Elino University in U.S in the 1930s and was the president of Lingnan University (Lingnan Daxue 岭南大学) in Canton before 1952.

References

Fu, Wumen 傅无闷 and Yu Shukun 郁树锟 (eds) (1939), *Nanyang Nianjian* 南洋年鉴 (Chronicle of Southeast Asia), Singapore: Nanyang Shangbao.

Giles, H.A. (1923), *Fo Kuo Chi: The Travels of Fa-hsian,* Cambridge: Cambridge University Press.

Gu, Hai 顾海 (1990), *Dongnanya Gudaishi Zhongwen Wenxian Tiyao* 东南亚古代史中文文献提要 (Abstract of Chinese literatures related to ancient Southeast Asia), Xiamen: Xiamen University Press.

Hirth, Frederick and W.W. Rockhill (1911), *Chu Fan Chih, Chau Ju- kua, on the Chinese and Arab Trade,* St. Petersburg: Imperial Institute of Sciences.

Ma, Huan 马欢 (1451), *Yingya Shenglan* 瀛涯胜览, annotated by Wan Ming 万明 and published in Beijing: Haiyang Press, 2005.

Medhurst, W.H. (1840), *Chronologische geschiedenis van Batavia, Tijdschrift voor Neerland's Indie*, 3-2, pp. I- 1 45.

Mills, J.V.G. (1970), *Ying Yai Sheng Lan: the Ocean's Shore,* Cambridge: Cambridge University Press.

Pelliot, P. (1902), *Chen La Feng Tu Chi: Mernoires sur les coutumes du Cambodge*, in *BEFEO*, Vol. 2.

Rockhill (1915), *Tao I Chih Lioh* (Notes on the Relation and Trade of Chinese with the Eastern Archipelago and the Coast of the Indian Ocean during the Fourteenth Century), in *Tong Pao*, Vol. 16.

Takakusu, J. (1896), *A Record of the Buddhist Religion as Practised in India and the Malay Archipelago,* Oxford: Clarendon Press, reprinted in Delhi: Munshiram Manoharlal, 1966.

Wang, Dayuan 汪大渊 (1349), *Daoyi Zhilüe* 岛夷志略, annotated by Su Jiqing

苏继廎 and published in Beijing: Zhonghua Shuju 中华书局, 1981.

Xingzhou Ribaoshe 星洲日报社 (ed.) (1931), *Xingzhou Shinian* 星洲十年 (Ten Years of Singapore), Singapore: Xingzhou Ribaoshe.

Zhang, Zhidong 张之洞 (1928), *Zhang Wenxiang Gong Quanji* 张文襄公全集 (Collections of literatures of Zhang Zhidong), Memorials, Beijing: Wenhua Zhai.

Zhao, Rukuo 赵汝适 (1225), *Zhufan Zhi* 诸蕃志, annotated by Feng Chengjun 冯承钧 and published in Shanghai: Shangwu Yinshuguan 商务印书馆, 1940.

Zhong, Shuhe 钟叔河 (ed.) (1985-1987), *Zouxiang Shijie Congshu* 走向世界丛书 (The collection of works: from east to west, Chinese travelers before 1911), Changsha: Yuelu Press.

Zhou, Daguan 周达观 (about 1300), *Zhenla Fengtu Ji* 真腊风土记, annotated by Xia Nai 夏鼐, published in Beijing: Zhonghua Shuju 中华书局, 1981.

Zhou, Qufei 周去非 (1178), *Lingwai Daida* 岭外代答 , reprinted in Beijing: Zhonghua Shuju 中华书局, 1999.

Politics and Foreign Policy

China's Changing Political Economy with Malaysia: A Regional Perspective

*Samuel C.Y. **Ku***

Introduction

Malaysia was the first major country in Southeast Asia that changed its relations with the People's Republic of China (PRC) when both countries exchanged diplomatic recognition on 31 May 1974. As a rising power, China has, since the early 1980s however, attracted grave attention from Malaysia, Southeast Asia, and from other major countries in the world.

China was actually hostile against its neighbours in the South during the first three decades after the Chinese Communist Party took over Mainland China in October 1949. During the period of China's confrontational relationship with major countries in Southeast Asia, the weak Asian giant was associated with former Soviet Union in fighting against the United States, then its enemy. The PRC was even in alliance with rebel Communist movements in Southeast Asia in the 1950s, 1960s and even in the early part of the 1970s.[1] In Malaysia, when the Communist Party of Malaya (CPM) initiated resurrection against the ruling government of Malaya in 1948, the then British colonial government started a twelve-year-long state of emergency and finally suppressed communist guerrillas in 1960.

When China broke off with the Soviets in the late 1960s, the still weak Asian giant then changed its policy from relying upon the Soviets to seeking an alliance with the United States, the other superpower. This was a turning point for Communist China in entering the global community, particularly after China's accession to the United Nations in October 1971. China made another significant change in December 1979 with the implementation of an open-door policy, partly because of its gradually increasing connections with the capitalist world, and partly because of its weak economy, which was urgently in need of foreign assistance. The new policy not only opened the Asian giant's door to the world but also changed China's relations with the world, including Malaysia and Southeast Asia. Since then, China has been perceived as a swiftly changing society, with changes beyond those of any period in Chinese history.

China's political economy with Malaysia has continued to change since the early 1980s, and has changed speedily since the late 1990s. In addition to frequent exchanges of high-level visits between the two countries, China has also greatly expanded its economic relations with Malaysia. For example, China's trade volume with Malaysia for the first time exceeded US$20 billion in 2003, and this figure further reached US$26.2 billion in 2004.[2] According to the Chinese statistics, Malaysia has become China's eighth largest trading partner around the world and has since 2003 overtaken Singapore as the largest in Southeast Asia.[3] China's relations with Southeast Asia have in the meantime improved, politically and economically.

Three key questions are then raised. What are the drives behind the changing political economy between China's relations with Malaysia and with Southeast Asia? What are the programs fostering the changing political economy between China and Malaysia and Southeast Asia? The most important question is: Is China's changing political economy with Malaysia in particular, or it is just part of China's overall relations with the region of Southeast Asia?

This paper argues that China's recent increasing political economy with Malaysia and Southeast Asia is actually being pushed forward by three important policy initiatives that started in the early 1980s, although a variety of factors are involved.[4] This paper also argues, on a regional perspective, that China's changing political economy with Malaysia is not a particular one; rather, it is just part of China's overall strategy towards Southeast Asia. This means that the Asian giant has also in the meantime strengthened its political economy with other countries in Southeast Asia since the early 1980s. This paper will examine these arguments by exploring China's three policy initiatives that started in the early 1980s, i.e. (1) the open-door policy, (2) the good-neighbour policy, and (3) the "go global" strategy, which construct the three main sections of this paper. This paper will then conclude that China's increasing political economy with Malaysia and with Southeast Asia will sustain, at least in the next decade, as China continues its "going global" policy.

The Open-door Policy since 1980

Studying the political economy of contemporary China, most scholars will agree on the importance of the open-door policy that was introduced in

December 1979. The open-door policy not only changed the modern development of China's political economy, but also the directions of international political and economic orders. For many Chinese on the mainland, the open-door policy was perceived as an opportunity for many changes, including the improvement of their daily lives due to gradual economic progress, access to foreigners due to the coming of international investors and visitors, observation of changing global development due to a wider usage of the Internet, the development of cross-Strait relations due to frequent exchanges across the Taiwan Strait, changing relations with major countries and neighbouring countries, going overseas for study, visitation, and tourism, and, probably most important of all, a chance to watch and experience the rise of the ancient kingdom.

For many countries around the world, the open-door policy was also perceived as an opportunity for many changes, including delving into Chinese society to get a better understanding of the Asian giant, to adapt to Chinese culture, behavior, and way of life; chances to engage China in an appropriate way whether it be containment or partnership in the international system or in other ways, to admit China in regional and international institutions, and, probably most important of all, to assess the strength and power of the Asian giant that is changing and rising.

Accordingly, the open-door policy is a comprehensive policy, which has generated impact on all areas of China's domestic and international affairs, politically, economically, and even socially. Although the open-door policy does not concentrate on China's relations with any specific country like Malaysia, it was a political initiative that changed China's foreign relations with most countries around the world. Prior to the implementation of the open-door policy, China's relations with Malaysia were actually not stable, in spite of the exchange of diplomatic recognition of the two countries on 31 May 1974.[5]

Things have gradually changed, however, since China's practice of the open-door policy in 1979. Economically speaking, the PRC did not have much trade with Malaysia in the 1950s, 1960s, and 1970s, but both countries began to expand their bilateral trade since the early 1980s. Although the volume of trade between China and Malaysia was not significant in the 1980s and not in Malaysia's favour, the market of the mainland was gradually opened to Malaysian enterprises and to other countries as well.

China's economic relations with Malaysia have improved since the late 1980s, due to a series of events between the two countries. The year 1988 was a crucial point, during which China and Malaysia signed two official documents, i.e. (1) the Investment Protection Agreement and (2) the

the early 1990s, paving the foundation for the upgrade of the bilateral relations between the two countries. Mr Jiang Zemin, then Chinese President, was also invited to visit Malaysia in 1994. In addition, Mr Zhu Rongji, Mr Li Peng's successor, was invited to visit Malaysia in 1997 and in 1999, whereas Mr Hu Jintao (then Vice President) also paid a visit to Kuala Lumpur in 2002. Recently, Chinese Premier Wen Jiabao paid an official visit to Malaysia on 11 December 2005 for the 9th ASEAN-China Summit, the 9th ASEAN Plus Three Summit (i.e. China, Japan and South Korea), and the first East Asia (EAS) summit in Kuala Lumpur.[10]

Similarly, Malaysia's Prime Minister Dr Mahathir Mohamad made a significant visit with a large delegation to China in June 1993 after his first trip to Beijing in 1985, and afterwards Dr Mahathir paid another three visits to China in May 1994, in August 1996, and in August 1999. The outcome of the visit of August 1999 was to sign a Memorandum of Understanding with China, which China promised to make an investment of US$1 billion on a pulp and paper plant in Sabah, the largest of Chinese investment outside of the mainland at that time (Liow, 2005: 288). Earlier in September 1994, Mr Anwar Ibrahim, then Malaysia's Deputy Prime Minister, also paid a visit to China, taking a number of joint-venture projects home.[11] In May 1999, Malaysian Foreign Minister Syed Hamid Albar, paid a visit to China, signing a Joint Statement of Future Bilateral Cooperation with his Chinese counterpart Mr Tang Jiazuan, not to mention the exchanges of visits among other cabinet ministers between the two countries.

The 1990s soon came to be seen as an era of increasing exchanges of visits of high-level officials between China and Malaysia, and a series of agreements, memorandums, declarations, and statements were signed among these high-level officials during their visits. These political initiatives laid a foundation for the expanding economic activities between China and Malaysia in the 1990s, including trade, investment, foreign aid, and tourism. Without doubt, the first Joint Committee on Trade and Economic Cooperation between China and Malaysia in 1991 was also credited for the expanding bilateral economic relations of the two countries in the 1990s. The volume of bilateral trade between the two countries jumped from US$910 million in 1988 to US$2.2 billion in 1994 and to US$4.2 billion in 1999.

Regionally speaking, China's upgrading political economy with Malaysia in the 1990s was, again, not a particular case, because China has in the meantime strengthened its relations with other countries in Southeast Asia. China's political economy with Indonesia, for example, has also begun to change since the beginning of the decade when both countries restored their full diplomatic relations in August 1990. Afterwards, China established full diplomatic relations with Singapore in October 1990 and with Negara Brunei Darussalam in October 1991. The year 1991 was particularly significant for both China and Indonesia, because Indonesia dispatched 17 cabinet ministers to visit China, whereas the latter, in addition to Chinese President Yang Shangkun's visit to Indonesia in June 1991, sent 13 cabinet ministers to visit the Muslim state.[12] Also, China and Indonesia began the first Joint Committee on Trade and Economic Cooperation in 1991,[13] laying a foundation for further economic cooperation between the two Asian giants in the 1990s. China shares a similar story on its increasing political economy with other countries in Southeast Asia.

Apparently, China has undergone the greatest change in its economic relations with Southeast Asia since the onset of the 1990s. Prior to its open-door policy, China only maintained a very minor volume of trade with Southeast Asian nations. It was only since the late 1980s that China began to officially set records in its trade volume with different regions around the world, including Southeast Asia. Starting from 1988, China's trade with Southeast Asia has shown great progress. In 1988, for example, the volume of bilateral trade between China and Southeast Asia was US$3.8 billion, but this figure kept expanding dramatically from US$4.3 billion in 1990 to US$10.6 billion in 1993 and to US$19.4 billion in 1995, so was this figure's share in China's entire trade. One more thing to be noted is that bilateral trade prior to 1995 was generally in favour of China, despite the gradual narrowing of the gap between the two.

Since 1996, China's trade with Southeast has significantly changed, not only because of the expanding trade volume between the two but also because of China's increasing deficits in its trade with Southeast Asia. The volume of bilateral trade has dramatically enlarged from US$20.39 billion in 1996 to US$39.52 billion in 2000, to US$78.25 billion in 2003, and to US$105.9 billion in 2004. China's economy has kept thriving since the turn of the century, and the share of China-ASEAN trade in China's entire trade volume has also kept increasing, from 7.0 per cent in 1996 to 8.2 per cent in 2001 and to 9.2 per cent in 2004, showing closer economic relations between the two.

It is apparent therefore that China's increasing political economy with Malaysia in the 1990s was not particular; China also improved its political economy with other Southeast Asian countries during the decade.

The "Go Global" Strategy since 2002

Chinese leaders proposed the strategy of "Going Global" in 2002 that was aimed at bringing Chinese enterprises overseas, in contrast to the open-door policy that invited foreign capital into the Chinese market. This is mainly because of China's growing economy since the implementation of the open-door policy, and has become stronger since the early 1990s and even stronger since the beginning of the new century.

The average of China's economic growth rate in the 1990s was 10 per cent, and it was 7.5 per cent in 2001, 8.3 per cent in 2002, 9.3 per cent in 2003, and 9.5 per cent in 2004. China's foreign reserves by mid-2005 soared to US$710 billion to become the world's second largest, only after Japan. Regarding foreign direct investment (FDI), China's receipt of FDI in 2003 (US$54 billion) for the first time exceeded that of the United States (US$30 billion), although China' receipt of FDI in 2004 (US$62 billion) fell behind that of the U.S. (US$121 billion).[14] In 2004, the U.S. and China were the two largest receipt of FDI around the world. 2002 was also the first year after China's entry into the World Trade Organization (WTO). This gave China more opportunities to construct a closer relationship of political economy with other countries under the framework of the institutionalized WTO.

According to China's Ministry of Commerce, several measures were taken in 2002 in promoting the "Go Global" policy, such as (1) enacting laws and regulations for enterprises' overseas investment, (2) improving the administration of the employment on foreign contract workers, (3) helping enterprises to undertake large-scale projects in key countries,[15] (4) fulfilling the achievements of the leaders' visits to foreign countries, and (5) assisting enterprises to develop foreign investment and cooperation in various ways.[16]

While the "Go Global" strategy continues to target African countries – China's traditional partners, this policy has also put much weight on China's neighbouring countries in Southeast Asia, in which Malaysia is a part. As a result, China's political economy with Malaysia and Southeast Asia has taken several steps further since the beginning of the new century. Malaysia continues to conduct its high-level visits to China, including former Malaysian supreme heads of state Sultan Salahuddin Abdul Aziz Shah in April 2001 and his successor Tuanku Syed Jamalullail in March 2005. After assuming the post of Malaysia's Prime Minister on 31 October 2003, Mr Abdullah Ahmad Badawi paid his first official visit China in May 2004 to celebrate the 30th anniversary of establishing full diplomatic relations of the two countries. Similarly, Chinese leaders were also kept being invited to visit Malaysia, including Mr Hu Jintao (then Vice President) in 2002, and, recently, Chinese Premier Wen Jiabao on 11 December 2005 for the 9th ASEAN-China Summit, the 9th ASEAN Plus Three Summit, and the first East Asia Summit in Kuala Lumpur.

China's economic relations with Malaysia continued to expand since the beginning of the new century. China's approved investment in Malaysia, for instance, grew from US$1 million in 2002 to US$3.19 million in 2003,[17] although it is not significant. It should be noted that Malaysia's investment in China is much larger than that of China's investment in Malaysia. Malaysia's investment in China grew from US$202.8 million in 2000 to US$262.9 million in 2001 and to US$367.8 million in 2002, in spite of a little decline in 2003 (US$251.1 million).[18] In addition, bilateral trade between the two countries expanded from US$4.2 billion in 1999 to US$18.4 billion in 2003 and to US$26.2 billion in 2004. From Malaysia's record, it had overtaken Singapore as China's largest trading partner in Southeast Asia in 2003.

Once again, from a regional perspective, China's improved political economy with Malaysia since the beginning of the new century is not exclusive, because China has also improved its political economy with other countries in the region. Taking the Sino-Vietnamese relationship as an example, most Chinese leaders have visited Vietnam since the turn of the century, and some of them even visited the Communist Party-led Socialist neighbour more than once. Former Chinese President Mr Jiang Zemin, for example, paid a visit to Vietnam in February 2002, while his Premier Mr Zhu Rongji visited Vietnam in December 1999. Before becoming China's President, Mr Hu Jintao (then China's Vice President) visited Vietnam twice in December 1998 and in April 2000. After assuming China's top leadership post in March 2003,[19] Mr Hu recently paid his first state visit to Vietnam on 1 November 2005.

As for Vietnam, almost all of its leaders have paid a visit to China during the last couple of years, including Prime Minister Phan Van Khai in October 1998, in February 2000, in May 2004 and in June 2005, former Secretary General of the Communist Party of Vietnam Le Kha Phiew in February 1999, and State President Tran Duc Luong in December 2000 and in July 2005. Mr Nong Duc Manh, the present Secretary General of the Communist Party of Vietnam, visited China twice in November 2001 and in April 2003, after taking the highest post in Vietnam.[20]

Regarding China's economic relationship with Southeast Asia as a whole, it has significantly augmented. China's trade with Southeast Asia has been indicated earlier, but China's investment in Southeast Asia is a little controversial, because statistics from both China and ASEAN is different. According to ASEAN's statistics, China's investment in Southeast Asia was only US$136.7 million in 1996, and this figure has gradually declined a little since then to US$62.5 million in 1999, to US$60.8 million in 2001 and to US$12.8 million in 2003 (ASEAN Secretariat, 2004: 142).

According to China's official statistics, the Chinese investment in Southeast Asia has increased, however, much larger than those of ASEAN's statistics. By the end of 1997, China had reached a total investment of US$870 million, including joint ventures or joint management ventures, in seven countries in Southeast Asia, of which US$320 million came out of China.[21] By the end of 2000, the amount invested by Chinese enterprises in Southeast Asia totaled US$893 million, of which US$458 million was from China.[22]

In recent years, Chinese official reports continue to show an increase in its investment in Southeast Asia. By the end of 2002, the Chinese enterprise invested a total amount of US$1,201 million in Southeast Asia, and US$716 million of which came out of China.[23] In the year 2002 alone, the Chinese enterprises made a total investment, including joint ventures or joint management ventures, of US$109 million in Southeast Asia, US$66.4 million of which was from China.[24] In 2004, China contributed to a total of US$224 million of investment in Southeast Asia, bringing China's entire investment in Southeast Asia up to US$775 million by the end of 2004.[25]

One thing more should be noted is international arrivals from China to Southeast Asia have greatly increased during the last one or two decades, another indicator showing the closeness of the two sides. Visitors from China to Southeast Asia have gradually increased since the early 1990s, and China has become the fourth largest country of origin of international visitors to Southeast Asia since 1999, next to Singapore, Malaysia, and Japan.[26] If Singapore and Malaysia, the two Southeast Asian countries, are excluded, the number of China's visitors to the region is next only to Japan since the turn of the new century.

Similarly, Malaysia has also made a significant contribution to China on the number of its tourists to the mainland. Malaysia's visitor arrivals to China began to show an increase since the early 1990s, and Malaysia has become the fifth largest origin of country in the number of visitor arrivals to China. In 2005, for example, China received 899,643 visitors from Malaysia, next to South Korea's visitors to China (3.5 million), Japan's (3.3 million), Russia's (2.2 million), and America's (1.5 million).[27] Yet, on the growth rate of visitor arrivals to China in 2005, Malaysia was the third highest (21.26 per cent), only next to that of South Korea (24.6 per cent) and that of Russia (24.1 per cent).

Finally, China has also, since the early 1990s, actively participated in the activities of the Association of Southeast Asian Nations (ASEAN), the largest and the most important organization in the region. China was, for the first time, invited to participate in ASEAN in July 1991 for the Twenty-fourth

ASEAN Post-Ministerial Meeting as a consultative partner, and Mr Qian Qichen, China's Foreign Minister then officially introduced the policy of Good Neighbourliness to its neighbours in the South. Three years later in July 1994, China and ASEAN established two committees, i.e. the ASEAN-China Joint Committee on Economic and Trade Cooperation, and the ASEAN-China Joint Committee on Science and Technology. Also in July 1994, the PRC joined and became one of the founding members of the ASEAN Regional Forum (ARF),[28] agreeing to have consultations on political and security issues of common concern with ASEAN countries.

In July 1996, China's linkage with Southeast Asia has taken a step further by its being accepted as a full dialogue partner of ASEAN. The outbreak of the Asian financial crisis gave China another opportunity to upgrade its relations with ASEAN, when the First ASEAN-China Summit (known as the "10+1" Summit) was convened in November 1997 and it has continued to be so to the present.[29] China then provided a loan of US$1 billion to Thailand under the framework of the IMF and also offered preferential loans to Burma, Vietnam, and Laos in 1997, not to mention China's grants in economic aid to Burma, Vietnam, Laos, Cambodia, and Indonesia also in the same year.

China's linkages with ASEAN continue to expand at the turn of the century. In November 2000 at the Fourth ASEAN-China Summit,[30] Mr Zhu Rongji, then Chinese Premier initiated a proposal to strengthen China's trade and economic relations with ASEAN, to establish a free trade area (FTA) between the two sides. After a series of talks among high-level officials between China and ASEAN, this proposal was officially announced in the November 2001 ASEAN-China Summit, and was enacted on 4 November 2002 at the Sixth ASEAN-China Summit in Phnom Penh, Cambodia, when Chinese Premier Zhu Rongji and ASEAN leaders signed the "Framework Agreement on Comprehensive Economic Co-operation between the ASEAN and the PRC". This framework laid the foundation for the eventual establishment of an ASEAN-China FTA by 2010 for ASEAN's older members and 2015 for the new members,[31] and this agreement went into force on July 1, 2003.

When China initiated the "Go Global" strategy in 2002, China and ASEAN started the First Economic and Trade Meeting for Economic Ministers in September 2002, in which Economic Ministers of both sides agreed on the "Framework Agreement on Comprehensive Economic Cooperation between the ASEAN and the PRC", which made the signing of this agreement possible later on 4 November 2002 at the summit. Also in September 2002, China and ASEAN started the First Meeting for Ministers of Transportation, showing a closer bilateral cooperation on transportation and communication related affairs. Later at the Sixth ASEAN-China Summit on 4 November 2002, leaders of China and ASEAN also publicized the Joint Declaration of ASEAN and China on Cooperation in the Field of Non-Traditional Security Issues, which set up priorities on bilateral cooperation on combating trafficking in illegal drugs, people-smuggling including trafficking in women and children, piracy on the high seas, terrorism, arms-smuggling, money-smuggling, money-laundering, international economic crime and cyber crime.[32]

China's linkages with ASEAN have continued to strengthen in recent years. China, for example, endorsed the Instrument of Accession to the Treaty of Amity and Cooperation (TAC) in Southeast Asia, which was originally enacted in 1976. Also in October 2003, leaders of China and ASEAN publicized the Declaration on Strategic Partnership for Peace and Prosperity, which was enforced by the signing of another Declaration on the Plan of Action to implement the above Declaration at the Eighth ASEAN-China Summit in November 2004.

China's recent economic linkages with ASEAN are particularly significant. During the Eighth China-ASEAN Summit on 29 November 2004 in Laos, leaders from both sides signed another three important documents, i.e. (1) Agreement on Trade in Goods, (2) Agreement on Dispute Settlement Mechanism of the Framework, and (3) Agreement on Comprehensive Economic Cooperation between ASEAN and PRC for China-ASEAN Free Trade Area. Both sides actually have started their tariff concession process since the beginning of July 2005 and the tariff of most products will be reduced to zero from 2005 to 2010, implying further economic cooperation and integration between the two.

It should be also noted that the ASEAN Plus Three (known as "10+3") was expanded to the East Asian Summit (EAS) when the EAS was first held in Kuala Lumpur on 14 December 2005. The EAS, including sixteen members, will be convened once every other year, which will give China another opportunity to play a larger role on the development of political economy in the entire region.

Conclusion

This paper has shown China's changing political economy with Malaysia and Southeast Asia as a whole, which started with China's three key policy initiatives. The open-door policy, introduced in 1979, was a comprehensive mechanism that changed China's overall relations with the world. The Good Neighbour policy of 1990 was directed at China's neighbours, and Southeast

Asia (including Malaysia) is regarded as one of China's most important neighbours. The "Go Global" strategy of 2002 aimed at bringing China's investments and enterprises abroad, in contrast to the open-door policy that brought in international capital into the Chinese market.

China experienced a confrontational relationship with Malaysia and Southeast Asia in the 1950s, 1960s, and 1970s, but because of the implantation of these three policies, China has changed its political economy with individual countries like Malaysia and also with the region as a whole. This paper has examined China's changing political economy with Malaysia and with Southeast Asia, from a low-key political economy to an extensive political economy with expanding economic relations and frequent political interactions.

Given the three policy initiatives from China and the ongoing developments between China and Malaysia as well as Southeast Asia since the late 1980s, it is apparent that China has changed its political economy with its neighbours in the South. Although some problems still exist between China and Southeast Asia (e.g. territorial disputes over the South China Sea, the threat of China's increasing military strength in the region) (Lee, 1993: 1095-1106), the Asian giant has abandoned its confrontational relationship with Southeast Asia, and a new page of accord with countries in Southeast Asia has been turned. Given China's sustained economic growth and the ongoing "going global" policy, it is predictable that China's political economy with Malaysia and Southeast Asia will continue to expand in the years ahead.

Notes

1. On the Communist-led coup in September 1965 in Indonesia, for example, Mr Adam Malik (former Foreign Minister of Indonesia) accused Beijing of complicity in the 1965 coup, in spite of Mr Malik's long support for the normalization of relations with the People's Republic of China. For details, see van der Kroef (1968).
2. China's trade volume with Malaysia was US$910 million in 1988.
3. Based on China's statistics, Malaysia is China's second largest trading partner in Southeast Asia.
4. These factors include the changing order of international political economy particularly after the end of the Cold War, China's domestic political and economic changes, and the changing economic order in the Asia-Pacific. For a comprehensive study on China's overall foreign policy, see Robison and Shambaugh (1995).
5. Mr Tun Razak, then Malaysia's Prime Minister paid an official visit to China in late May 1974, signing a joint communiqué of exchanging diplomatic recognition with the PRC.

6. By 2005, both countries have completed six meetings on joint economic and trade affairs.
7. For a comprehensive study on China's changing relations with Malaysia, see Liow (2005).
8. Mr Ghazali Shafie made a keynote speech at the Conference on "ASEAN: Today and Tomorrow" at Fletcher School of Law and Diplomacy in Boston, 11 November 1981.
9. In the *Yearbook of China's Diplomacy 1991*, China for the first time mentioned the focus of its diplomacy in 1990 was on the development of its relations with neighbouring countries, which initiated the so-called Good Neighbour Policy.
10. The EAS includes sixteen members, i.e. China, Japan, South Korea, India, Australia, New Zealand, and the ten ASEAN member states.
11. "Malaysia Assumes Larger, More Vital Role in Regional Affairs," *Straits Times*, 15 September 1994.
12. *Almanac of China's Foreign Economic Relations and Trade 1992/1993*, 1992: 426.
13. Indonesia also removed the restrictions on its citizens to visit China in 1991.
14. " World FDI Flows Grew an Estimated 6 per cent in 2004, Ending Downturn," UNCTAD Press Release. 11 January 2005. *<http://www.un.org/News/Press/docs/2005/tad2003.doc.htm>*
15. For instance, railway building in the south of Malaysia and a cement mill in Burma were two of the major projects undertaken in 2002. (*Yearbook of China's Foreign Economic Relations and Trade 2003*: 53.)
16. *Yearbook of China's Foreign Economic Relations and Trade 2003*: 52-53.
17. The figure of 2002 is from the *Yearbook of China's Foreign Economic Relations and Trade 2003*: 778, while the figure of 2003 is from the *China Commerce Yearbook 2004*: 668.
18. *China Statistical Yearbook 2002:* 630, and *China Statistical Yearbook 2004*: 732.
19. Mr Hu Jintao actually succeeded Mr Jiang Zemin as Secretary General of the Chinese Communist Party at the 16th National Party Congress in mid-2002.
20. Mr Nong Duc Manh became the new leader of the Communist Party of Vietnam at the Ninth National Party Congress in April 2001.
21. *Almanac of China's Foreign Economic Relations and Trade 1998/1999*, 1998: 420.
22. *Almanac of China's Foreign Economic Relations and Trade 2001*: 547.
23. *Yearbook of China's Foreign Economic Relations and Trade 2003*: 257-258.
24. *Yearbook of China's Foreign Economic Relations and Trade 2003*: 257.
25. *China Commerce Yearbook 2005*: 123.
26. According to *ASEAN Statistical Yearbook*, international arrivals refer to visitors from one country of residence to another. Based on this definition, Singapore visitors to Malaysia, for example, are counted as international arrivals.
27. *http://www.cnto.org/chinastats.asp#Stats* (30 April 2006).
28. Founded in July 1994, the objectives of the ARF are: (1) to foster constructive dialogue and consultation on political and security issues of common interest

and concern; and (2) to make significant contributions to efforts towards confidence-building and preventive diplomacy in the Asia-Pacific region. (*http://www.aseansec.org/3530.htm*, 21 July 2005)

29. The ASEAN Plus Three Summit (the three refers to China, Japan and South Korea) was also, for the first time, convened in November 1997, and China has been participating in the "10+3" Summit since then.
30. The Sixth ASEAN Summit was held at the same time.
31. The old members of ASEAN include Thailand, Malaysia, Singapore, Indonesia, the Philippines and Brunei), whereas ASEAN's new members are Vietnam, Cambodia, Laos, and Burma.
32. For details, visit *http://www.aseansec.org/13185.htm*

References

Almanac of China's Foreign Economic Relations and Trade 1992-93. Beijing: China's Foreign Economic Relations and Trade Publishing House.

Almanac of China's Foreign Economic Relations and Trade 1998-99. Beijing: China's Foreign Economic Relations and Trade Publishing House.

Almanac of China's Foreign Economic Relations and Trade 2001. Beijing: China's Foreign Economic Relations and Trade Publishing House.

ASEAN Secretariat. (2005) *ASEAN Statistical Yearbook, 2005*. Jakarta: ASEAN Secretariat.

ASEAN Secretariat. (2004) *ASEAN Statistical Yearbook, 2004*. Jakarta: ASEAN Secretariat.

Cheng, Joseph Y.S. (1999) " China's ASEAN Policy in the 1990s: Pushing for Regional Multipolarity," *Contemporary Southeast Asia* 21 (2), August, pp. 176-204.

Cheng, Joseph Y.S. (2001) "Sino-ASEAN Relations in the Early Twenty-first Century," *Contemporary Southeast Asia* 23 (3): 420-451.

China Statistical Yearbook 2002. Beijing: China Statistics Press.

China Statistical Yearbook 2004. Beijing: China Statistics Press.

Deng, Yong. (1992) "Sino-Thai Relations: From Strategic Cooperation to Economic Diplomacy," *Contemporary Southeast Asia* 13 (4), March, pp. 360-374.

Editorial Board of the China Commerce Yearbook. (2005) China Commerce Yearbook 2004. Beijing. China Commerce and Trade Press.

Editorial Office of Diplomatic History. (1991) *Board of Yearbook of China's Diplomacy 1991*. Beijing: World Knowledge Publisher.

Lee, Lai To. (1993) "ASEAN-PRC Political and Security Cooperation: Problems, Proposals, and Prospects," *Asian Survey* XXXIII (11), November, pp. 1095-1106.

Liow, Joseph Chinyong. (2005) "Balancing, Bandwagoning, or Hedging? Strategic and Security Patterns in Malaysia's Relations with China, 1981-2003" in Ho Khai Leong and Samuel C. Y. Ku, eds., (2005) *China and Southeast Asia: Global*

Changes and Regional Challenges. Singapore: Institute of Southeast Asian Studies.

Liow, Joseph Chin Yong. (2000) "Malaysia-China Relations in the 1990s: The Maturing of a Partnership," *Asian Survey* XL (4), July/August, pp. 672-690.

Muni, S. D. (2002) *China's Strategic Engagement with the New ASEAN*. Singapore: Institute of Defense and Strategic Studies, IDSS Monograph No.2.

Nam, Mak Joon. (1991) "The Chinese Navy and the South China Sea: A Malaysian Assessment," *Pacific Review* 4 (2): 145-158.

Robison, Thomas W. and David Shambaugh. (1995) *Chinese Foreign Policy: Theory and Practice*. Oxford: Oxford University Press.

Van der Kroef, Justus. (1968) "The Sino-Indonesian Rupture," *China Quarterly* 33: 20-35.

Yearbook of China's Foreign Economic Relations and Trade 2003. Beijing. China's Foreign Economic Relations and Trade Publishing House.

4

Sino-Malaysian Diplomacy in the Post-Cold War Period: A Regional Analysis

Li Yiping

Both Malaysia and China lie in East Asia, the most active area in the present world economic development. The political, cultural, economic relations and trade between these two countries have been extensively developed since they established the diplomatic relationship in 1974. As it came to the 1990s, Sino-Malaysian relations began to enter a new developing stage. Friendly exchanges and cooperation are being comprehensively outspread in all the realms.

China's Changes and Development in Solving the Issue of Its Relationship with the Surrounding Countries in the Post-Cold War Period

After the Cold War, China has shown more concerns on its relationship with the surrounding countries (*zhoubian guanxi* 周边关系) and taken real actions to improve it. It is the relationship between China and Southeast Asian countries that China first concerns and considers to improve so that this relationship could become the breakthrough in the improvement in relationship with the surrounding countries. At first, China became a conversational partner of ASEAN, and then gradually developed a generally better relationship with the Southeast Asian countries. Actually, there used to be quite a lot of problems in China's relationship with Southeast Asian countries, not only including disputes in territorial sea and islands, but a long-time difference on the political aspect, which is even more important. However, through great efforts, the comparatively trustful cooperative relationship between Southeast Asian countries and China has been gradually established.

In improving China's relations with Southeast Asia, it is the first time for China to realize that to develop its relationship with the surrounding countries is significant to the improvement of China's external environment in general.

Cooperation, Agreement on Agriculture Cooperation, Agreement on Space Cooperation and the Peaceful Use of Outer Space, Memorandum of Understanding on the Cooperation in the Employment of Chinese Workers, Memorandum of Exchange on Executing Malaysian Record Remote Sensing Cooperation Program, etc. In January 2004, Chairman Wu Bangguo of the Standing Committee of the NPC met with House Speaker Mohammed Zahir Ismail who came to China to attend the annual session of the Asia-Pacific Parliament Forum. In May of the same year, Malaysian Prime Minister Abdullah Ahmad Badawi visited China. He first held talks with Premier Wen Jiabao, President Hu Jintao, then together with Vice Premier Huang Ju attended the reception celebrating the 30th anniversary of the establishment of diplomatic relations between China and Malaysia. The series of agree ments signed by the two countries during his visit are: *Memorandum of Understanding between the Government of the People's Republic of China and the Government of Malaysia on Cooperation in the Field of Foreign Affairs and International Relations Education, Memorandum of Understanding between the Government of the People's Republic of China and the Government of Malaysia on Cooperation in the Field of Public Health and Plant Health* and *Memorandum of Cooperation Between China Mayor Association and Malaysia China Business Council.* Both sides reached important consensus on strengthening bilateral relations, agreed to boost strategic cooperation between the two countries and identified the direction to deepen bilateral relations, thus brought relations between the two sides to a new level, injecting new vitalities in cooperation in various fields of both countries. In October, State Councilor Tang Jiaxuan visited Malaysia, meeting separately with Prime Minister Abdullah Ahmad Badawi and Vice Prime Minster Najib Tun Razak. In November, while attending a series of meetings by Chinese and ASEAN leaders in Laos, Premier Wen Jiabao met with Prime Minister Abdullah Ahmad Badawi.

In March 2005, Malaysian Supreme Head of State Sultan Salahuddin visited China. In April, Chairman Jia Qinglin of the CPPCC met in Hainan with Malaysian Prime Minister Abdullah Ahmad Badawi, who attended the annual session of Bo' ao Asian Forum. In May, Chairman Wu Bangguo of the Standing Committee of the NPC paid an official goodwill visit to Malaysia. In September, at the invitation of Vice Premier Huang Ju, Malaysian Vice Prime Minister Najib Tun Razak paid a state visit to China. In December 2005, at the invitation of Malaysian Prime Minister Abdullah Ahmad Badawi, Chinese Premier Wen Jiabao of the State Council paid an official visit to Malaysia, where the two officials co-issued *Joint Communiqué Between the People's Republic of China and Malaysia.*

Exchanges of high-level visits have been playing an important part in boosting the development of bilateral relations.

Furthermore, the two countries hold identical or similar standpoints and views in many important global and regional issues such as the United Nations reform, East Asian cooperation, and coordinate well. Both believe that people in each country should determine their own affairs and world affairs should be equally negotiated between countries; that cultural diversity should be respected; that competing ones should learn from other's strong points to make up for their own deficiencies, and to achieve co-prosperity by seeking common ground while reserving differences; that economic globalization should benefit all developing countries, and should positively push forward South-South cooperation and North-South dialogue as well as regional cooperation to realize co-prosperity. China, which appreciates and supports Malaysia's standpoint and attitude of actively participating in regional and global affairs, in opposing hegemony, in doing justice to all and boosting actively the cooperation and development of developing countries in international relations, participated first ASEAN-China, then ASEAN+3 and East Asian Summit organized by Malaysia. Former Prime Minister Mahathir Mohamad for many times publicly refuted the so-called "China Threat Theory". Prime Minister Abdullah Ahmad Badawi also pointed out explicitly that "the development of China is rather an opportunity than a threat to Malaysia. We regard China as a reliable friend."(Ministry of Foreign Affairs of PRC, December 15, 2005) On issues like human rights, democracy and China's peaceful reunification, Malaysia explicitly demonstrated their support for China, and played an important role in boosting China-ASEAN cooperation. The two countries have been cooperating in issues involving regional and bilateral securities of anti-terrorism, preventing and checking acute diseases from spreading, anti-drug campaign, and cracking down on cross-border crimes. Even though they have disputes over the ownership of some islands in the Nansha Archipelago, they could proceed from maintaining peace and stability of the South China Sea, expressed many times that the disputes should be solved by friendly consultants and negotiations with other countries concerned to implement the follow-up actions of the *Declaration on the Conduct of Parties in the South China Sea*, according to established principles of international law.

In military cooperation, with the establishment of military attaché offices in both countries in 1995, China and Malaysia have witnessed growing contacts and exchanges of visits between their military circles. China's navy formation fleet visited Malaysia in 1997 and 2000. In August 2002, Malaysia's fleet visited China for the third time. In September 2002, Vice-

Chairman of the Central Military Commission, State Councilor and Minister of Defense Chi Haotian made a stopover in Malaysia and had a meeting with the Malaysian Minister of Defense Najib. In September 2003, Chief of the General Staff of the People's Liberation Army Liang Guanglie met with Prime Minister Mahathir Mohamad, Minister of Defense Najib and Chief of Defense Forces General Mohd Zahidi Zainuddin during his visit to Malaysia. In September 2004, Vice-Chairman of the Central Military Commission Guo Boxiong made a stopover in Malaysia and met with Deputy Prime Minister and Minister of Defense Najib. In September 2005, the ministries of defense of both countries signed the *Memorandum of Understanding in Defense Cooperation*, in which both countries agreed that Sino-Malaysian Defense Security Negotiation regime should be established as soon as possible under the framework set by this memorandum of understanding. The Malaysian side also welcomes China's positive contribution for the security of the Malacca Strait as a major user of this strait.

Shifting our focus from bilateral political relations and security contacts to economics and trade, very rapid development is witnessed in the recent bilateral economic and trade relations between China and Malaysia. The total volume has been such that it ranks among top in each country's foreign economic and trade relations, which have become the foundations and links of the stable development between the two countries.

Statistics on the Chinese side shows that bilateral trade volume has expanded 21 times from 1990 to 2004. The trade volume between China and Malaysia takes up one quarter of that between China and ASEAN. The trade volume between China and Malaysia in 2001 totaled 9.425 billion US dollars; the figure in 2002 has exceeded US$10 billion to US$14.271 billion, an increase of 51.4 per cent. Malaysia for the first time overtook Singapore to become the first trade partner in ASEAN. The trade volume between the two countries in 2003 even exceeded US$20 billion, to US$20.13 billion, up 41 per cent the previous year, of which China's exports registered US$6.14 billion and its imports US$13.99 billions, up 23 per cent and 50 per cent respectively. Malaysia again ranked first in ASEAN nations' trade to China. The trade volume of the two countries in 2004 was up to US$26.26 billion. During the same period, China's position in Malaysia's foreign trade is also elevating, after the United States, Japan and Singapore, ranking the fourth as trade partner. By 2010, trade volume between the two countries is expected to amount to or exceed US$50 billion. Mutual investment also constitutes an important part in bilateral economic and trade relations. In 2003, there are 350 Malaysian investment projects in China with a total commitment of US$960 million, up 20.8 per cent, of which US$250 million has already been realized, down 31.8 per cent. In the first 10 months of 2004, there are 278 Malaysian investment projects in China with a total commitment of US$969 million, up 15.2 per cent, of which US$359 million has already been realized, up 75 per cent. As of October 2004, there are 3166 Malaysian investment projects in China with a total commitment of US$8.13 billion, of which 3.45 billion has been realized. Compared with ASEAN nations' investment to China, the absolute sum of investment from China to Malaysia is relatively small, but with greater potential and rapid growth. In recent years, with the implementation of the Going Global Strategy, more and more Chinese enterprises actively invest abroad. As China's peripheral neighbours, Southeast Asian countries, abundant in resources, their economy being complementary with China's economy, thus become the key area for the Chinese enterprises to go global. As of June 2003, China has set up 101 wholly China-owned enterprises with a total commitment of US$38.42 billion. The development in Sino-Malaysian trade structure demonstrated that bilateral economic and trade relations are deepening and exploiting new fields. China is the main importer of Malaysian's electronic products, palm oil and rubber, etc. The cooperation in a series of key fields set by the two sides such as agriculture, high-tech, resource development and infrastructure construction, etc. is in full swing with no signs of slowing down. Cooperation projects launched have achieved initial success. Tourism and education cooperation experienced rapid development. There are over 100 round-trip airlines every week between China and Malaysia. The number of yearly personnel traveling between the two countries reached more than 1 million person-times. Over 13,000 Chinese students are now studying in Malaysia, while the number of Malaysian students in China exceeds 1,000. China has been one of Malaysia's major sources of overseas tourists and students.

The rapid development in the political, economic and trade relations between China and Malaysia is facilitated by favourable conditions in many ways.

First, as developing countries and close neighbours, the two countries both hope for peaceful surroundings, regional and international, so that they can dedicate themselves to social and economic developments. In the post-Cold War settings in which international relations set-up is undergoing significant changes, both China and Malaysia feel the urge to maintain peace and stability in East Asia, while cooperating for the implementation of economic cooperation and development in this region and with other countries. Both sides uphold the Five Principles of Peaceful Coexistence as the principles in promoting bilateral relations, while adamantly pursuing foreign policies that facilitate good neighbourliness and mutual trust. Above are the important factors that have accelerated Sino-Malaysian relations.

Second, leaders of both countries have been paying close attention to the development in bilateral relations. To quote a speech made by the former Malaysian Ambassador to China Abdul Majid Ahmad at the Asia-Pacific Forum held by the Institute for Research on Asia Pacific of the Chinese Academy of Social Science in July 17, 2003: "The visits to Malaysia and other Southeast Asian countries paid by Mr Deng Xiaoping and the changes in China's foreign policy would help to modify Malaysia's opinions on China... Malaysian Prime Minister Datuk Seri Mahathir bin Mohamad's dynamic foreign policy and his assertion to actively contact China, and the assertion in which he urged Asia to play a more important role in international affairs, made Malaysia realize the importance of strengthening and expanding Sino-Malaysian relations" (Abdul Majid Ahmad, 2003). On the one hand, frequent visits by leaders of both countries inject vitalities in the development of bilateral relations; on the other hand, senior officials in both countries have been able to attach importance to bilateral relations from the strategic altitude and in the long run, therefore the development of Sino-Malaysian friendship has been greatly boosted.

Third, economic development has been good in both countries; especially the high growth rate the Chinese economy has sustained has laid a solid foundation for the economic and trade relations between the two sides. China has quickened its pace in opening to the outside world since 1992. Its economy has been taking the lead, which maintained a high growth rate of not less than 7 per cent, even during the East Asian financial crisis. Not only that, its trade volume experienced a rapid and corresponding expansion as well. By 2005, China's gross domestic product (GDP) has attained as much as 18.2321 trillion Rmb (renminbi), its volume of foreign trade totaled US$1.42212 trillion, an increase of 23.2 per cent of which its exports registered US$762 billion and its imports US$660.12 billion (up 28.4 per cent and 17.6 per cent respectively), which is 2.8 times that of 2001. China's foreign trade has experienced a growth rate of over 20 per cent in four consecutive years since 2002, the volume of which remained the third in the world. In the first 11 months of 2005, China-ASEAN trade volume has totaled US$117.24 billion, up 23.5 per cent from the same period of the previous year, of which its exports registered US$49.83 billion and imports US$67.41 billion, up 31.1 and 18.4 per cent respectively. ASEAN continued to be the fifth trade partner, the fifth export market and the fourth source of import to China (Department of Foreign Investment Administration, Ministry of

Commerce of the People's Republic of China, 2006). The huge market scale and the potentiality of sustained development China enjoys furnish various opportunities for the rapidly expanding bilateral economic and trade relations between China and Malaysia. Although the Malaysian economy was under huge impact from the East Asia financial crisis, it quickly got rid of the negative effects the crisis brought and has been in recovery and back to the track again by the Malaysian government's effective reactions.

Fourth, bilateral economic and trade relations has gradually achieved regularization and legitimization. The two countries signed over 10 economic and trade cooperation agreements, such as, *the Agreement on Avoidance of Double Taxation, Trade Agreement, Agreement on Investment Protection, Shipping Agreement* and *Air Transport Agreement, Memorandum of Understanding on Aviation Cooperation*, etc. In 1999, the two countries signed the *Joint Statement on Framework for the Future Bilateral Cooperation*, which furnished gradually improved and regulated institutional environment for the development of bilateral relations. Moreover, both countries set up a Joint Committee of Economy and Trade. In 1992, *Scientific and Technological Agreement* was signed and a joint committee of science and technology was set up. In 2002, a bilateral business council was established. The establishment of these agencies and institutions has become important bilateral institutional arrangement for the negotiations and communications between these two countries.

Fifth, the import and export composition of the two countries is in continual optimization; the status of high-tech products in bilateral trade has been on the rise yearly, on the basis that the complementarity of products in bilateral trade benefits the stable development of bilateral trade. Of China's trade volume with Malaysia, almost 40 per cent of products are evidently complementary, of which China's exports – mainly grain, food and cooking oil, fruits and vegetables, local cattle, light textile products, while vessels, iron and cements, etc. – grew rapidly in the last two years. China's imports are mainly resource products, such as palm oil, lumber, rubber, etc. The remaining 60 per cent of bilateral trade is machinery and electronic products, of which what China imported – electronic components, such as integrated circuits, etc. – took up a very large portion, while its exporting machinery and electronic products to Malaysia are relatively abundant in general machinery products. These structural differences and continual optimization also formed certain complementarity. Although of the total volume in Sino-Malaysian trade, resource products take up a large portion, with very low actual tariffs, the China-ASEAN Free Trade Area would greatly reduce the management costs. At the same time, the increase in demand led by China's economic development will bring about further strengthening of trade and other economic relations.

Sixth, China and Malaysia participated together in multi-level international political economic cooperation. The interests and standpoints of both sides are basically identical. As the effects of geopolitical and geo-economic factors are on the rise, countries like China and Malaysia regard peace and development as their strategic priorities for nation building. To develop mutual political and economic cooperation has been the urge and common necessity for China and Malaysia to pursue socioeconomic development. In international political and economic cooperation, both sides advocate the democratization of international relations, the reduction of the limits to international trade and investment activities. Therefore, the two countries adopt similar standpoints when participating in multilateral cooperation organizations of different spheres, such as the United Nations, the World Trade Organization, the Asia Pacific Economic Cooperation Organization, etc. It is notable that both countries collaborate with other members of ASEAN in pushing forward the negotiations of establishing China-ASEAN Free Trade Area, actively promote the liberalization and facilitation of the process of trade and investment. These multidimensional cooperation in various spheres not only furnished wider ranges of institutional guarantee for both side to participate in activities in the international society, but the achievements of these cooperation also directly boosted the rapid development of bilateral relations.

To predict the trend of future development, the above-mentioned active factors will continue to play important parts. Therefore, the prospects for the bilateral development will be positive and stable.

However, the development of bilateral relations still rests on the continual exploitation and perfection from the two parties. As the manufacturing industry of the two countries expand and upgrade, the similarity of the product composition in bilateral trade will go up, relatively reducing the complementarity. Thus product competition between the two countries will to some extent escalate, which involves both parties to elevate each enterprise' competitiveness, while under open market situation. From 1991 to 2002, Malaysia had been in favourable balance of trade for 12 consecutive years, the sum of trade surplus amounted to US$18.393 billion (Liao, 2005). For the Chinese side, the trade deficit it suffered had been too large, which means Chinese enterprises should increase product competitiveness as quickly as possible, trying their best to exploit the Malaysian market while the Malaysian market is to be more open. For the Malaysian side, China will further open up its market to fulfill commitments on its entry into the World Trade

Organization, and at the same time more foreign investment brought into China would develop more new industries and products, which will constitute huge competitive pressure on Malaysian products. This also requires Malaysian enterprises to make their products more competitive in order to maintain their share in the Chinese market.

Moreover, since the 1990s, nongovernmental contacts between China and Malaysia have been increasingly frequent, greatly facilitating the development of bilateral relations. This situation has also been exploited by lawless intermediaries and criminal gangs. Negative incidents happen repeatedly, such as China nationals being illegally detained in Malaysia, and China students studying in Malaysia and China tourists in Malaysia being swindled. These specific problems of civil disputes and crimes due to the increased bilateral cooperation and contacts have aroused attention from the senior officials in both countries. As long as both governments could treat them seriously, take effective measures, create conditions for normal contacts between the two countries, these unpleasant episodes would not hamper regular developments of bilateral relations.

Conclusion

The regional strategy of Malaysia is to keep equilibrium among great powers in this area and to enforce the cooperation between great powers and ASEAN members so that regional stability and Malaysian national interests could be preserved. China also thinks that stable surroundings can offer important conditions for its peace and development. This has resulted in "double win" on Sino-Malaysia relations after the Cold War.

As for future Sino-Malaysian relations, Malaysia believes that the prosperity and development of China will bring about positive multidimensional influence on Malaysia and this area. So Malaysia does hope that these two countries could establish closer economic and trade relations, enlarging trade, increasing two-way investment and enforcing mutual cooperation in energies, finance and so on. In December 2005, when Premier Wen Jiabao visited Malaysia, he also expressed himself like this: "The Chinese side would like to work with the Malaysian side to strengthen the cooperation in the following areas: first, maintaining high-level contacts and enhancing mutual understanding and trust; second, the two foreign ministries should work together to formulate joint action plans for China-Malaysian strategic cooperation and make concrete arrangements for the cooperation in every area; third, further expanding bilateral trade, promoting energy cooperation and discussing the common exploration of the gas and oil resources in South China Sea; fourth, strengthening the coordination and collaboration in the East Asian cooperation process and pushing for constant growth of East Asian cooperation. " (Ministry of Foreign Affairs of PRC, December 15, 2005)

The development of Sino-Malaysian relations is becoming a successful example for China to develop its relationship with the surrounding countries. The constant development of Sino-Malaysian relations will facilitate the peace and prosperity of this area.

References

Abdul Majid Ahmad 阿卜杜勒·马吉德·阿哈迈德 (2003), "Zhong-Ma Guanxi yu Malaixiya de Duiwai Zhengce 中马关系与马来西亚的对外政策" (Sino-Malaysian Relations and Malaysia's Foreign Policy), *Dangdai Yatai 当代亚太 (Contemporary Asia-Pacific Studies)*, September, No. 105, pp. 3-6.

Department of Foreign Investment Administration, Ministry of Commerce of the People's Republic of China (2006), "2005 Nian Zhuangao: Zhongguo-Dongmeng Jingmao Hezuo Jinru Quanmian Fazhan Xin Jieduan 2005 年专稿: 中国-东盟经贸合作进入全面发展新阶段" (Special Publication of the year 2005: "China-ASEAN Economic and Trade Cooperation into a New Stage of General Development"), January 9, 2006, *http://finance.sina.com.cn/roll/20060109/1036486260.shtml/*

Huang, Lin 黄琳 (2005), "Jiedu Zhongguo Xin Waijiao Zhanlüetu: Quanfangwei Heping Waijiao Chuxian Jinzhan 解读中国新外交战略图: 全方位和平外交出现进展" (Comprehension of China's New Diplomatic Strategic Chart: Progress in All-Direction Diplomacy), November 9, 2005, *http://news3.xinhuanet.com/world/2005-11/09/content_3756767.htm/*

Li, Peng 李鹏 (1993), "Zhengfu Gongzuo Baogao 政府工作报告" (Government Work Report), *Renmin Ribao 人民日报 (People's Daily)*, Overseas Edition, April 2, 1993.

Liao, Xiaojian 廖小健 (2005), "Lengzhan Hou Zhong-Ma Guanxi de Hudong yu Shuangying 冷战后中马关系的互动与双赢" (The Interaction and Win-Win Condition of Sino-Malaysian Relations in the Post-Cold War Period), *Dangdai Yatai 当代亚太 (Contemporary Asia-pacific Studies)*, April, No. 124, pp. 56-59.

Ministry of Foreign Affairs of the People's Republic of China (2005), 双边关系 (Bilateral Relations), *http://www.fmprc.gov.cn/chn/wjb/zzjg/yzs/gjlb/1256/default.html/*

Ministry of Foreign Affairs of the People's Republic of China (2005), "Wen Jiabao yu Malaixiya Zongli Badawei Huitan 温家宝与马来西亚总理巴达维会谈" (Premier Wen Jiabao Holds Talks with Malaysian Prime Minister Abdullah Badawi), December 15, 2005, *http://www.fmprc.gov.cn/eng/wjdt/wshd/t227520.htm/*

5

The Globalization Impact on Malaysia-China Political Relations

K.S. Balakrishnan

Introduction

Globalization is not a recent phenomenon. Historians and anthropologists can relate it back to the ancient era. However, contemporary perspectives on globalization revolve mainly around the economic, political, security, social and technological spheres.[1] Where Malaysia-China political relations are concerned, one can trace interactions and policies that are mainly grounded on some of the above fields. Malaysia's political relations with China have improved significantly in the last two decades or so. While the initial establishment of diplomatic relations served mainly the security and internal political interest, recent developments portray the rise of economic globalization influenced mainly by the trade and investment relations in line with the global capital and liberalization agenda. Will it bring about harmony remains to be seen. What seems to be more promising is that political relations between the Communist China and the democratic Malaysia have improved in an unprecedented manner. This paper will examine the new developments in political relations and offer some analysis.

Early Historical Context and the Current Constructive Engagement Strategy

Political relations between China and the Malay world can be traced back to the Han Dynasty, 206BC-220AD. This was a period popularly known for trading and the tributary system very well covered in many scholarly writings. The second crucial period of political and diplomatic contact was popularized by the Ming Dynasty, 1368-1644. The arrival of Admiral Zheng He (Cheng Ho) during the 15th century marked an important version of maritime diplomacy and political contact. It was also a period whereby scholars are debating that the Chinese discovered America first and later by Columbus. The debate on China's naval expeditions to Southeast Asia was benign or militaristic is still ongoing. However, to find the right answer, one has to analyse the tributary system that was established. The idea of small states offering tribute to big power under the feudal international system can be generally argued in the context of fear and respect. Numerous naval expeditions can send signals to the sultanates on potential threats.

However the arrival of Admiral Zheng He to the Malay land, especially in Malacca must be viewed from two perspectives. The first is from the perspective of a Muslim Admiral arriving to establishing hegemony and influence. Second is the fact that smaller international trading ports like Malacca viewing it positively in the context of enriching the sultanates and its future survival. In both scenarios, the idea of fear and friendship had dominated politico-security thinking of the epoch. The survival strategy of the Malacca sultanates in that epoch vis-à-vis the rise of Chinese influence can once again be equated in analysing politics, diplomacy, and foreign policy of a post-modern Malaysia. It is indeed not too far fetched that it is national interests, survival and fear dominates patterns of smaller states' political relations with great power. In a civilised world where norms of international relations dominate inter-state relations between the big China and small Malaysia, it is indeed a fashion for leaders to use common terms such as "pragmatism, mutual interests and benefits" in explaining the nature of political bilateral relations. Leadership in Kuala Lumpur is no exception. The realization to engage the rising China in a positive way is perhaps the best possible strategic option available for Malaysia, despite its historical animosity after several decades of threat-based relationship caused by the communist uprising, ideological differences, insurgency and continuous Beijing support for the Malayan communist party. It is also important to note that, the visit of Tun Abdul Razak in 1974 did not halt Beijing's support for the CPM in any significant way.

Notwithstanding these strategic and historical impediments, Malaysia's foreign policy statements and implementations in the decades of Mahathir's rule and followed by his successor can be regarded as the most successful one. The strategic policy of "constructive engagement" and promoting national interests via economic pragmatism has prevailed all along since end of Cold War. And of course the peace agreement that resulted in CPM ending their armed struggle in 1989 paved the right climate for fostering the stronger relationship with China both politically as well as in the economic field. While these factors may appear influential in foreign policy decisions of Malaysia, the most glaring one is still based upon "economic pragmatism" whereby the overall gain outweigh the perceived and actual problems hinge upon the nature of bilateral relations. The peaceful rise of China's economy following Deng's modernization has a significant impact on Malaysia's perception. The years of late 1980s and 1990s have portrayed the strength and potential of China's social market economy to the world on what it is capable. Because of its prudent policy Malaysia too benefited significantly by increase its trade with China tenfold. While problems exist in various areas, it is important to point out that the overall results of the "constructive engagement" strategy has been phenomenal.

Tun Abdul Razak's Historic Visit and Its Impact Upon Political Relations

All Malaysian prime ministers had visited China except for, Tunku Abdul Rahman. Malaysia's foreign policy under Tunku was often explained by scholars as pro-western and very much anti-communist. The arrival of Tun Abdul Razak at the pinnacle of national politics after the 1969 riot resulted in major policy shift not only in managing the internal national security problems but also that of the external environment. The link between the internal and external threat cannot be looked in isolation. Malaysia has a substantial Chinese population in which case the offering of an olive branch in establishing diplomatic relations with China would also means making peace with the Chinese both inside and outside Malaya. From a strategic point of view, it means "winning the hearts and minds" of the guerrillas and ensuring that CPM's membership recruitment inside Malaysia would reduce. It will also be consistent with some of the policies to thwart the spread of communist activities which may increase if left unchecked due to the racial riot that caused significant lost for the non-Malays in Malaysia in that year. The establishment of the formal relations could also enhance the prestige of the government in the context of the oncoming election. In fact the result was tremendous for Tun Abdul Razak and the National Front which swept 135 of the 154 federal seats contested in 1974.[2] The effect of the visit in a way managed to decommunalise politics at certain level for gaining massive support for the National Front formula and consociational politics at that time. Other domestic considerations for establishing an Embassy was also crucial given the presence of non-citizen Chinese. Tan Sri Michael Chen who was part of the ping pong diplomacy in the early 70s and followed Tun Razak in 1974 highlighted the importance of resolving some 200,000 Chinese who were red identity card holders then. In his view the work towards improving relations started in 1971 via Malaysia's ping pong diplomacy in which case Tun Razak gave a letter to thank Premier Zhou Enlai much earlier. In those years, the salient point was not economy. Malaysia had a more serious concern for the communist threat and the domestic political considerations in line with ensuring stability and gaining the support of the Chinese population within. Friendship with the mainland was crucial.

From the perspective of international relations, Tun Razak created some new dimensions in Malaysia's foreign policy. The visit to China in 1974 cannot be contextualized if not for the adoption of a neutralization approach towards great powers in the region. The creation of the Zone of peace, freedom and neutrality (ZOPFAN) in 1971 in Kuala Lumpur boosted the role of ASEAN and Malaysia's foreign policy with a realization it was important to avert the region and country from great power rivalry. Tan Sri Ghazali Shafie explained neutralization in the context of an "act which brings about a state of neutralism" which can be referred to foreign policy of state or region. In October 1971, he explained the importance of both the United States and the Soviet Union coming to terms with China.[3] From a foreign policy point of view, Tun Razak's administration was quite clear about the importance of engaging China by 1971. The principle for the significant shift in foreign policy then was heavily based on both neutralization and non-alignment. Unlike the other Southeast Asia neighbours, Malaysia was in fact far ahead in thinking and ensuring that China cannot be avoided but vital to be engaged.

One of the fundamental reasons for moving away from heavily relying on the west was mainly due to the withdrawal of United Kingdom from providing the necessary security umbrella. The Australians too was ambivalent in their role in providing sufficient support after the 1969 riot. And most importantly, the arrangements with Western allies via the Five Power Defence Arrangement (FPDA) in 1970 only resulted in forming a security alliance which did not guarantee that Malaysia will be defended by its colonial friends. The timing was also crucial given China's assistance to Vietnam and the emerging strength of the communist in mainland Southeast Asia. Amidst all these strategic changes, the role played by the United States in a way helped Malaysia to be confident in its move to engage China and establish diplomatic relations. US foreign policy under President Nixon popularly known as the Nixon Doctrine emphasized on relaxation of tension with the communist world. Nixon visited China in February 1972 and struck an understanding to increase economic, cultural and scientific cooperation as well as to send a senior United States representative to Peking from time to time for enhancing consultations and normalization of the bilateral relations.[4]

In sum Tun Razak's vision and implementations of political relations with China were mainly influenced by the desire to manage Malaysian foreign policy prudently. Foreign policy of Malaysia at that time was tailored to address issues that were mainly geostrategic and security challenges. Strengthening political relations with China was inevitable and necessary for national survival especially for Malaysia when its armed forces were not well equipped. Normalizing relations with China was an essential political and security strategy in the wake of the communist uprising. It was also further influenced by the US normalization strategy in a way especially by the Nixon doctrine. While the globalization process of the epoch can be discussed from the security and ideological perspective, Tun Razak's initiative was not based on economic or trade objectives. Cold War and ideological differences were paramount in restoring relations. Despite establishing diplomatic relation in May 1974, bilateral relations did not improve much for many years because of security suspicion.[5] Political relations with China were not all that warm. However the continuity of the bilateral was not severed. Deng Xiaoping visited Malaysia in 1979 and the visit was later reciprocated by Tun Hussein Onn. Despite the exchange of visits, it cannot be argued that Malaysia enjoyed a warm or strong bilateral relation with China during that period. As for Malaysia, those visits were crucial to send very clear messages to the domestic audience and the external powers that it seeks peace and harmony from within and internationally. The result of this grand strategy could only be reaped in tenfold as Malaysia marched into the 1990s and at the dawn of the 21st century.

Diplomatic Reinforcement and Political Relations Under the Mahathir Administration

A new wave was clearly seen in the early days of Prime Minister Dr Mahathir's administration. He made an official visit to China in the year of 1985. This trip paved a path in terms of economic relations. Though economic cooperation existed previously, both nations only increased multidimensional economic cooperation after the Economic and Trade Joint Commission was formed in 1992.[6] Delegation wise, Mahathir's visit to China in 1985 had a smaller number of delegates compared to the big delegation that accompanied him during his June 1993 trip. In fact the June 1993 trip opened a new chapter in Malaysia's policy towards China. Since that visit, a larger group of Chinese high-level officials visited Malaysia. Mahathir himself led five official trips after his trips in 1985 and 1993. His deputies, Datuk Seri Anwar Ibrahim and Datuk Seri Abdullah Ahmad Badawi have also made official visits while serving under the Mahathir administration.

Prominent leaders from China have also visited Malaysia during the Mahathir era. President Jiang Zemin visited Kuala Lumpur in November 1994. Other high-ranking officials such as Li Peng and Zhu Rongji are among the influential officials who have visited Malaysia. The new President of China Hu Jiantao has also visited Malaysia during the Mahathir era in April 2002. On the whole, the Mahathir period is the most successful period in strengthening diplomatic relations. China's ambassador to Malaysia, HE Mr Hu Zhengyu opined that Mahathir knew several generations of Chinese leaders and formed what can be termed as personal chemistry with China. It was further solidified through visits by HRH Sultan Azlan Shah, Tuanku Jaafar and Sultan Sallahuddin in 1990s.[7]

Enhancement of bilateral diplomatic relations was made through various policies, initiatives and through additional delegations. Each delegation that visited China with Mahathir consisted of key ministers, leading business figures and media representatives. Apart from that, International Trade & Industry Minister, Datuk Rafidah Aziz also visited China on different occasions with groups of businessmen and investors. In addition, there were also trips made by the Transport Minister and Tourism Minister. Mahathir also ensured that bilateral relations are further strengthened through special initiatives and clearer policies so that misunderstandings and strains in the Malaysia-China relations can be monitored and solved amicably.

Apart from the 1992 Trade and Economic Joint Commission, another popular initiative was undertaken when Mahathir signed the Joint Statement on framework for Future Bilateral relations on 31st May 1994.[8] The joint statement signing ceremony has opened a larger scope in further widening bilateral relations in line with the needs and demands of the twenty first century. The introduction of foreign policy in this particular signifies that intelligent strategic moves are vital in reducing forthcoming tensions that would escalate due to a difference in political stands or security policies over a variety of issues such as the Taiwan and Spratlys issues.

Apart from the policy initiatives stated above, Mahathir has also encouraged the role of the private sector from various perspectives. He has clearly encouraged Malaysia-China Friendship Society (MCFS). This organization has been active in increasing cooperation at the societal and private sector level. It is also supported by Malaysian Chinese Chamber of Commerce and Industry (MCCCI). The role of these agencies in increasing bilateral relations through various activities such as organising conferences, conventions and major expos in Malaysia and China is a good combination in Mahathir's policy that frequently prioritises the role of private sector in national development. From an analytical view it exemplifies the role of civil society in influencing foreign policy so that profit can be enjoyed by the nation and its people. China has also encouraged the roles played by its private sector and relevant associations.

Generally, Mahathir's policy toward China signifies several common key factors within the context of Malaysia's relations with the developing world.[9] As a developing nation with progressive policies towards the rise and development of East Asia, Kuala Lumpur has clear, defined and indivisible stand to witness the rise of China in a positive context. Even though several Western nations and small nations are worried about the rise of China, the Malaysian government, especially Dr Mahathir has called upon the United States and Japan to see China as an opportunity instead of a foe on several occasions. This similar stand has also been taken by Datuk Seri Abdullah Ahmad Badawi since taking over the administration in October 2003. Mahathir also often advised other nations to cooperate with China as it was more profitable than seeing China as an enemy. These policies have brought positive results to the extent that China has become Malaysia's fourth largest trading partner.

The outcome of Mahathir's pragmatic and positive foreign policy has created advantages at the international level. A glaring example is China's support towards Mahathir's foreign policy initiatives. China has been rendering its full support towards realising the idea of East Asia Economic Group (EAEG).[10] Though EAEG has not materialized, this institution has been formed through ASEAN Plus Three meetings where Japan, South Korea and China are key members. China's role in these initiatives to develop the East Asian economic and political interest is in line with Malaysia's policy. China has also formed a Davos version of the World Economic Forum that gives emphasis on towards Asian and Asia Pacific interests.[11]

During the Asian economic crisis, China continued to support capital and currency control policy introduced by Malaysia. In fact China was steadfast in their stand to maintain their currency value in spite of external pressure. This policy helped to stabilise East Asian economies. China has also been positively looking at ideas to create the East Asian Monetary Fund that is supported by ASEAN and other East Asian nations. As far as Malaysia is concerned, it has supported China's entry into the World Trade Organization (WTO) in 2002. Presently, both China and Malaysia feel that ASEAN and China must speak in a concerted voice to defend the interests of developing nations in the WTO. Apart from that ASEAN and China have agreed to form

ASEAN-China Free Trade Area (ACFTA) in 2010. The formation of ACFTA would intensify Malaysia-China bilateral trade relations if it is carried at the top most level. This is because, even though China is a member of the WTO, liberal economic policies have not been exercised thoroughly. Many practices at the national and domestic levels can still be improved especially in the realm of tax and trade tariffs. China's ability to monitor and control certain sectors of the economy as well as its continuity of political authoritarianism has influenced economic liberalization policies and thus cannot be denied.[12] While challenges continued trade between Malaysia and China increased from RM1 billion in 1980 to RM76 billion (US$20 billion) in 2003. By 2002, Malaysian investment in China reached RM11.4 in 2500 projects. China too began to invest in billion dollar projects.[13] In sum economic globalization had strengthened bilateral political relations in an unprecedented way.

Political Relations under the Abdullah Administration

The bilateral political relations between Malaysia and China under Prime Minister Abdullah Ahmad Badawi have flourished in a significant way. Malaysia's national interest was enhanced in strategic areas by courting China in a positive manner. Noting the fact that Malaysia would host the East Asia Summit in 2005, a pet project of the previous administration popularly know as the EAEC or EAEG under Dr Mahathir, Mr Abdullah Ahmad Badawi and his Deputy, Datuk Seri Najib Tun Razak played pivotal role in ensuring China fully support Malaysia's gigantic diplomatic project for setting up the East Asian Economic Grouping. Though EAEG still operates under the ambit of ASEAN consensus, it is globally known that the idea was mooted by Dr Mahathir to counter the weight of Western influence through APEC and other projects. Mahathir's success of witnessing ASEAN Plus Three emerging as an East Asian Summit after 15 years under his protégé Prime Minister Abdullah Ahmad Badawi in a way manifest consistency that Malaysia-China political relations has truly matured.

Mr Abdullah visited China in May 2004. The visit was extremely significant because Beijing became the first capital outside ASEAN for the Prime Minister since assuming office in 1 November 2003. The visit signifies where and at what level Malaysia positions China in its foreign policy priorities. More or less, one could argue that China has truly become an important component of Malaysia's Look East foreign policy which earlier emphasized on Japan and South Korea in the 80s. As both Japan and South Korea was slow in responding to EAEC, the Asian financial crisis led the two join ASEAN Plus Three. China's consistent support for EAEG and the

East Asian summit was a victory for Malaysia being the first host nation of the summit and ended positively involving others like Australia and India. Like Dr Mahathir, Abdullah seems to have developed close political link with Beijing. Describing Abdullah's previous visit, Dato Muhammad Noh, acknowledged that the personal chemistry was very good with leaders of China.[14] Abdullah was also accorded more time by Chinese leaders during his visit in 2004.

Bilateral trade with China had increased from US$14.1 billion in 2003 to US$18.8 billion in 2004 and by 2005 it surpassed US$20 billion.[15] There is now a prediction that if current momentum persists trade with China will reach US$50b by 2010. With such optimism, Malaysia political goals are quite clear. Economic aims via trade and investment will the guiding impetus for political relations in the age of globalization. China has invested thus far more than US$1.1 billion. Malaysia's investment has reached more than US$3.1 billion making the country as the 16th largest investor in China. Malaysia is also ASEAN's number one trading partner to China.

Malaysia's engagement strategy is also in line with an emerging China which for the last 25 years had economically grown at an average of 9.6 per cent. It has also overtaken the United States as the largest and top destination of FDI (foreign direct investment) globally in 2003 valued at US$53.5 billion. China's entry into the World Trade Organization (WTO) is also expected to bring FDI worth US$800 billion by 2010. This explains well on why all countries are observing and wanting to be a part of the China boom. Its consumer base is ever growing with some 130 million of middle class population. Another more than 100 million are moving into the urban areas which will result in an ever-growing consumer base. China is also comprised of 75 million Muslims. Overall, economic pragmatism tend to guide political relations. For several decades, this trend will continue, unless Malaysia finds a valid reason detour from the principles and path which it had been walking in the last three decades. As for China, it is important to build strong relationship with Malaysia given it has to confront with smaller ASEAN who can be suspicious of Beijing actions and intention. The fear over China is still there and that cannot be erased in just two decades of engagement.

Challenges of Globalization to Malaysia China Relations

Globalization has its inherent benefits and repercussion. Malaysia's constructive engagement policy has a sound basis from the economic pragmatism approach. The boom in China and its effects on bilateral political and economic relations are all not that rosy. While the positive trends indicate the benefits outweighing the challenges, a smaller nation like Malaysia will still confront unpredictable events and circumstances that can affect if not deteriorate political relations. Malaysia's pursuance of unhindered positive and constructive policies are not without setbacks.

While the government is strongly advocating trade and investment with China, will trade imbalance be beneficial to Malaysia in long-term remains to be seen. China's investment is still less than Malaysia's investment there. Similarly, the numerous MOUs signed need also be examined in the context of actual success rates. There is no doubt that jobs are going more to China. Many multinationals have moved out from Southeast Asia. Where trade is concerned Malaysia exported only RM28.19 billion (Jan-Oct, 2005) and imported RM41.13 billion (Jan-Oct, 2005) for the same period.[16] Although trade growth is ever increasing, Malaysia has to deal with this reality of imbalance favouring China. Malaysia is also facing a serious challenge of the dumping of low quality products from China. It is not surprising that China goods are available in a big way in almost every town in Malaysia. While it appears cheap, Malaysians can lose in terms of the quality of living and throwing wastage at a faster rate which can put stress on environment.

As Malaysia promotes tourism and welcome tourists from China, the challenges are many. Tourist arrival from China dropped by 45 per cent in 2005 in comparison with the year 2004. Measures are taken to improve the situation with the hope that 2006 will be a better year. The treatment of Chinese tourists has become a political issue. The nude squat incident had tarnished the image of the police although the woman involved happened to be a Malaysian. Chinese travellers had faced many difficulties at different entrance point in Malaysia resulting in temporary detention. Overstaying of Chinese nationals was reported to reach 180,000 at one time. Some of those who enter on social visit visas had been found to be involved in vice activities. Similar cases were found among some students. While the incidents and issue were manageable, its impact people's perception on tourist from China has yet to change. The media has been highlighting the issues. During the nude squat incident, the media in China was also aggressive in promoting negative reports on Malaysia. The question of do Malaysia really welcome the arrival of the Chinese tourist remains debatable. Its nexus to internal politics cannot be erased though the economic benefits are positive.

The promotion of the many aspects of social cooperation between Malaysia and China in recent years tends to portray great success. Education, for example, is seen as an area to woo the Chinese students. However, Malaysia has yet to recognised some of China's top universities. It reveals that, Malaysia has a long way to win the hearts of the Chinese. Cooperation cannot be based on one-sided perspective for long.

While the economic and social dimensions reveal some critical areas of problems in Malaysia-China political relations, the analysis on China threat from the military point of view is an interesting one. Mahathir was the first leader in Asia to say that China is not a threat but full of opportunity. As such policy holds ground and bears positive result, it is indeed difficult to believe that an authoritarian communist regime which suppresses its own people will always be a benign power. The 1995 Mischief Reef incident near Philippines had an effect on several ASEAN countries to increase their military capabilities in the maritime zones. China's unlawful drawing of maritime baseline and its continued insistence on indisputable sovereignty will not in any manner compromise some of its military position. The situation near the Taiwanese Strait is ever explosive. The US and its allies in East Asia have all increased military cooperation in recent years. Malaysia too relies on the western intelligence support. While politically it differ with the US, military to military cooperation is certainly growing and remain very strong. Malaysia has signed the Memorandum of Understanding on defence cooperation with China but it is nowhere near the way it cooperates with the Australians or the US. China's defence budget is ever growing and its military modernization and reach will remain a serious concern for smaller countries like Malaysia. Although China has been a positive member of the ASEAN Regional Forum (ARF) for more than 10 years now, it is difficult to state that Beijing has won the confidence of all ASEAN members. China threat is real but not discussed extensively in Malaysia for pragmatic reasons. Taking care of China's sensitivity is in fact an important part of Malaysia's diplomatic approach.

Other forms of threats do come in different ways. Contagious killer diseases such as SARS (severe acute respiratory symptom), bird flu and any potential new diseases that may spread from one country to another must be closely monitored. The experience of SARS from China for the first time witnessed the real effect of globalization. If China sneezes, its repercussion can be felt globally. Similarly, the overheating of China's economy can affect many countries. Malaysia will not be spared.

Politically, China holds the key for further democratization in East Asia. Beijing's strong support for Myanmar and Vietnam has ensured that these regimes remain authoritarian and continue to abuse human rights. Myanmar's survival this far despite the international pressure has a lot to do with China's support. Being the strongest ally for Yangon, Beijing will never put pressure on democratization. In East Asia, China's support for North Korea is openly known. The US and its allies have yet to get the full support of China for putting pressure on the North Korean regime where all negotiations result in stalemate. As China's economic growth can be viewed as the driving momentum for others in the region, this cannot be said in the political realm. It is believed, the situation will remain same for several decades and Beijing's political, economic and military support for authoritarian regimes will continue unhindered.

China's role in various international organizations including the UN needs to be scrutinised. While in many areas China may favour the developing world and be in line with Malaysia's foreign policy, it is unlikely that Beijing will put any human rights condition on its development assistance and business dealings with many authoritarian regimes world around. Whereas Malaysia and ASEAN are beginning to portray otherwise in the case of Myanmar, differences can also be found in the way Malaysia and China deal with the big powers like the United States and Japan. In many occasions both the countries have slightly differing positions on how to deal with the two. For Malaysia, Japan and the US are democracies and important source of capital. The two are not enemies. However, this may not be the same for China especially so when it is becoming a contender in the global power configuration.

Conclusion

Malaysia's political relations with China have improved in a significant way driven by the pragmatic constructive engagement policy. During the Cold War, the diplomatic relations was established to avert China threat and appease internal political turmoil caused by the 1969 riot. Globalization at that time can be viewed from the ideological differences perspective and the quest for security. The Mahathir era witnessed for the first time the challenge and the need to engage China. The economic motivation could be clearly seen. Both Mahathir and Abdullah have been vocal on viewing China positively. While the economic reasoning is glaring, it will not resolve all that Malaysia could aim. Engaging China in recent decades will likely to face important challenges. Trade deficit, political differences, social perception and security problems are main areas in which engaging China can be equally challenging. For the time being it is fulfilling Malaysia's national interest to a greater extent. Can this last long needs careful investigation and China's economy has yet to experience a major tremor for us to evaluate further.

Notes

1. For some theoretical perspectives on globalization see Balakrishnan (2003a). See also Higgot (2000).
2. Goh (1994: 20).
3. Ghazali Shafie (1992).
4. Wolf (1977: 82).
5. Dato Muhammad Noh, Undersecretary of East and South Asia, presentation made at the Conference on "Malaysia-China Relations: Strengthening Partnership", Hotel Nikko, 27 April 2004.
6. Reports on various visits by high ranking officials can be obtained from *Sunday Star*, 15 December 2002; *Sunday Star*, 21, September 2003; *New Straits Times*, 21 September 2003; and *New Straits Times*, 24 April 2001.
7. For further information on JSFF see *New Straits Times*, 20 August 1999.
8. Balakrishnan (2003b).
9. For discussions on EAEG see Noordin Sopiee (1994). See also Mahathir Mohamad (1997).
10. *New Straits Times*, 1 December 2000.
11. See M.D Nulapat (Professor), "Authoritarianism and Growth", *Far Eastern Economic Review*, 16 January 2003.
12. On China's military doctrinal change, see Lampton (ed.) (2001). Also see Swain (1995).
13. Balakrishnan (2004). See also Balakrishnan (1997).
14. Dato Muhammad Noh, Undersecretary of East and South Asia, presentation made at Conference on "Malaysia-China Relations: Strengthening Partnership", Hotel Nikko, 27 April 2004.
15. Trade figures from the Ministry of International Trade and Industry, Malaysia.
16. Trade figures from Department of Statistic, Malaysia, and the Ministry of International Trade and Industry, Malaysia.

References

Balakrishnan, K.S. (1997), "Malaysia-China Relations: Moving Beyond Ideological Barriers, Marching Towards Smart Partnership", *Asian Defence and Diplomacy*, October, pp. 21-26.

Balakrishnan, K.S. (2003a), "Globalisation and Malaysia's Foreign Policy", in Khairulmani and Kantasamy (eds), *Malaysia and Globalisation: Issues and Challenges in the 21st Century*, Kuala Lumpur: University of Malaya, pp. 397-429.

Balakrishnan, K.S. (2003b), "Malaysian Foreign Policy in the Age of Globalisation: Theoretical Relevance and Practical Responses", *Journal of Diplomacy and Foreign Relations*, Vol. 5, No. 1, June.

Balakrishnan, K.S. (2004), "Hubungan Malaysia-China Dalam Era Mahathir", in

Obaidellah (ed.), *China: Isu Dan Hubungan Luar*, Kuala Lumpur: Institute of China Studies, University of Malaya, pp. 147-171.

Ghazali Shafie (1992), "Neutralisation of Southeast Asia", in B.A. Hamzah (ed.), *Southeast Asia and Regional Peace*, Kuala Lumpur: ISIS Malaysia, pp. 39-46.

Goh, Cheng Teik (1994), *Malaysia Beyond Communal Politics*, Petaling Jaya: Pelanduk Publication.

Higgot, Richard (2000), "Back from the Brink: The Theories and Practice of Globalization", in Mely C. Anthony and Jawhar Hassan, *Beyond Crises: Challenges and Opportunities*, Kuala Lumpur: ISIS Malaysia.

Lampton, David (ed.) (2001), *Major Power Relations in East Asia*, Tokyo: Japanese Center for International Exchange.

Mahathir Mohamad (1997), "Building a New East Asia", Perdana Papers, ISIS Malaysia.

Noordin Sopiee (1994), "EAEC: Fact and Fiction", Opinion Paper, ISIS Malaysia.

Swain, Michael D. (1995), *The Role of Chinese Military Doctrine in National Security Policy Making*, Santa Monica: Rand Corporation.

Wolf, Alvin (1977), *Foreign Policy: Intervention, Involvement or Isolation?*, Englewood Cliffs: Prentice Hall.

6

Indonesia, Malaysia, and Singapore's Relations with China: A Comparison

Ho Khai Leong

Introduction

There is long history of trading links between Indonesia, Malaysia, Singapore and China. There are records of contacts between China and the Indonesian Islands and Peninsular Malaya (including Singapore) going as far back as the early 15th century. The 19th century heralded a period of booming trade as a flood of migrant workers left their homeland for the "South Seas" to make their fortunes. While many of these immigrants returned to their homelands, some chose to stay behind. These trade links were maintained through the turbulent 1949s and 1950s despite the Chinese Communists takeover of China and the communist parties' active involvement in Indonesia's political affairs and colonial Malaya's political insurgency. Despite ideological differences, these countries' newly formed governments continued the colonial policy of trading with China in the 1950s.

Unfortunately, the evolution of foreign relations of Indonesia, Malaysia, and Singapore with China is not extensively documented and researched. Given the physical proximity[1] and close bilateral relations between the three neighbouring states of Malaysia, Singapore and Indonesia, their foreign policies towards China merits further analysis. After all, China has become increasingly important to these countries in the last two decades. They are all watching a rising China with much political, economical and strategic concern. This paper seeks to compare and contrast the issues involved and uncover the factors contributing to the recent developments in the bilateral relations. In so doing, the following questions were raised: What are the similarities and differences in Malaysia's, Singapore's, and Indonesia's response to a rising China? How can these similarities and differences be explained? Why does China regard Indonesia as a "strategic partner" over Malaysia and Singapore? How is China's singling out of Indonesia significant?

Indonesia-China Relations

Indonesia's foreign policies toward China have come a long way. Since the People Republic of China (PRC) was established in 1949, Sino-Indonesian bilateral relations have been plagued by ideological differences. These differences encountered a brief respite in the Bandung conference in 1954, when Chinese Premier Zhou Enlai led a Chinese delegation to Indonesia as part of his plan to promote Third World unity. Indonesia signed its first bilateral trade agreement with China in 1953, after officially establishing diplomatic ties with China on April 13, 1950. In the 1960s, Indonesia's suspicion of China was fuelled by the Chinese support of the Indonesia Communist Party (PKI). President Suharto believed that the PKI was behind the attempted coup in 1965. Despite the PRC government's strong denial of any involvement in Indonesia politics, Indonesia severed diplomatic ties with Beijing in 1966. Thus, Sino-Indonesian bilateral relations soured for almost two decades.

PRC-Indonesian diplomatic relations were re-established in 1990. Trade relations, however, were already re-connected in 1985 when the Indonesian Chamber of Commerce and the China Council for the Promotion of International Trade (CCCPIT) signed a memorandum of understanding (MoU). Some analysts interpret the prior re-establishment of trade relations vis-à-vis diplomatic relations "as a sign that both countries regarded economic relation as one of the most important – if not the least contentious – factor in their relationship."[2] In 1999, President Wahid sought to further improve ties with China in all areas. Indeed, after the 1999 elections, President Wahid's foreign policy ushered in a new era of cooperation between the two countries. In 2000, a memorandum of understanding was signed in the fields of politics, economics, science and tourism. President Wahid also made China the destination for his first official trip abroad.

In 2002, President Megawati visited China thereby marking a major milestone, for she made Indonesia-PRC relations a top priority in her foreign policy. There were closer educational exchanges and economic relations (for example, the Indonesia-China energy Forum). On China's side, Petro China, one of the largest state-controlled oil and gas exploration and production companies in China, also attempted to secure the rights to oil fields in Indonesia.

In early 2000, China showed an increased interest in Indonesia because of her need for energy at home. As China's energy needs are expected to increase dramatically in the future, it is actively sourcing for energy from major energy-producing regions such as the Middle East and Africa.

Observers believe that Indonesia's massive reserves of liquefied natural gas in West Papua could help supply China's increasing energy needs.

In 2004, leaders of China and Indonesia signed a "Joint Declaration on Strategic Partnership" which covered bilateral cooperation in political and security, economic and development, and socio-cultural and other areas. During President Susilo Bambang Yudhoyono's visit to Beijing in July 2005, he declared, "We want to be part of China's economic success and we also want China to be part of Indonesia's economic success." According to the Indonesian Chamber of Commerce, bilateral trade between China and Indonesia will reach 15 billion US dollars to 20 billion US dollars by 2008.

Malaysia-China Relations

Malaysia has gradually readjusted its policy toward China. Its relation with China has evolved from a suspicious and hostile one (during Tunku Abdul Rahman's tenure as Prime Minister), to a period of normalization (when Abdul Razak was Prime Minister), and finally cooperation (in the regimes of Mahathir and Abdullah Badawi).[3] Malaysia's political leaders have always been proud of the fact that Malaysia was the first country in ASEAN to establish diplomatic relations with China in 1974. Malaysia's Prime Minister Tun Abdul Razak visited China in May 1974 and issued a Joint Communiqué with Premier Zhou Enlai at the end of his visit. The Joint Communiqué emphasised the "mutual recognition and the establishment of diplomatic relations."[4] Trade relations were not mentioned.

Prime Minister Mahathir's 1985 China visit provided another impetus for improving Malaysia-PRC relations. Indeed, a series of important events followed. These included the Sino-Malaysia Direct Flight Agreement (1986) and Sino-Malaysia Trade Agreement (1988). The PRC's Premier Li Peng also visited Malaysia in 1991. This visit may be considered the most encouraging and significant sign of the changed relations between China and Malaysia. The momentum of these improving relations was further enhanced when Mahathir led a 290-member delegation to China in his 1993 trip there. Mahathir described his 1993 China trip as "the most successful delegation" he has led in his then twelve-year-old administration.[5] During the visit, both parties signed various agreements, the most important of which was the Avoidance of Double Taxation Agreement.

Prime Minister Mahathir's perception of China has changed significantly in his political career. By the late 1980s, he no longer saw China as a threat. He was convinced that economic issues should be the basis of Malaysia-PRC bilateral relations.[6] The Abdullah Badawi administration continues this train of foreign policy. The end of Cold War, the demise of the Communist Party of Malaya, the PRC government's commitment towards economic reform, and more importantly, the ASEAN states' investments in China, contributed to the accelerated development of Sino-Malaysian economic relations.

Since the ascendance of the Abdullah Badawi administration, both countries have been rapidly developing in the economic sphere. This led observers to express one concern: Chinese and Malaysian enterprises increasingly occupy similar market niches and have targeted similar products, such as automobiles, for market development. Although the authorities have looked into this issue, it has yet to be resolved. However, Sino-Malaysian bilateral economic relations are on the right tracks. Malaysian officials argue that opportunities to improve Malaysia-China economic relations are abound. If tariff and non-tariff barriers could be brought down under the existing ASEAN-China Free Trade Agreement, then trade relations between Malaysia and China are poised for even more dynamic growth.

Singapore-China Relations

Singapore was the last ASEAN country to establish diplomatic relations with China in 1990. This was largely out of deference to Indonesia. Singapore's political leaders were fully convinced that during the country could not afford to be labelled as "the Third China" during the Cold War. Even though it had no political relations with China, Singapore had a cordial trading relationship with China. Singapore also maintained good economic relations with Taiwan. This Taiwanese-Singaporean economic relation would eventually become a sour point in Singapore-PRC relations.

Ironically, one significant development in Singapore-PRC relations occurred in China during Deng's southern tour or *nanxun* 南巡 in 1992. During the tour, Deng cited Singapore as a model for development. That remark initiated the momentum for improving Sino-Singapore bilateral relations. As a result, the Suzhou Industrial Park (SIP), Singapore's flagship project in the PRC was established in 1994. It is the only PRC industrial park established at an inter-governmental level. Since its establishment, Singapore businesses, both government-linked as well as private ones have expanded beyond the traditional investment fields of real estate and manufacturing into service industries such as legal consultancy, management consultancy, insurance and finance.

Despite their close trade relations and bilateral cooperation, the Taiwan issue is still a sour point between Singapore and China. Deputy Prime Minister Lee Hsien Loong's visit to Taiwan in 2004 provided China with an opportunity to show its long-held displeasure over Singapore's close relations with Taiwan. China's protest of Lee Hsien Loong's visit to Taiwan is a classic case of the Chinese government's exertion of negative pressure so as to influence policies.

Some Comparisons

One can argue that the initial obstacle to the establishment of economic relations between Indonesia, Malaysia, Singapore and China was the absence of formal channels and diplomatic relations. Diplomatic relations between China and Indonesia were cut off in 1966 and China-Malaysia diplomatic relations were non-existent before Tun Razak's visit in May 1974. China-Singapore diplomatic relations were only established in 1990. Why was it so difficult for China and these three countries to establish diplomatic relations? The limitations imposed upon Sino-relations with these countries can be analyzed systematically as there were two sources of pressure.

First, the PRC had been active in supporting the revolutionary movements throughout Southeast Asia. For instance, the North Kalimantan Unitary State Revolutionary Government in North Kalimantan, the Malayan National Liberation League and the Malayan Communist Party (MCP) in Malaya and Singapore received public Chinese support. As far as the Malayan Alliance government was concerned, the Communist insurgency constituted a serious treat to regime stability and legitimacy of the newly independent nation. The Malayan government was suspicious of China in light of its open support for the MCP. As China also supported the Indonesia Communist Party (PKI), the Suharto government regarded China as serious PRC intervention in Indonesian domestic affairs. When the PKI supposedly attempted a coup d'état in September 1965, the blame was laid at Beijing's door.

The second source of contention arose from the question of dual nationality and the allegiance of the ethnic Chinese in these countries. This has been a thorny issue as a large number of ethnic Chinese residing in Indonesia and Malaya (including Singapore) during the 1950s and 1960s were not citizens in those countries. The indigenous population did not regard the ethnic Chinese's close cultural and ethnic ties with the mainland as conducive to nation-building. Although the Malayan Chinese Association (MCA) attempted to obtain citizenship for many non-citizen Chinese, the question of dual nationality and political allegiance remained a largely unresolved issue.[7] The situation was exacerbated by the fact that the PRC did not have a consistent and clear policy on the status of Chinese residing overseas.

China's closed-door policy of the 1950s and 1960s also contributed to the problem. During these periods, Mao Tse-tung adopted an isolationist policy. The Chinese economy was inward-looking and its foreign relations with the rest of the world were almost at a standstill. Mao advocated a policy of self-reliance so as to reduce China's dependence on world markets. China only drastically changed its views on foreign trade and investment in 1978. Chinese policymakers realised that China's export expansion should be encouraged. Such a move provided propelled China's open-door policy in the post-Mao era.

In the late 1980s, China's open-door policy and its commitment to economic reform began to impact the ASEAN countries' perception of the Communist giant. In November 1985, Prime Minister Dr Mahathir led a large delegation to visit the PRC, marking the turning point in Sino-Malaysian economic relations. In the early 1990s, Singapore was the first Southeast Asian country to invest in China. Its example led to a surge of ASEAN investment in China. With the disbandment of the CPM in 1989, the Malaysian government appeared to have resolved the issue of China's support of revolutionary movements. The resolution of the political huddle enabled economic relations to take off.

However, one question still remains – that of the Malaysian, Singaporean and Indonesian Chinese's allegiance. The radical factions of Malaysia's Malay community have always doubted the Malaysian Chinese's loyalty to the Malaysian state. Practically all Malaysian Chinese leaders have made public declarations of the Chinese community's total allegiance to the Malaysian state. Singapore's leaders have repeatedly stated that all its citizens (regardless of race) are required to pledge absolute allegiance to the sovereign state of Singapore. While there is some official discrimination against ethnic Chinese in Indonesia, the Indonesian government has lifted many Suharto era cultural restrictions on the ethnic Chinese in the early 2000. However, the ethnic Chinese are still regarded as a trading class. As a racial minority, the Indonesian Chinese are still discriminated against and are likely targets during the country's riots and periods of unrest.

Internal and external factors have led to the establishment of closer economic relations between China and Indonesia, Malaysia and Singapore. China's internal economic reform under Deng Xiaoping and its open policy certainly have contributed to the large volume of investment from the Asian states, especially Malaysia and Singapore. Policymakers in these Southeast Asian states realise that sustained economic growth in their respective countries are dependent on a diversified China. Singapore was among the first ASEAN states to realise the potentials of the huge Chinese market.

Malaysia and Indonesia have only recently begun to invest in China. Indeed, China's huge market and its potential prompted these countries to expand their economic relations with the mainland.

It is clear that the rapid growth of trade and investment between China and these three Southeast Asian states was driven predominantly by economic considerations. All the investment decisions were geared towards profit-making. However, there were some political considerations as well.

China seems to be eyeing for a closer relationship with Indonesia in the long run. Both face separatist movements at home and China has made it known that it supports Indonesia's efforts to safeguard its sovereignty, as well as its campaign against "internal terror". Such support is welcome because Indonesia faces separatist challenges from Aceh and West Papua. In return, Indonesia has reassured Beijing that it supports the "One China Policy." Thus, Indonesia became the friendliest ASEAN country to China. Given the long history of suspicion and mistrust, Indonesia's change of attitude may be interpreted as a Chinese diplomatic triumph in Southeast Asia.

Singapore's close relations with Taiwan and United States limit Chinese friendly overtures to Southeast Asia. Singapore has traditionally been closer to US, and Singapore-US trading relations reached a new level with the signing of the Singapore-US FTA. Singapore belong to a different group of nations with close ties with the United States (such as South Korea, Japan, Taiwan); Malaysia and Indonesia foreign and security policy postures are much more composed. Malaysian and Indonesian strategic and security considerations are less prioritized than economic relations with China; Singapore pays equal attention to both. One analyst observed that Singapore "recognizes that China will be a great military power in Asia within the next few decades, and that it will have the wherewithal to resolve its territorial claims by force. Singapore thus supports a balance of power in the Asia-Pacific region among China, Japan and the United States."[8]

Malaysia and Indonesia policymakers emphasized the fact that approximately 60 to 75 million of China's total population are Muslims, suggesting that such a religious/ethnic made-up of the population could certainly bring closer ties. Malaysian leaders also highlighted this as a trading issue, emphasizing the huge *halal* (food prepared accordingly to the Muslim way) market in China is an opportunity for Malaysian businesses. Malaysian government has consistently urged Malaysian businesses to export *halal* food and other *halal* products such as cosmetics, toiletries and skin care products to China.

Singapore has much more to worry where economies of scale are concerned. Indeed, Malaysia with a population of 24 million, and Singapore

(4 million) are on the losing end in the economies of scale in comparison to Indonesia (207.4 million) vis-à-vis China with a population of 1.3 billion. All these Southeast Asian states expect their trade volumes to increase in the near future.

In recent years, all the three Southeast Asian countries have consistently emphasized the importance of Chinese tourists and students. China's out-going tourist market is rapidly growing. When the Chinese government approved the first batch of outbound private travel destinations which including Thailand, Singapore, Malaysia, the Philippines, and the Hong Kong and Macau special administrative regions in 1997, 5.32 million trips were made that year. That number increased to 16.6 million in 2002, 20.22 million in 2003 (despite the severe acute respiratory syndrome epidemic) and 28.85 million in 2004, according to the National Tourism Administration (NTA). Southeast Asia is the most popular destination for the majority of these Chinese tourists. Undoubtedly, the number and spending power of Chinese tourists herald increased revenues for these countries' hotel and catering industry.

Conclusions

In the last five years, China's diplomatic olive branch in Southeast Asia has been welcomed by government leaders in the region. However, the Southeast Asian leaders are wary of China's hegemonic ambitions in the region. Presently, Indonesia, Malaysia and Singapore regard China as a source of economic opportunity rather than a strategic concern or military threat. While advocates of a China threat scenario have long argued that China desires regional hegemony in the region, political leaders and policymakers in the region are more sanguine. A comparison of the three countries relations with China suggests that internal and external problems of the past which once acted as obstacles to better diplomatic relations have receded into the background. China is now positively perceived by these states, and its recent advances in the region are but a first move to another "long-march" of diplomatic relations with its southern neighbours.

Notes

1. They can be grouped as Island Southeast Asia, which includes the Indonesia, Malaysia, the Philippines, and Singapore. This is also a region known for its diversity and long history as a crossroads of international commerce.
2. Raymond Atje and Arya Gaduh, "Indonesia-China Economic Relations: An Indonesian Perspective," CSIS Working Paper Series, Jakarta, Indonesia, 1999.

3. Shee Poon Kim, "Malaysia and China: Economic Pragmatism and Cooperation", in Shee Poon Kim, *China and The Maritime Southeast Asian States: From Hostility to Rapprochement and Cooperation*, forthcoming.
4. "China-Malaysia Joint communiqué, 31 May 1974," in R.K. Jain (ed.), *China and Malaysia, 1949-1983*, New Delhi: Radiant Publishers, 1984, pp. 221-222.
5. *The Star*, 22 June 1993.
6. Stephen Leong, "Malaysia and the People's Republic of China in the 1980s", *Asian Survey*, Vol. XXVII, No. 10, 1987, pp. 1109-1126.
7. See, for example, Cheah Boon Kheng, "Malayan Chinese and the Citizenship Issue, 1945-48," *Review of Indonesian and Malayan Affairs*, Vol. 12, No. 2, 1978, pp. 108-117.
8. Ian Storey, "Singapore and the Rise of China: Perceptions and Policy," in Herbert Yee and Ian Storey (eds), *The China Threat: Perception, Myths and Reality*, London: RoutledgeCurzon, 2002, p. 222.

References

Cheng, Joseph (1999), "China's ASEAN Policy in the 1990s: Pushing for Regional Multipolarity", *Contemporary Southeast Asia: A Journal of International & Strategic Affairs*, Vol. 21, Issue 2, August, pp.176-198.

Godley, Michael (1981), *The Mandarin-capitalist from Nanyang: Overseas Chinese Enterprise in the Modernization of China 1893-1911*, Cambridge: Cambridge University Press.

Goh, Evelyn (2005), "Singapore's Reaction to a Rising China: Deep Engagement and Strategic Adjustment", in Ho Khai Leong and Samuel Ku (eds), *China and Southeast Asia: Global Changes and Regional Challenges*, Singapore: Institute of Southeast Asian Studies.

Ho, Khai Leong (1993), "The Changing Political Economy of Taiwan-Southeast Asia Relations", *The Pacific Review*, Vol. 6, No. 1, pp. 31-40.

Ho, Khai Leong (1995), "The Political Economy of Malaysia-China Relations", in Leo Suryadinata (ed.), *Southeast Asian Chinese and China: The Politico-Economic Dimensions*, Singapore: Times Academic Press, pp. 230-248.

Ho, Khai Leong (2001), "Rituals, Risks and Rivalries: China and ASEAN in the Coming Decades", *Journal of Contemporary China*, Vol. 10, No. 29, November, pp.683-695.

Ho, Khai Leong and Samuel Ku (eds) (2005), *China and Southeast Asia: Global Changes and Regional Challenges*, Singapore: Institute of Southeast Asian Studies.

Leong, Stephen (1987), "Malaysia and the People's Republic of China in the 1980s", *Asian Survey*, Vol. XXVII, No. 10, pp. 1109-1126.

Liow, Joseph (2005), "Balancing, Bandwagoning or Hedging? Strategic and Security Patterns in Malaysia's Relations with China, 1981-2003", in Ho Khai Leong and

Samuel Ku (eds), *China and Southeast Asia: Global Changes and Regional Challenges*, Singapore: Institute of Southeast Asian Studies.

Shee Poon Kim (1987), "Peking's Foreign Policies Towards Malaysia", *Issues and Studies*, Vol. 23, No. 8.

Storey, Ian (2002), "Singapore and the Rise of China: Perceptions and Policy", in Herbert Yee and Ian Storey (eds), *The China Threat: Perception, Myths and Reality*, London: RoutledgeCurzon.

Stuart-Fox, Martin (2004), "Southeast Asia and China: The Role of History and Culture in Shaping Future Relations", *Contemporary Southeast Asia*, Vol. 26, No. 1, pp. 116-139.

Wang, Gungwu (2005), "China and Southeast Asia: Changes in Strategic Perceptions", in Ho Khai Leong and Samuel Ku (eds), *China and Southeast Asia: Global Changes and Regional Challenges*, Singapore: Institute of Southeast Asian Studies.

Zha, Daojiong (2000), "China and May 1998 Riots of Indonesia: Exploring the Issues", *The Pacific Review*, Vol. 13, No. 4, pp. 557-575.

7

China's Nationality Laws, Dual Nationality Status and the Chinese in Southeast Asia

*Leo **Suryadinata***

Introduction

Nationality or citizenship has always been a sensitive issue in Southeast Asia, constituting one of the problems that many Southeast Asian states faced with the People's Republic of China (PRC). However this problem appeared to have been resolved with the promulgation of the 1980 PRC Nationality Law, though not in its entirety as the issue of dual citizenship resurfaced recently. Interestingly, the ones who raised this issue were not Southeast Asians, but the Chinese in China. In 1999, during the National Overseas Chinese Affairs Working Committee Meeting held in Qingdao, Shandong Province, a Chinese leader from the "Overseas Chinese Affairs Office" under the State Council called for the dual citizenship status of Chinese overseas to be revived.

In the same year, during the second session of the 9th People's Political Consultative Conference (PPCC), Chen Duo, Ye Peiying[1] and 10 other committee members made a proposal (No. 2172), suggesting that "the dual nationality status of Chinese nationals should not be abrogated."

In 2004, during the second session of the 10th PPCC, another proposal (No. 0222) was made to amend that the part of the Constitution of the PRC relating to the citizenship law, so that Beijing "can selectively recognize the dual nationality status" (Zhou, 2005: 241-243). In response to such developments, Hong Kong TV channels and Internet websites hosted a debate on the issue of the Chinese dual citizenship status which had been temporarily put aside even though it had not been completely resolved then. If the dual nationality status is revived, what will its impact be on the ethnic Chinese in Southeast Asia in general and Malaysia particularly? This is an interesting topic for discussion and study. First of all, let us look at the developments of Chinese nationality law from the Qing dynasty to Republican China in order to understand the current situation.

The 1909 and 1929 Nationality Laws[2]: Dual Nationality Status for Chinese Overseas

The 1909 Law

China's first "nationality law" was issued in 1909 at a time when the Qing dynasty was facing tremendous difficulties, especially in dealing with the "overseas Chinese". It was argued that the law was a reaction to the Dutch government which intended to declare the Chinese in the Dutch East Indies (Colonial Indonesia) Dutch subjects. Fearing tremendous pressure on them to become Dutch subjects, many China-born migrant Chinese appealed to the Qing government to promulgate a nationality law which would enable them to remain as Qing's subjects under the protection of the Qing dynasty.

In fact, the Qing government had earlier realized the importance of the "overseas Chinese". Prior to the appeal of the Chinese in the Dutch East Indies, it had already negotiated with the Dutch authorities on their rights in the Indies. Nevertheless the pressure of the Chinese officials in Colonial Indonesia hastened the process where the Qing nationality law came into being. In 1909 it promulgated the first nationality law, stipulating that all Chinese born in and outside China were the "nationals" (subjects) of the Imperial China.

Because of this law, the Dutch hurriedly issued the Netherlands Onderdaanschap (Dutch subject-ship law) in the following year, making it mandatory for all Chinese born in the Dutch East Indies (mainly *peranakan*[3]) to be classified as Dutch subjects. Therefore, both the Chinese and Dutch governments were claiming jurisdiction over the Chinese in the Dutch East Indies. Negotiations between China and the Netherlands, which had begun in 1908 but soon stopped, were resumed in The Hague. The talk led to a Consular Treaty between the Netherlands and Imperial China in 1911, with China acknowledging that the Dutch East Indies-born Chinese in the Netherlands and its territories were subject to Dutch Law. But they were free to choose either Chinese nationality or Dutch subject-hood if they left the Dutch territories. In return, the Dutch agreed to the establishment of a Chinese consulate in the Dutch East Indies, which would primarily serve as a commercial agency.

At this stage China had not completely abandoned its claim over the overseas Chinese, but merely agreed to the application of the Dutch law to the *peranakan* Chinese when they were in the Dutch East Indies for practical purposes. By then the Dutch East Indies-born Chinese were holding dual nationality. It should be noted that strictly speaking, subject-ship was not really citizenship, but a position with a lower status than citizenship or nationality. The Dutch Indies-born Chinese were thus Dutch subjects, but not Dutch nationals. This was also the case with the Straits-born Chinese in Malaya and Singapore who were British subjects but not British nationals. Nevertheless to simplify the matter, when discussing Chinese nationality during the colonial period, we often do not differentiate these two concepts. As in the case of the *peranakan* Chinese in Java, the Straits-born Chinese held dual "nationality" (subject-ship) status.

However, the Qing dynasty did not have much time to implement the 1909 "nationality law" as it was overthrown during the 1911 revolution; nevertheless the law served as a basis for the subsequent nationality law in Republican China.

The 1929 Law

There is no doubt that the 1914 law and the 1929 law were all based on the 1909 law where the 1914 nationality law had been in force before the unification of southern and northern China. Many overseas Chinese hence held dual nationality, the case in point being the Indies-born Chinese. It was not a problem as long as the person concerned stayed within the Dutch territory. But when he/she went to China, the person would automatically be subjected to Chinese law. A notable case concerned Oen Keng Hian, a *peranakan* Chinese who committed a crime in Java and fled to China. Oen was arrested in China and the Dutch government attempted to have him extradited to the Indies to be tried under Dutch laws there, but the Chinese government rejected the request as Oen was a Chinese national according to the Chinese law. China won the case and Oen could only be tried in the Chinese court in Shanghai.[4]

The 1929 law was the first Guomindang law after Chiang Kai-shek succeeded in unifying China. It used the *jus sanguinis* (blood) rather than *jus soli* (birth place) as the principle of Chinese nationality law. Under this nationality law, "no Chinese could divest himself of his nationality without first obtaining a certificate of denationalization from the Ministry of the Interior, and such a certificate was rarely gained" (Chan, 2002: 488).

A number of factors contributed to the *jus sanguinis*-based nationality law. Guomindang China, like its predecessor, was aware of the value of the overseas Chinese. It intended to make them remain culturally and politically loyal to China. Chinese schools as part of Chinese education were supported by the Guomindang throughout Southeast Asia and Chinese nationalism was encouraged. However, so long as Southeast Asian countries remained under colonial rule where they could be portrayed as struggling against Western imperialism, they provided Chinese nationalism the opportunity to co-exist with Southeast Asian nationalism. (The exception was Thailand where there was a clash between Chinese nationalism and Thai nationalism.) Nevertheless, Chinese nationalism posed a challenge to Southeast Asian nationalism after independence.

The 1955 Afro-Asian Conference and the PRC Nationality Law (1980): From Dual Nationality to Single Nationality

The People's Republic of China (PRC) was established on 1 October 1949 but until early September 1980, there was no PRC nationality law. In the absence of this new law, it seemed that the 1929 Guomindang law was still in use, although it would come to be modified. 31 years later. However, on 10 September 1980, suddenly the PRC Nationality Law was adopted by the Fifth National People's Congress.

In discussing the 1980 law, Johannes Chan forcefully argued that it "reaffirms the principles of the *jus sanguinis* and non-recognition of dual nationality." On de-nationalization, it adopted a more liberal approach. "While maintaining the general principle of no-denationalization without government consents, it allows, for the first time, automatic loss of Chinese nationality for those who have acquired a foreign nationality for those who have settled abroad and have acquired a foreign nationality of their own free will" (Chan, 1992: 489).

In fact, the principles used in the 1980 law were practised by the PRC as early as 1955 when Premier Zhou Enlai introduced his good-neighbour policy, which intended to solve the dual nationality problem. Aware of the suspicion of the new Southeast Asian governments, Zhou was willing to sign the dual-nationality agreement with Southeast Asian countries which had sizeable Chinese communities. Once such an agreement was signed, local Chinese could only have one nationality. In other words, an ethnic Chinese was required to choose one nationality and renounce the other, but only Indonesia signed such a treaty. This was during the Cold War and many non-communist and anti-communist Southeast Asian countries were still strongly suspicious of the PRC until during the early 1970s when the normalization between Washington and Beijing took place.

Nevertheless, it took another few years before Malaysia, Philippines and Thailand established diplomatic ties with the PRC. It is important to note that in all communiqués, China requires the signatory country to recognize a One-China Policy while China did not recognize dual nationality (dual citizenship). In the case of Malaysia, for example, the communiqué clearly stipulated the followings:

> Both the Government of the People's Republic of China and the Government of Malaysia declare that they do not recognize dual nationality. Proceeding from this principle, the Chinese Government considers anyone of Chinese origin who has taken up of his own will and acquired Malaysian nationality as automatically forfeiting Chinese nationality....[5]

In other words, Beijing denounced its judiciary power over the Chinese who chose foreign citizenship in order to show to the Southeast Asian governments that it would like to establish friendly relations with them. During that period, many Southeast Asian states were newly independent, and were at the stage of "nation-building". They were suspicious of the PRC who was not only different ideologically but also projected a revolutionary image. However, Chinese leaders such as Zhou Enlai considered the so-called "Chinese problem" as a historical legacy which should be resolved in order to promote good relations with local governments. It seemed that Zhou was sincere and his government encouraged local Chinese to choose local citizenship and integrate themselves into local societies. This policy of rejecting dual nationality was continued without issuing any Chinese nationality law. Only after the resurgence of Deng Xiaoping in 1978 and the occurrence of the Sino-Vietnamese War in 1979, was the first PRC nationality law promulgated in 1980.

The promulgation of the 1980 nationality law only reaffirmed the existing national status of the Chinese in Southeast Asia. This has officially resolved the dual nationality problems between China and Southeast Asian countries with significant ethnic Chinese minorities.

However this new policy was questioned by some "domestic returned overseas Chinese" who preferred dual nationality for Chinese overseas. They thought that many Chinese in reality had dual nationality or multi-nationality. China should not be afraid of offending other countries and it should not introduce a single nationality policy. However, this view was overruled by Deng Xiaoping (Suryadinata, 1985: 87; Hooker, 2002: 178).

In the early 1990s, there was again a discussion on Chinese nationality among these "domestic overseas Chinese". Although they no longer directly made demands for dual nationality status, they urged the Beijing Government to make it easy for foreign Chinese to become Chinese nationals again. They also argued that the PRC Nationality Law had been issued at a specific time for Southeast Asia where the majority of overseas Chinese had been domiciled. However to date, the situation had changed in that the centres of the ethnic Chinese were no longer concentrated in that region but had expanded to North America and Europe (Mao and Lin, 1993: 312; 402). With the rise of new "Overseas Chinese Centres" it was necessary for China to have a new policy towards the ethnic Chinese. However, to my knowledge it was never put forward officially in the People's Congress before 1999. It was only in 1999 that the proposal of re-examining the 1980 Nationality Law was raised in the People's Political Consultative Conference.

Why Dual Nationality?

Why did some of the overseas Chinese officials in China raise this issue at this time? This is related to the new wave of Chinese migrants, often known as *xinyimin*. In addition, it has something to do with the re-emergence of Chinese nationalism in China together with the rise of China as a new economic giant. Originally, the voices came from these *xinyimin* or the first generation Chinese migrants from Canada, New Zealand, the United States, [6]and of course some Chinese leaders in Beijing.

Those who agreed with the dual national status for the Chinese overseas argued that there are benefits for both the PRC and the Chinese:[7]

1. Beneficial to attract a large number of talents, technology and capital and experience. Because those with dual-nationality can enter and leave the country freely, they will bring more business, remittances and taxes.
2. With dual nationality, the Chinese overseas will be oriented towards China, to defend the national interest of China; he or she can be invited back to be a member of People's Congress as a Chinese citizen, to express his/her views and contribute to the development of China.
3. They will foster the unification of China and go against Taiwan's indepen-dence. They can support the unification of China as Chinese nationals.
4. Easy for China to manage these Chinese. If they commit crimes in China, they can be tried in accordance with Chinese law which will not jeopardize the interest of China.
5. Many countries in the West (e.g. the USA, Canada and Australia) recog-nize dual nationality status.

In short, this group argues that dual nationality would bring both political and economic benefits to China and provide the Chinese overseas an emotional sentiment for their traditional motherland. If we examine the above argument, it is clear that China's domestic point of view was strongly reflected, and it represented the idea of the new Chinese migrants to the West rather than old migrants in Southeast Asia. In addition, the benefits that the group mentioned may not necessarily true. The implementation may jeopardize Beijing's foreign policy interest. Below are the pitfalls of the above-mentioned arguments:

1. The first point assumes that the majority of the Chinese overseas with skills and capitals want to obtain dual nationality (one of them was that of the PRC). In fact, many Chinese overseas may not be interested in having PRC nationality at all. The argument that dual nationality will give the overseas Chinese the freedom to move around in China is false. The "green card" (PR status) policy, which has already been implemented in 2004, will serve this purpose; one does not have to change his/her nationality status. Therefore, the argument that a dual nationality policy will bring more business, remittances and taxes may be considered dubious in this case.

2. This argument is also based on the assumption that the majority of overseas Chinese are interested in participating in China's politics; that may not be the case at all.

3. The Chinese overseas are not a homogeneous group and they have different ideologies. Many are loyal to their adopted country. It is also a fact that Mainland China and Taiwan are still separated, and the Chinese overseas are also divided in their views. It is unrealistic to expect that the Chinese overseas will support only Beijing.

4. The Chinese nationality status for the "overseas Chinese" would enable the Chinese government to arrest and try "Chinese overseas" who have committed all sorts of crimes (including "political crimes") in China. It is also possible that the Chinese government would use the nationality issue as a foreign policy tool. But it may not be without a problem (see the opposition argument below). To use the nationality issue to intervene in other country's domestic affairs would not be welcome by the country concerned.

5. Every country has a different historical background and China does not have to follow other countries if this is neither in the national interest of China nor in the group interest of the Chinese overseas. In fact, the United States began to review the dual nationality status of the people from some countries after the 911 incident.

Those Who Oppose the Dual Nationality Status

However, those who disagreed are people from Southeast Asia, or "returned overseas Chinese" scholars who came from the Southeast Asian region. They maintained that the dual nationality status would harm the Chinese individuals, China and inter-state relations; they are reflected in the following:[8]

1. It would jeopardize China's relations with friendly states; they would begin to suspect the motives of China of reintroducing dual nationality.
2. It would also create problems for the Chinese individuals with regard to their rights and obligations.
3. He/she might receive discriminatory treatment from one country, but could not ask the protection from another country as the two countries have equal rights.
4. He/she has to give his/her allegiance to two countries, and this would put him/her in a very difficult position.
5. Also, the dual nationality status often gives rise to diplomatic problems and conflicts: for instance, a Chinese with dual nationality status who committed a crime escapes to a third country to avoid arrest, it may also create problems for the third country.

The opposition arguments also consider the points of view from both China and the Chinese overseas. Nevertheless, it appears that the reasoning is more convincing than the first group. In fact many argue that since the PRC has been gaining benefits from practising the single nationality policy, why should this be changed at this moment as it continues to serve the interest of the PRC? Furthermore, it is also in the interest of the majority of the Chinese in Southeast Asia and beyond.

Some of the scholars, including Professor Wang Lingchi (Berkeley) and Professor Zhou Nanjing (Peking University) argued that those overseas Chinese who wanted to have dual nationality are small in number. They are either new migrants or Chinese businessmen who would like to have their cake and eat it. But they do not represent the majority of the Chinese overseas. Their attitude and interests should not prevail at the expense of the majority interest.

What Will Happen If China Revived the Dual Nationality Status for the Chinese Overseas?

The majority of Southeast Asian states do not recognize the dual nationality status for their citizens, especially the citizens of Chinese descent. They introduce a single nationality policy. Those Chinese who became the nationals of one of these countries had been required earlier to give up their other citizenship (including PRC citizenship). It is an offence to hold dual nationality. If China reintroduces dual nationality to these Chinese, it will not be welcome by both the ethnic Chinese and the country concerned. The so-called indigenous population will have more excuses to discriminate their fellow citizens of Chinese descent.

Nevertheless, not all Chinese in Southeast Asia are Southeast Asian nationals. There are still significant numbers of alien Chinese in Southeast Asia, and they are Chinese nationals who will not be affected by the dual nationality status. They have single national status: either the PRC, Taiwan or other countries (see Table 7.1).

Table 7.1 Number of Alien Chinese in Southeast Asia by Country (c. 1990)[9]

Country	No. of ethnic Chinese	No. of alien Chinese
Brunei	40,621	31,228
Burma/Myanmar	466,000	Minority
Cambodia	50,000	Minority
Indonesia	400,000	92,717
Laos	10,000	Minority
Malaysia	5,261,000	220,000?
Philippines	850,000	40,000
Singapore	2,102,800	48,200
Thailand	4,813,000	270,766
Vietnam	962,000	Minority

Source: Suryadinata, 1997: 13.

However, in the era of globalization, due to more intensive interactions between Southeast Asia and China, increasing numbers of Chinese migrants begin to enter and reside in Southeast Asia. According to one estimate, during the 1970s and 1990s, between 50,000 and 70,000 Chinese migrants entered Southeast Asia, of which the majority was undocumented or illegal migrants (Zhuang, 2001: 353). Even if they receive permanent resident status, they are still alien Chinese, not Southeast Asian citizens, unless they have succeeded in getting local citizenship. Therefore the majority do not have a "dual nationality" status.

However, the number of Chinese new migrants is much larger in the USA, Canada and Australia than in Southeast Asia. Between 1980-1999, about 1 million Mainland Chinese migrated to the developed countries, of which 450,000 went to the USA, 200,000 to Western Europe, 150,000 to Australia and 140,000 to Japan (Zhuang, 2001: 356). A significant number of these new migrants have also become the citizens of Western countries. Some of them may not be able to integrate themselves into local society and might feel alienated; they thus want to regain PRC citizenship. These individuals might form a very small minority. But, to be sure, a survey should be conducted in order to determine their number.

The problem of dual nationality is complex and for many ethnic Chinese who live in Southeast Asia, it will only bring more problems for them. They will encounter more difficulties in the local setting. With regard to China, I do not think it would bring any benefits. The fear of the "China threat" and "fifth column" will become stronger if China amends the nationality law and recognizes the dual citizenship status – the status which it had abandoned since the Afro-Asian conference.

Conclusion

The citizenship issue is one of the major problems in China-Southeast Asia relations. In the past, both the Qing dynasty and the Guomindang government declared that all ethnic Chinese born in China or abroad were Chinese nationals (citizens). The colonial powers in Southeast Asia also recognized local-born Chinese as their subjects. This is the origin of the question of dual citizenship status of Chinese overseas. The PRC established in 1949, has continued the old "overseas Chinese" policy, giving rise to suspicions on the part of Southeast Asian governments as regards the real motive of Beijing.

Sensing the concern of the Southeast Asian governments, Beijing offered to sign a dual-citizenship treaty with their countries to resolve the citizenship issue during the Afro-Asian conference in 1955. Only Indonesia signed the treaty. In 1980, China unilaterally issued the first PRC "nationality law, " which recognizes only single citizenship. All Chinese abroad who acquire foreign citizenship voluntarily lose their Chinese citizenship automatically. The issue of citizenship for the ethnic Chinese is thus settled.

However, in the wake of the rise of China in a globalizing world, a small group of Chinese decision makers who are not specialists on "Chinese overseas" has begun to feel that China should follow the United States and Canada in introducing the "dual citizenship law. " They may have been influenced by new Chinese migrants (*xinyimin*) in Western countries who would like to have the "best of both worlds." They seem to be unaware of the history of the dual citizenship law and the world situation, especially in Southeast Asia where between 75 to 80 per cent of the "Chinese overseas" live.

Nevertheless, the above "Chinese nationalist view" is not shared by older migrants or the local-born. A leading Chinese American scholar, Professor Ling-chi Wang, argues that, "restoring the dual citizenship law will harm both

China and Chinese abroad" (Zhou, 2005: 352-361). Those Chinese who live in Southeast Asia and know the situation well still favour the single citizenship law as the so-called indigenous population still harbour suspicions against China and the ethnic Chinese. It is important to note that Beijing has not yet made a move to amend the constitution, as the present citizenship law is perceived as still beneficial to China. Nevertheless, the possibility of adjustment and amendment is there, depending on who is in power.

Notes

1. Chen Duo 陈铎 is from the literary circle while Ye Peiying 叶佩英 is from Qiaoban. See Zhou (2005: 175-176).
2. For a detailed description and analysis of the 1909 law and the 1929 law, see my article entitled "China's Citizenship Law and the Chinese in Southeast Asia" (Hooker, 2002: 169-202).
3. *Peranakan* refers to local-born and Indonesian speaking Chinese.
4. For a discussion of Oen's case, see Suryadinata (1980: 26-27).
5. *Peking Review*, 23 (June 1974), p. 8. It should be noted that if the Chinese was forced to become a foreigner, he or she would remain as Chinese national. The case in point was that of Vietnam in 1976 after the reunification. But apart from Vietnam, it appears that ethnic Chinese have become Southeast Asian nationals on their own free will.
6. Liang Yingming 梁英明 , *Shuangchong Guoji Bu Fuhe Haiwai Huaren Sheng-cun Fazhan de Changyuan Liyi* 双重国籍不符合海外华人生存发展的长远利益, see Zhou (2005: 413-425).
7. For the arguments, see "Huaqiao Huaren Guoji Wenti Zhouyi 华侨华人国籍问题诌议 (1)", *Zhongguo Ribao Wangzhan Huanqiu Zixun* 中国日报网站环球咨询, 3 March 2006.
8. See "Huaqiao Huaren Guoji Wenti Zhouyi 华侨华人国籍问题诌议 (1) ", *Zhongguo Ribao Wangzhan Huanqiu Zixun* 中国日报网站环球咨询, 3 March 2006.
9. It is difficult to obtain the numbers of ethnic Chinese who have settled in Southeast Asia but are still holding alien status. Most governments do not release these figures. Therefore the above information is based on estimates or calculated guesses. See Suryadinata (1997: 13). For the figure on Thailand, see *Statistical Yearbook* (1993), p. 49.

References

Chan, Johannes (1992), "Nationality", in Raymond Wacks (ed.), *Human Rights in Hong Kong*, Hong Kong: Oxford University Press.

Hooker, Barry (2002), *Law and the Chinese in Southeast Asia*, Singapore: Institute of Southeast Asian Studies.

Mao Qixiong 毛起雄 and Lin Xiaodong 林晓东 (eds) (1993), *Zhongguo Qiaowu Zhengce Gaikuang* 中国侨务政策概况 , Beijing: Huaqiao Chubanshe 华侨出版社.

Statistical Yearbook, Thailand, no. 43 (1993), published by National Statistical Office, Office of the Prime Minister.

Suryadinata, Leo (1980), *Chinese Politics in Java 1917-1942*, Singapore: Singapore University Press.

Suryadinata, Leo (1985), *China and the ASEAN States: The Ethnic Chinese Dimension*, Singapore: Singapore University Press.

Suryadinata, Leo (1997), *Chinese and Nation Building in Southeast Asia*, Singapore: Singapore Society of Asian Studies.

Zhou Nanjing 周南京 (ed.) (2005), *Jingwai Huaren Guoji Wenti Taolun Ji* 境外华人国籍问题讨论辑 , Hong Kong: Xianggang Shehui Kexue Chubanshe 香港社会科学出版社.

Zhuang Guotu 庄国土 (2001), *Huaqiao, Huaren yu Zhongguo de Guanxi* 华侨、华人与中国的关系 , Guangdong: Guangdong Gaodeng Jiaoyu Chubanshe 广东高等教育出版社.

Economic Relations

8

China-ASEAN Relations: Towards Global Stability, Peace and Sustainable Growth

Chia Oai Peng

Introduction

China has the world's largest population totalling 1.3 billion and land area is 9.6 million sq. km. China is currently the world's third largest trading country. Exports in 2005 totalled US$772 billion, while imports totalled US$660.1 billion. Trade surplus in the same year is US$102 billion.[1] In 2005, domestic private economy accounts for 49.7 per cent of GDP on the mainland, while foreign funded enterprises and businesses invested by China's Hong Kong, Macao and Taiwan business persons account for 15 per cent.[2] China's GDP in 2004 is US$1.972 trillion following an average economic growth rate of 9.4 per cent over the past 27 years. The GDP in 2003 is US$1400 billion as compared to US$147.3 billion in 1978 (Zhang, 2004: 55). China hopes to double the GDP and raise per capita GDP to US$3000 by 2020.[3] China's central bank reveals that foreign exchange reserves totalled US$818.9 billion at the end of 2005, an increase of 34.3 per cent year on year. China's offshore debts, not including those in Hong Kong, Macao and Taiwan, totalled US$267.46 billion at the end of September 2005,

Table 8.1 China's Economic Performance (in US$)

	GDP	Total Trade Volume	FDI	Forex Reserves
2020 (projection)	4 trillion			
2004	1.972 trillion			
2003	1.4 trillion	851.2 billion	679.6 million	403.3 million
1978	147.3 billion	20.6 billion	0	0.167 million

up 8.07 per cent from the end of 2004. New foreign debts over the first nine months in 2005 totalled US$208 billion, an increase of 67.63 per cent on a year on year basis.[4]

The People's Republic of China was formed in October 1st 1949. Since then China was behind bamboo curtain until 1978, the year that marked the end of the Cultural Revolution, and the beginning of liberalization. For the past 27 years, China is in the stages of modernization, in transition from planned economy to market economy, and the foreign policy also amended from time to time in response to the international community. China is experiencing ongoing transformation. China's fast progress and ascendance in the 1980's was interpreted as threat to world order. Such interpretation is the consequence of the rise of European countries and US through expansionism, colonialism and war. Germany, Italy and Japan followed the path of rising using expansionism and invasion but ended in defeat. However, the reconstruction of Germany, Japan and Europe and their peaceful rise to strong economy in the past 60 years, has set models of peaceful development. China being a large developing nation and socialist country, her path to dynamic economic development that holds close to two-digit annual growth rate for 27 years, needs to gain international trust and confidence. China's ascendance to fast economic growth and a seemingly perpetual close to two-digit growth for almost three decades and the years to come is thus not unprecedented.

ASEAN being one of China's immediate neighbours has close relations with the latter. Beginning from 1997, China participates in ASEAN + 1 and ASEAN + 3 forums held annually to promote understanding and cooperation among member nations. China-ASEAN and China-Japan relations have hurdles to be solved. The conflicts over claim of sea and island sovereignty pose as potential threat in the region.

This article intends to study the relations between China, a nation with the fastest growing economy in the world, with ASEAN, a ten-member organization with dynamic economic activities. This study will look into various perspectives like economic, political, social and cultural aspects.

Association of the Southeast Asian Nations (ASEAN) is founded in 1967. Its members are Indonesia, Malaysia, Singapore, Thailand, Philippines, Brunei, Vietnam, Laos, Cambodia and Myanmar. ASEAN nations have a total area of 4.5 million square km, and a total population of 530 million. The total GDP is US$700 billion while total trade volume is US$600 billion. ASEAN-China FTA forms a huge market with 1.85 billion consumers and a combined GDP of almost US$2.5 trillion. Trade between China and ASEAN grew by 23.5 per cent in the first 11 months of 2005 to US$117.24 billion.

China is ASEAN's fourth largest trading partner, after Japan, US and Europe. The region is very rich in natural resources and occupies strategic position in global geo-politics. ASEAN nations are very diverse in terms of ethnicity, culture, languages and religion. ASEAN members are also new nations where their politics and economy are very much dominated by external forces. The ascendance of China in the past two and a half decades has gradually reshuffled the world order. ASEAN nations with their geographical proximity to China are now with an alternative to establish regional cooperation with China with the aim to reduce over-dependence on certain countries. The regional peace, security and sustained development in ASEAN and China are tied to the mutual commitment of ASEAN and China to the issue. Thus, it is a challenge for China to reassure her neighbours, especially ASEAN nations, of China's good intentions, that a strong China is no threat or obstacle to any nation, and that China's fast economic growth undermines no nation. Contemporary East Asian cooperation is characterised by development in economic cooperation growing by leaps and bounds, while security cooperation is moving slowly, bilateral cooperation develop better than multi-lateral cooperation. This is attributed by the differences in the political systems and unbalanced economic development in the region, and the influence of US in Asia Pacific region.

Peaceful Rise and Driving Force for World Economy

Is China a Threat (to Regional Security)?

The models of rise to development, strength and prosperity of Europe, US and Japan are acquainted with colonialism that is characterised by invasion, occupation, expansion and the use of military and force. China in her ascendance to development and prosperity inevitably attracts suspicion of fear that China would follow the same path of her predecessors. Developed countries interpret China's ascendance as challenger and competitor to their existing interests. For US who has been dominant in international affairs since the Second World War, there is the constant fear that China would follow the same path to contest for international dominance. Before the ascendance of China, Japan is the head of the flying geese in East Asia. China's ascendance inevitably attracts resources tangible and non-tangible, markets, influence and friendship from the region. For this, Japan has several times made remarks that China is a threat to regional security. Comparing the military expenses which are US$25.6 billion for China in 2004 and US$41.4 billion for Japan while China's population is ten times that of Japan, and

China's land size is twenty five times that of Japan, the remark seems not convincing. Japan's huge military expenses for her relatively small population and land size as compared to China illustrate that China is far from being a threat to regional security. Following a military trimming program that completed on schedule, China downsized the military by 200,000 in 2005. Troop numbers had been reduced to 2.3 million as compared to 3.2 million in 1987. The 11th Five-year Plan (2006-2010) is increasing defence and military expenditure by 14 per cent to modernize the People's Liberation Army (PLA).

Table 8.2   Comparing Military Expenses, Population and
            Land Sizes of China and Japan

	Military Expenses in 2004 (US$ billion)	*Population Size (billion)*	*Land Size*
China	25.6	1.3	9,600,000 sq. km.
Japan	41.4	0.13	384,000 sq. km.

China is gaining influence and friendship in Southeast Asia, as seen in the inaugural ASEAN Summit, a position and status enjoyed by Japan in the past three decades. After signing a joint communiqué in December 2005, Malaysia's Prime Minister Abdullah Ahmad Badawi and China's Premier Wen Jiabao gave high remarks on both nations' celebration of the 600th year of Chinese Admiral Zheng He's visit to Southeast Asia. Both leaders noted that China's southward visit was friendly as in contrast to those from the West that was to conquer and colonise. The remark acknowledges that China at her prime in history was no threat to regional security. China's friendly gesture and diplomatic policy has gained increased bilateral trade volume and upgraded China-ASEAN relations in the past decade.

A favourite question often asked by experts on China is: where would China head to and what would China want to do?

"Peaceful Rise, Harmonious Society and Scientific Development"

China in her path of ascendance has set a three-tier goal of "Peaceful Rise, Harmonious Society and Scientific Development" in her development plan. The first goal of "peaceful rise" is a pledge of peace to the international community. The second goal is a promise of security to the nation. The third is to an undertaking of scientific approach to achievement national development. China's diplomacy is guided by the three goals and has since switched to foster closer relations with her immediate neighbours to create a relatively peaceful ambience for her ascendance.

China proposed "peaceful rise" in response to "China threat". Chinese Premier, Wen Jiabao in his December 2005 visit to France explained the choice of "peaceful rise", "Having suffered enormously from foreign invasions, China know the price of peace. This choice is a logical choice, dictated by China's history and culture." Responding to widespread fears and accusations in France that China's low costs of production are attracting foreign investments and economic activities, resulting in unemployment in Europe, Wen stated that growing domestic demand in China has led to opportunities for the world.

China's model of ascendance follows after Japan and the Asian four dragons, with quite a similar path, that is, intense FDI, high saving rate, labour intensive, export oriented, low cost of production and evolving from low end to high end production. China's growth depends on high foreign investment rate and a 40 per cent saving rate for her capital formation. China's personal saving rose to US$1.74 trillion at the end of 2005 as compared to US$1.56 in 2004.[5] Her economy begins with export driven low value added production and switches to high value added production. The difference is China has a huge population to propel prowess sufficient domestic demand for her fast economic growth and has abundant supply of cheap labour for her labour intensive economy at the initial stage creating an almost perpetual 8-9 per cent growth rate.

In a comprehensive national ranking carried out in 2005 by China's top think tank, China ranks 6th after US, UK, Russia, France and Germany. The findings were published in the annual Reports on International Politics and Security. The ranking using econometrics perspectives for measurement was made from ten major countries, using their economic, demographic and territorial size as criteria. The researcher, Wang Ling, took into consideration the economic power, military and diplomatic capacities and "national power resources" of each country and government's macro-control capacity to determine the aggregate national strength.[6] The World Economic Forum in its global competitiveness report for 2005-2006, ranked China 49th out of 117 economies. The International Management Development World Competitiveness Yearbook 2005, placed China 31st in the overall ranking. The Strategic Assessments Group of Rand Corporation in its latest report, assessing national power by GDP, population, defence spending and technology innovation, estimated that China held about 14 per cent of the global power, the same percentage as the European Union.[7]

Table 8.3 National Power Ranking

Country	Score	Country	Score
US	91	China	59
UK	65	Japan	57.8
Russia	63	Canada	57
France	62	ROK	53
Germany	61.9	India	50

Source: Reports on International Politics and Security.[8]

From historical perspective, China's ascendance resembles the regaining of her national strength including economy, politics, military, and culture, after foreign invasions and internal feuds in the 19th and the 20th century.

" Peaceful Development "

To dispel the suspicion and caution of threat from the international community, China in the 1990's follows a policy of "peaceful rise" and non-expansionism. In the 15th China Communist Party Congress held in 1997, the then President, Jiang Zemin, stressed that China opposed hegemonies and super power politics. As a result of lingering international suspicion and fear, China has refined her development policy in the last four years. In the 16th Congress held in 2002, Jiang noted the increase of uncertainties affecting world peace and development. He placed existing and new security threat that had led to the rise of terrorism in priority of importance. He attributed the widening North-South disparity, and conflicts driven by ethnic, religion and border disputes as factors leading to global instability. He proposed mutual trust, mutual benefit and cooperation as the crux for promoting global security in pursue for the benefits of mankind (Jiang, 2002). Jiang's 2002 policy speech is made with consideration of the 2001 New York September 11 attack, showing that Chinese government recognised the necessity of mutual trust and cooperation among nations to work towards an understanding global community and thus mutual benefit will be vital to achieve the goal. As such the criticism on opposing hegemonies and super power politics was no longer highlighted.

In 2003 China declared her policy of "Peaceful Rise, Harmonious Society, and Scientific Development". In 2004, the emphasis was on "Peace and Development". In 2005, the emphasis is changed to "Peaceful Development". China's President, Hu Jintao's speech at the 60th Anniversary of the United

Nations highlighted China's determination to promote "long lasting peace and harmonious world". At the inaugural East Asia Summit held at Kuala Lumpur in December 2005, China Premier Wen Jiabao in his speech again assured participating leaders that China would stick to a path of peaceful development. He said that China will never seek domination in East Asia, and that China will not develop at the expense of others, and that China's development will not threaten any other country. These refinements show that China is sensitive and responsive to international views and works towards constructive measures promoting a more conducive environment for trade, development and diplomatic relations. China's replacement of "rise" which causes uneasiness among the international community for "development" demonstrates matured leadership in careful planning and insightful development policy. The leadership is also actively engaging with the international community. In the past decade, China is involved in dynamic international dialogues to gain international community's trust in her ascendance, extending her spheres of regional cooperation into environment protection, fighting and preventing global epidemic like SARS and avian flu, anti-narcotics, human rights, intellectual property rights, fields of non-proliferation and security, global development and cultural exchanges. On the last day of 2005, China issued "White Paper On Peaceful Development: China's Road Map" to further explain China's determination to develop in a peaceful environment and is of no intention to domination. The theme of the paper is in consistence with Wen's speech at the East Asia Summit.

At a welcoming 2006 New Year reception where 400 foreign diplomats and Chinese officials were present, China's Foreign Minister, Li Zhaoxing at his speech remarked that China will follow peaceful development and would adhere to an independent foreign policy of peace, development and cooperation in the coming year. China's President, Hu Jintao, in his 2006 new year speech reiterated China's determination of openness and policy of peaceful development and the building of harmonious global society. On the Taiwan issue, he emphasised that China would not allow the "independence" or separation of Taiwan. Hu's speech had carefully coined "peaceful development" to replace "peaceful rise" that was much discussed in the past three years.

Driving Force for World Economy

Towards the last quarter of 2005, "stagflation" (the combination of stagnation and inflation) is brewing in Europe and drawing concern over economic performance. The surge in oil prices, from US$10-15 a barrel in 1998 to

China is a peaceful China. In China, there is growing economy and a growing middle class. China's ascendance has significant impact on nations worldwide. China's fast development has aroused anxiety in certain countries about their giant neighbour. The US and Japan perceives China as a competitor for energy, market and international domination. This is further aggravated by the imposed image of China as a threat posed by China's military modernization and robust economy.

Table 8.8 Actual Foreign Direct Investment in China (in US$ billion)

2005 Jan-Oct	2004	2003	2002	2001	2000	1999
48.4	60.6	53.5	52.7	46.9	40.8	40.4

Source: Ministry of Commerce (*China Daily*, 15 November 2005, p. 9).

The volume of SMS text messages sent by Chinese illustrates the market opportunity generated by China's huge population. During Spring Festival (also known as Chinese New Year) in 2005, 11 billion text messages were sent during the 7-day vacation. For the first eleven months in 2005, a total of 274 billion messages were sent, generating about 27.4 billion yuan (approximately US$3.42 billion), 40 per cent higher than the same period in 2004. Between December 31st 2005 and January 1st 2006, over 180 million text messages were sent in Shanghai and more than 150 million (US$1.86 million) in Beijing.

China is improving her logistics and public transport system, including modernizing her railways. New highways and railway lines are built connecting to the northwest and southwest of China, areas targeted for development. ALSTOM, a French world-leading supplier of transport system technology and equipment, is making optimum opportunity in China's railway transport system.

Commitments to International Community

China has committed to the international community by taking part in the humanitarian mission to help nations hit by natural disaster in the past few years. In the 2004 tsunami, China donated US$49.3 million (400 million yuan) to Indonesia, including US$7.4 million for reconstruction and rehabilitation in Acheh Province. China also donated cash and kinds to the massive earthquake in Pakistan and Katrina in New Orleans.

Domestic Problems and Challenges

China's fundamental problem is her dependence on growth combined with a widening gap between rich and poor. Though China is a big, growing and strong economy, the populous nation is faced with several domestic affairs that need to be addressed for her sustainable development. China's dramatic economic growth and rapid transition to a market economy have imposed an urgent need for social and political reform. On 19 October 2005, China issues its first white paper on political democracy entitled "Building of Political Democracy in China", and vows to push forward political system reform. In the 11th Five-Year Programme (2006-2010), priorities are given to building harmonious society to ensure domestic stability and sustainable development as the economy is riding excessively on increased foreign investment and material input. Other agenda given high priorities are education, medical care, employment and defence.

The fifth national demographic census conducted in 2000, shows that the illiteracy rate in China was 5.22 per cent among the 15 years and above age group in the urban areas and townships. The figure was 11.55 per cent in the rural regions (Wang, 2006). 91 per cent of the rural labour force received only junior high school or primary education. China in her 11th Five-Year Programme has pledged to provide education in some rural areas and make education affordable to more.

Medical care in China is a costly commodity and this has partly attributed to the high saving rate in China.[16] Wang (2006), a researcher from the Macroeconomics Research Institute under the National Development and Reform Commission, pointed out that the number of hospital beds and doctors for every 1000 citizens in 1978 were 1.93 and 1.07 respectively. In 2004, these had only increased to 2.4 and 1.5 respectively. Medical care is unevenly distributed, where 80 per cent of medical services are provided in the urban areas. The rural areas make up 70 per cent of the population but are not provided with adequate medical care. It is a challenge for China to provide affordable medical care to her rural population and the urban poor.

China has to create about 25 million job opportunities each year for her 1.3 billion population. In the summer of 2006, China would have 4.1 million fresh college graduates entering the job market. In 2005, figure from the Ministry of Education shows that 27 per cent of the fresh college graduates are unemployed. Unemployment rate in 2004 stood at 4.3 per cent.

China has been a peasant country at large whereby peasants make up about two-thirds of the population, spreading over vast rural regions. Agriculture attributes to 13.1 per cent of GDP in 2004, industry 46.2 per cent and tertiary trade (the service sector) 40.7 per cent. The peasants' low income has made rural and agricultural regions the weakest links in China's fast economic and social development. Rural poverty has turned many peasants into migrant workers flocking to the urban areas. To reduce rural poverty and narrow urban-rural disparity, in 2004 Premier Wen Jiabao announced that the government would gradually reduce agricultural taxes. Beginning in 2006, China moves further abolishing her 2600-year old agricultural tax. These measures are China's efforts to boost agricultural production and growth and to raise income of the 800 million-peasant populations, to ensure stability and sustainable growth, and to achieve food security for her huge population. Besides agricultural tax abolition, China is undertaking plans to improve rural infrastructure including irrigation and transportation network, subsidise rural education and improve affordable rural health care.

China has about 150,000 street children in 2002, as revealed by statistics from the Ministry of Civil Affairs. Four-fifths of these children came from poverty stricken areas. About 70 per cent of them are boys. These children left home and lived on the streets because of domestic violence and neglect, according to Masahiro Ono, chief of Protection and Community Services Section of UNICEF (United Nation's Children's Fund) Office for China. China has set up about 130 rescue centres nationwide to cater for homeless children. From 2006 to 2010, UNICEF will contribute about US$100,000 each year to Zhengzhou, capital of Henan Province in central China, to help street children. Zhengzhou in the past five years had made achievements in reaching out and helping street children.

Another project that would help to reduce poverty is the building of highways linking major grain producing areas, regions with low income, old revolutionary bases and border areas. In 2006, China will be building 180,000 kilometres of rural highways. The network will be linking all administrative villages. At the end of 2005, UN praised China for the efforts in reducing poverty. Until 2004, China has helped 300 million of her people out of poverty (Zhang, 2004: 55).

China's population is still quickly increasing since implementing family planning policy in 1971. To curb the huge population increase, one-child policy was strictly carried out beginning in 1982. However, the rural peasants, minority groups and couples whose first child is disabled, are not bound by the one-child population policy. In Mainland China, 90 million families have adhered to the family planning policy. Under the current birth rate, the population is estimated to reach 1.37 billion in 2010, 1.46 billion in 2020 and 1.5 billion in 2033. The huge population poses intense pressure on China's economic development, environment, resources, medical care and education. China has pledged the one-child population policy to be a long-term state policy and incorporated into the 11th Five Year Plan (2006-2010) and beyond to curb the fast growing population and for sustainable development.

Cultural Factors in Chinese Diplomacy

Chinese leaders and academics adopt centuries old Chinese values to explain the importance of peace, harmony and stability for China to develop and grow. These values highlight mutual attitudes of consideration for self and others. The crux of the values is harmony as a pre-condition for self and others to prosper together.

Confucian philosophy has been prevalent and dominant in Chinese society and politics for over two thousand years. Though the philosophy was denounced and banished at the third decade until the 1980s, it regains vitality after China liberalized in 1978. The philosophy is deep rooted in Chinese society where the teaching is spread and passes down through long periods of time to the individuals via the family values and tradition. China under communism is no exception to Confucian influence. "Harmony" (*he* 和) is one of the pivotal Confucian teaching and Chinese value that is dominant in Chinese culture. In solving disputes, the Confucian principle is "harmony is precious" (*yi he wei gui* 以和为贵). In compliance to these teaching and principles is the Chinese family rule of "family harmonious everything prosper" (*jia he wanshi xing* 家和万事兴). Beginning in the early 1990s, China's foreign affairs illustrate influence of Confucian thinking embracing "harmony" (*he* 和) in her diplomatic policy. The speeches of President Hu Jintao and Premier Wen Jiabao at various international and domestic occasions put emphasis on China following a diplomatic path of "harmony" and her continuous efforts in promoting universal harmony in the global community.

Throughout Chinese history, Confucian scholars at different periods have laid down various principles regarding relationship with neighbours. One of these is "in harmony with neighbours and prosper together" (*mu lin fu li* 睦邻富里). In traditional Chinese peasant society where hardship was common, one would be in need of others' help for survival. Furthermore, traditional Chinese family and lineage structure has formed a close knitted society where individuals in a community are related to one another through blood ties, conjugal ties and other relations. Thus, living in harmony with the neighbours and prosper together was seemingly the choice. Another

Confucian neighbourliness principle is to "be partner of neighbours and do good to neighbours" (*yi lin wei ban, yu lin wei shan* 以邻为伴, 与邻为善). One of Confucius' teachings is "do not do to others what one does not want" (*ji suo bu yu, wu shi yu ren* 己所不欲, 勿施于人. The principle of "do good to neighbours" is in unity with Confucius teaching. These principles were diplomatic relations with her neighbouring countries in Eastern Europe, South Asia, ASEAN and East Asia, are practising "in harmony with neighbours, prosper together with neighbours, and assuring the neighbours" (*mulin, fulin, anlin* 睦邻, 富邻, 安邻). China treats US as one of her immediate neighbours because of the latter's strong economy and dominance that make it significant.

In 2005, China has designated Xi'an (capital city of Shaanxi province in northwest China) as the site for Euro-Asia Economic Forum. The Forum is to promote understanding and greater cooperation between 5 European (Russia, Kazakhstan, Kyrgyzstan, Tajikistan, Uzbekistan) and 8 Asian (Iran, Nepal, Pakistan, India, Mongolia, China, Republic of Korea, Japan) countries to explore opportunities for mutual growth, prosperity and stability among the 13 nations thus helping development in some of the member nations. China's initiative to form and host the Euro-Asia Economic Forum is exemplary of China's policy of "in harmony with neighbours, prosper together with neighbours, and comforting the neighbours". China has established Nanning, the capital city of Guangxi Province, as the permanent site for promoting and strengthening China-ASEAN relations and trade.

Diplomatic Policy and Relations

China's Foreign Policies

Since China declared her peaceful rise (*heping jueqi*) in 2003, China has committed herself to international roles in (1) promoting world peace, (2) realizing world prosperity, and (3) contributing to denuclearization in the Korean Peninsula. In 2005, China's President Hu Jintao, Premier Wen Jiabao and other top officials had very busy schedule receiving world leaders and making official visits to US, Europe, East and Southeast Asia. China shares her land boundaries with 15 nations and has 8 sea-neighbouring nations. China's consideration in the making of foreign policy centres on her domestic development and security interests. China's 1.3 billion population and huge disparity in income with uneven domestic development, needs internal stability and a peaceful environment for her rapid and continuing development. China's diplomacy aims to maintain a peaceful international environment for her domestic economic development, and to create a harmonious world, in which all countries, big or small, have equal rights to development in their own models. As such, China has established partnership relations with other countries.

The conflicts between China and other countries can be categorised into three major groups, namely conflicts (1) carried down from history, (2) unbalanced development between China and her neighbours, and (3) intervention from third party. The first includes border demarcation disputes, sovereign in disputed waters and continuing hurts from WWII atrocities that are not yet remorse. The second includes security interests, conflicts involving arms competition and modernization as well as defence expansion. The third is the result of economic and global influence competition. The three groups of conflicts are intertwining where there is intervention from third party in the first two major groups of conflicts.

China pursues a multi-lateral, friendly, mutual beneficial, peaceful, equal and close cooperation foreign policy with the Bandong declaration as the foundation. China divides the international environment into four kinds of countries, namely super power, developed countries, neighbouring countries and under developed countries. Her relations with these countries are accordingly strategic partnership, constructive partnership, harmonious and friendly partnership, and basic partnership. China-US relation is "constructive strategic partnership" (1997), China-Russia is "constructive partnership" (1994) and later changed to "strategic cooperation partnership" (1996), China-Japan is "peace and development friendly cooperation partnership" (1998), China-India is "constructive cooperation partnership" (1996) but in April 2005 qualitatively upgraded to strategic levels, China-Europe is "long-term stable constructive partnership" (1998), and China-ASEAN is "harmonious and mutual trust partnership" (1997) (Zhuang, 2002: 202-203). In October 2003, ASEAN and China became "security partnership". In April 2005, Indonesia and China agreed to set up "strategic partnership" to maintain and strengthen long-term mutual cooperation. During Hu's visit to Europe in November 2005, he signed "strategic partnership" with Spain, the fifth European country after UK, France, Italy and Germany. During Wen's visit to Portugal in December the same year, China and Portugal elevated their relation to "strategic partnership" to commit to stronger cooperation and political trusts. In January 2006, the Treaty of Friendship, Cooperation and Good-Neighbourly Relations, signed in April 2005 between China and Pakistan, came into effect. China's classification of the various relations and the elevation of ties illustrate her varying strategies and dynamism in her foreign policy. The choice of words in building partnerships lays China's navy and air force aroused suspicion and tension from her neighbours. On the other hand, China's increased spending and upgrading of her military, air force and navy also result in uneasiness from Japan. On China's oil and gas exploration and drilling activities in her waters, Japanese have made fuss and claimed to use force to safeguard the latter's maritime rights and interests. Japan's oil and gas exploration activities in disputed waters have also aroused tension between the two nations. Talks on the issue between the two countries took place in October 2005 and may resume in early 2006. The two countries had agreed in principle to develop the area jointly but have not yet touched upon any further details, including questions of investment and profits sharing concerning the proposed joint venture. The crux of cold political ties between the two nations is attributed by Japan's attitude of not acknowledging and apologised over the hurt inflicted upon the Chinese people during the period of 1894 to 1945. The situation is further worsened with distortions in Japanese textbooks about historical facts of Japanese invasion in China.

In October 2005, Chinese Premier Hu Jintao visited North Korea (DPRK) strengthening their relation and convincing North Korea to attend the resumption of the 5th round of six-party talks on the denuclearization of the Korean Peninsula and to normalize US-DPRK ties.[17]

China is the largest trading partner of the Republic of Korea (ROK). The bilateral trade volume between the two nations is estimated to reach US$100 billion for 2005. The figure is projected to double, reaching US$200 billion in 2012. On November 16, ROK has accorded China full market-economy status. In November 2005, Hu visits South Korea (ROK) and attends the APEC summit.

In the 2004 Asian tsunami and the 8 October 2005 7.6-magnitude earthquake in Pakistan-controlled Kashmir, China had demonstrated her role as one of the world leaders in disaster relief. China has been responding well to earthquakes and other emergencies. China is becoming a bigger and more predictable donor in international assistance work, and has the potential and obligation as a world leader to help in international relief efforts. The United Nations emergency relief co-ordinator, Jan Egeland says, "China did very well."[18]

China-ASEAN Relations

China-ASEAN relations have to be understood in the backdrop of a competitive global economy and dominance, and the ascendance of China coupled with her huge population and domestic problems and challenges. Guangxi is scheduled to be the centre to promote China-ASEAN relations. This is an effort to divert diplomatic activities and accompanying economic and political activities from the congested capital metropolitan Beijing to the developing southwest region as well as to enhance development and progress in the province of Guangxi.

China's rapid economic rise and seemingly perpetual average annual growth rate of 9 per cent, and increasing diplomatic activities, have aroused worries that China is ambitious to dominate the East and Southeast Asia region. However, the 1997 Asia financial crisis has brought to the closer cooperation of ASEAN members with China, Japan and ROK. During the inaugural East Asia and ASEAN summits in December 2005 at Kuala Lumpur, China Premier, Wen Jiabao reassured Asian leaders that China is committed to East Asia cooperation to foster a harmonious, secure and prosperous neighbourly environment. China's role in her relation with ASEAN is to be a major driving force than to dominate in ASEAN matters.

China's rapid growing economic development relies heavily on foreign investments and exports that are easily affected by overheating in some industries and trade protectionism. China ties up her economic and political agenda to her relations with ASEAN nations. Developing the less developed hinterland like the southwest and the northwest regions is part of China's policy and efforts to reduce illiteracy, poverty and instability as well as improving the status of women in these regions. Putting Guangxi and the Zhuang autonomous regions as the permanent venue for enhancing China-ASEAN relations has prompted dynamic economic opportunities for the region. The annual China-ASEAN EXPO and other related forums and activities held at Nanning, the capital city of Guangxi and Zhuang autonomous regions has brought delegates, businessmen, tourists, businesses, employment and development of infrastructure to the regions, thus making the regions a dynamic business hub and bringing prosperity to the people of the regions. The intended prosperity is necessary for the reduction of illiteracy, poverty, instability and improving the status of women.

Dialogues, interaction and cooperation with a common aim to develop the region into a place of peace, stability and growth signify China-ASEAN relations in the last decade. The change in trend is accelerated by the change in the new world order and the fast pace of development in China. The rise of China has provided an alternative market and demand for ASEAN produce and raw materials. China is also an alternative out-sourcing for ASEAN. The fast-increasing trade volume between China and ASEAN in the past few years well illustrates the situation.

The close relation between China and ASEAN lies in the political, economic, social and cultural ties. Malaysian Foreign Minister, Syed Hamid

China is Indonesia's fourth largest trading partner while Indonesia is China's 18th. The two nations have diplomatic relations since 1950. Indonesia supports one China policy in return for China's recognition for the unitary state of Indonesia. The two countries agreed to cooperate in marine security in the Malacca Strait. With the initiation of China-ASEAN FTA in 1992, trade barriers between the two nations are being gradually removed. Since then, bilateral economic and trade relations have experienced powerful driving force. Trade volume between China and Indonesia reached US$13.48 billion in 2004, up 31.8 per cent from previous year. Trade volume in the first five months of 2005 between the two nations stood at US$6.7 billion, indicating a rise of 37 per cent over the same period. In 2004, China's export volume to Indonesia totalled about US$6.3 billion, an increase of 39.6 per cent over the previous year. Chinese exports to Indonesia are mainly consumer and industrial goods like electrical appliances, electronic equipment, machinery, furnishings, textile and motorcycles, while Indonesian exports to China are mainly primary products like crude oil, natural gas, palm oil, paper pulp and timber. Chinese investment in Indonesia between 2000 and 2004 reached US$6.5 billion. Out of this amount, US$1.2 billion is invested in the energy sector alone. On the other hand, official statistics show that Indonesian investment in China has reached at least US$2 billion by the end of 2003.[19]

China and the Philippines have diplomatic relations since 1975. Total trade value between China and the Philippines were US$9.4 billion in 2003 and US$13.33 in 2004. The Philippines enjoyed a favourable trade balance of US$1.175 billion in 2002, US$3.212 billion in 2003, and US$4.09 billion in 2004. The hurdles in China-Philippine relations are the latter's occupation of 8 of the Spratly islands and the close military cooperation with US which China interprets as a threat to her security.

Singapore is one of the last in ASEAN to establish diplomatic relations with China. The relations were set in 1990. China is the third largest trading partner of Singapore. The two-way trade volume totalled US$33 billion in 2004, an increase of 44 per cent from US$22.84 in 2003. The trade volume in the first eight months in 2005 totalled around US$21 billion. Singapore is 6th largest source of overseas investment in China, with an accumulated sum of US$26 billion. At the end of September 2005, 88 companies based on Mainland China (an increase of 20 companies from 68 in 2004), 52 from Hong Kong and 12 from Taiwan are listed on the Singapore stock exchange. At the end of 2004, the number of Mainland Chinese companies investing in Singapore is 1493 (an increase of 893 companies from 600 at the end of 2002). The total sum of investment is US$616.52 billion at the end of 2003.[20]

Laos has diplomatic relations with China since 1961. In Laos, tourism accounted for18 per cent of the country's total revenue in 2004. There were more than 800,000 tourists in 2004. In the first 6 months of 2005, the number has reached 550,000. Statistics show that most of the tourists come from ASEAN countries, and 30 per cent from US and Europe. Tourists from China accounted for a total of 34,000 in 2004, ranking 5th. Tourism industry is significant to Laos in terms of revenue, and the nation has issued policies favourable for the promotion of the industry. In 2004, China has signed a memorandum with Laos to enhance cooperation between the two nations to promote Laos as a new international tourism destination for the Chinese.

Myanmar has diplomatic relations with China since 1950. The bilateral trade volume between China and Myanmar totalled US$1.15 in 2004. China is the 11th largest foreign investor in Myanmar.

Cambodia has diplomatic relation with China since 1958 and Thailand since 1975. Both nations have friendlier relations with China as compared to other ASEAN members. Malaysia has diplomatic relation with China in 1974 and Brunei in 1991, the last in ASEAN to have diplomatic relation with China. Both nations have sovereign disputes with China over islands in South China Sea.

China's fast growing economy has stimulated bilateral trade between ASEAN and China. The increasing trade and cooperation between ASEAN and China reduce the potential conflict and threat in Southeast Asia and the East Asia region. While China, Japan and ROK has continuing tension over Japanese Prime Minister Koizumi's annual Shrine visit since 1991 and Japanese textbooks distorting WWII history, trade disputes, and sovereignty claim over disputed waters and islands, ASEAN through the three ASEAN + 1 and ASEAN + 3 organizations is able to play the role of mediator to ease tension in the region.

Table 8.11 Dates of Diplomatic Relations between
         China and ASEAN Nations

Nations	Year	Nations	Year
Vietnam	1950	Malaysia	1974
Indonesia	1950	The Philippines	1975
Myanmar	1950	Thailand	1975
Cambodia	1958	Singapore	1990
Laos	1961	Brunei	1991

Economic Relations

The smooth political relations between China and ASEAN members in recent years has led to major progress in terms of cooperation in matters related to imports and exports, investment and contractual labour. In 2003, ASEAN announced moving towards building a common economic, security, social and cultural entity. The objective for 2020 is the free flow of goods, services and investments in the region.

China and most ASEAN countries' economy is export oriented, labour intensive and production requires semi-skilled labour. The difference is China has a huge domestic market to spur her economy while ASEAN countries' single largest determinant of growth is external demand. Thus ASEAN and China trade complements each other whereby the latter imports mostly primary products from ASEAN. Beginning from 1993, China has a trade deficit in her trade with ASEAN.

China is the fastest-growing major vehicle market compared to North America, Europe and Japan. There are two significant changes in the Chinese automobile market. The first is the Chinese passenger vehicle market has shifted from one predominantly controlled by sales to the public sector to one which sees the majority of sales going to the private sector. The second is that the strongest growth is coming from the small car segment, where most models sell for less than 60,000 yuan (US$7,400 or RM30,000). Such trend provides a niche-market for ASEAN-made passenger vehicles though China is also producing her own passenger vehicles. China's huge demand for automobiles provides export opportunities for some ASEAN members.

Table 8.12 China-ASEAN and ASEAN Trade Volume (US$ billion)

	China-ASEAN Trade Volume	ASEAN Trade Volume
2005 (Jan-Nov)	117.24	
2004	105.9	600
2003	76.24	
2000	40.0	783.7
1999	27.5	646.4
1998	23.5	
1996	20.0	
1993	10.7	
1990	6.0	
1980	2.064	
1975	0.523	

Sources: China-ASEAN Trade, Han (2002), pp. 213-214. ASEAN Trade, Wang (2002), p. 127. 2003-2005 figures are from *China Daily*.

Regional cooperation is part and parcel of the globalization process. While the EU has expanded its membership to 25 nations, there are other economic blocs, the NAFTA (North America Free Trade Area) for example. As ASEAN was formed in 1967 with an initial six members, the membership has been expanded to include Vietnam, Laos, Cambodia and Myanmar. China is tying up the development of southwest China to economic cooperation with ASEAN nations. Nanning, the capital city of Guangxi province and Zhuang Autonomous region is assigned to be the permanent centre for ASEAN meetings and forums. Yunnan province has joined the Mekong region for economic development and cooperation with Myanmar, Thailand, Vietnam, Laos and Cambodia.

CAFTA was initiated in 1992. China-ASEAN Business Council (CABC) was initiated in 2001 at Jakarta. CAEXPO was initiated in 2003. The CABC was initiated as a principal entity for the promotion of trade and investment between China and ASEAN members. The CABC has a role to strengthen ties between governments and enterprises, and promoting cooperation and economic growth for China and ASSEAN members. As most enterprises from ASEAN members are mainly SMEs lacking knowledge of investing and expanding their businesses in China, the CABC has a role to assist them through chambers of commerce and industry in the ASEAN nations. The CABC thus provides a platform for closer regional economic integration and construction towards achieving CAFTA scheduled for 2010.

At the 7th China-ASEAN leaders meeting in 2003, Chinese Premier Wen Jiabao proposed the launching of the China-ASEAN expo (CAEXPO), and proposed that it be an annual event. ASEAN leaders warmly welcomed the idea. In 2004, the first CAEXPO was held with success. In July 2005, China-ASEAN tariff reduction programme is launched signifying the start of the comprehensive implementation of a Free Trade Area (FTA). These show that China is seeking mutual economic development with ASEAN members. China is working closely to provide favourable conditions for the flow of business in the region. At the second CAEXPO in 2005, China strengthens economic ties with ASEAN, with an agenda to realise CAFTA as scheduled. Besides promoting products and cooperation in investment, the CAEXPO also provided a high-level forum for business and cultural exchanges.

In anticipation of the CAFTA, the "early harvest programme" (EHP) was launched on 1st January 2004. The EHP covers primarily more than 500 agricultural products; allow ASEAN members and China to benefit earlier from tariff reductions.

In 2004, the bilateral China-ASEAN trade volume reached US$105.9 billion, an increase of 38.9 per cent from 2003. In the first three quarters of

2005, trade volume reached US$94.54 billion, an increase of 25.3 per cent over the same period.[21] China and ASEAN members are looking into potentials in increasing bilateral trade volume, tourism and a more favourable mutual investment environment. The FTA once fully implemented will bring to a surge in trade and investment between ASEAN members and China.

Existing Cooperation and Problems

In preparation for the annual China-ASEAN expo (CAEXPO), the province of Guangxi alone has spent US$1.6 billion in 2004 to upgrade the transportation network. Out of that sum, US$1.3 billion was earmarked for highway development. At present the province has 60,000 kilometres of highways of which expressways account for 11,000 kilometres. In 2005, the province is building another 1,500 kilometres of highways in the region. Guangxi province is also upgrading its railway lines connecting major cities in China.[22] The upgrading of the railway network is scheduled to consume US$4.9 billion. At present, the highways and railway lines provide easier and convenient access to Guangdong and Yunnan provinces as well as Vietnam thus connecting to some of the ASEAN member nations.

During the second CAEXPO, temporary direct charter flights between Guangxi province and major ASEAN cities were arranged. However, direct flights still need to be launched to actualise the closer and bilateral economic and cultural relations between China and ASEAN members. Direct flight opening between Mainland China and Taiwan needs to be realised too as one of the steps to ease tension between the two sides.

In the effort to receive CAFTA in 2010, Guangxi is upgrading its present port facilities. In 2005, the province has 20 berths with a total handling capacity of about 30 million tons. The province is planning to develop a total of 61 berths with a handling capacity of 10,000 tons each by 2010.

Though ASEAN and China complements each other in their bilateral trade, both competes for foreign investment and market shares in US, EU and Japan. As there is still fear towards China's ascendance backed by one-fifth of the world population and a continuing fast growing economy, China is still working hard to reduce lingering suspicion and gain continuing trust from her neighbours, ASEAN.

Sovereignty disputes over Spratly Islands and surrounding waters between China and five of the ASEAN member nations were once a confronting issue. Vietnam has occupied 27 islands in the troubled waters, an island in the Beibu Bay and demanding sovereignty over Xisha islands, the Philippines occupies 8 of the Spratly islands and one of the Zhongsha islands. Malaysia occupies

9 of the islands and China 7 while Taiwan occupies one of the islands and controls Dongsha Islands (Chen, 2004: 284-285). With the general consensus and friendlier relations between China-ASEAN, the conflict has been put aside under the principle of "setting aside disputes and developing together". The challenge of this solution is the absence of concrete plans and dates for developing together the disputed islands and water, and there is no mention of technology and capital inputs, nor the individual proportion of sharing the development. At the mean time, fishing activities and oil and gas exploration activities continued in the disputed waters. The Philippines has several times detained fishermen from China (Chen, 2004: 285). The close military cooperation between Philippine and US poses threat to China's security.

Conclusions

The 2003 proposed "peaceful rise, harmonious society, and scientific development perspective" portrays China's determination to achieve stability in the country, direction of development and growth, and the pledge of peace to the global community. The proposal is explicitly illustrated in China's political, economic and cultural ties with other countries. As for the hurdles in diplomatic and political ties, it takes the understanding of parties involved to take into consideration mutual benefits, sustaining growth, common prosperity and universal peace and harmony in the global community.

As 2006 marked the beginning of China's 11th five-year plan, "peaceful development" is going to be the theme guiding China's relation with other countries. The same year also witnessed the hosting of Year of Russia in China and in 2007 Year of China in Russia, and for the first time, China-India Friendly Year. China and Spain have agreed to host each other's cultural year. In September 2005, both China and France had just concluded their mutual cultural year as a great success. By initiating and holding these pioneering cultural events, China is demonstrating to the global community her determination to promote mutual understanding achieving her principle of "in harmony with neighbours and prosper together" (*mu lin fu li* 睦邻富里).

China's "rise" may be interpreted more correctly as the re-ascendance to her grace and strength as was during the dynasties. China's ascendance follows a path of her own that has some similarities to that of Japan and the four dragons (ROK, Taiwan, Hong Kong and Singapore), that is, rapid growth that is spurred by excessive foreign investments and an export oriented economy. The variations are China's seemingly perpetual, close to two digit annual growth for the past 27 years and significant domestic demand created by the 1.3 billion populations. As the rise of any big nation attracts international attention, China's political ideology has attributed partly to attract attention. China's ascendance has reshuffled world order and dominance. In her switch from planned economy to market economy, China is undergoing tremendous social and political reform. In the process, China pursues for peace, harmony and stability with her neighbours and international community. The huge population where two-thirds are peasants who have no access or little access to education opportunities and medical care resembles severe challenge for China's sustainable development. China's pledge to peaceful development is assurance to her neighbours and the international community. China's peaceful development model is exemplary to the international community that is facing traditional and new security threats.

China's relations with ASEAN, a loose organization of mostly small nations, is initiated by trade but has upgraded to mutual closer cooperation extending into regional security cooperation. ASEAN is able to mediate in the adverse China-Japan relations, a role that would not arouse suspicion from big nations.

The increasing bilateral trade between China and ASEAN has led to closer and upgraded diplomatic ties. China and ASEAN have agreed to solve issues related to Spratly Islands and disputed waters through negotiations and cooperation for mutual benefits. China-ASEAN relations have proven effective in achieving regional stability and peace.

The creation of China-ASEAN FTA is to promote thriving bilateral trade. The trade complements each other's needs and provides opportunity for prosperity in the region. Cross border trade and tourism coupled with cooperation in energy supply, road construction, cultural heritage conservation projects and human resource training have enhanced regional relations. The existing model of China-ASEAN relations needs time and further study to evaluate its success in promoting regional stability, peace and sustainable growth that may be a model for global stability, peace and sustainable growth.

Notes

*   I would like to express my gratitude to Professor Yang Baoyun, Professor Liang Zhiming, Professor Zhao Jing and Professor Li Mou for their time to discuss with me on this topic. However, any shortcomings in this paper are the responsibility of the writer.

References used in this paper include books, articles, conference paper, magazines, *China Daily* and *Cankao Xiaoxi*, a paper formerly for internal circulation among China's Communist Party leaders only. Statistics printed in *China Daily* are taken as said issued by government departments. On January 5th 2006, it is reported that China will put all data survey teams under the direct management of the National Bureau of Statistics (NBS). Officials with the NBS said that the State Council has made public a decision to amend the rules on the implementation of the Statistics Law, so as to make the central government's statistics more relevant, guarantee more reliable data, improve the quality of national accounting standards and to meet the demand for reforming China's statistical work. The new rule is also to tackle the problem of local officials inflating economic figures for political gain, leading to a gap between the aggregate of local figures and those published by the central government, thus causing skepticism about the accuracy of China's data.

1. *China Business Weekly, China Daily*, 16 January 2006, p. 2.
2. *China Daily*, 14 December 2005, p. 2.
3. Figures for 1978 and 2003 are taken from Zhang (2004: 55), for 2004 and 2005 from *China Daily*, December 2005.
4. *China Daily*, 9 January 2006, *China Business Weekly*, p. 2.
5. Figure released by the People's Bank of China, the central bank. *China Daily*, 17 January 2006, p. 1. Chinese keep high savings for children's education, medical care, housing and old age.
6. Wang Ling is associate researcher with the Chinese Academy of Social Sciences.
7. *China Daily*, 6 January 2006, p. 1.
8. Wang Ling aggregated the factors and sub-indices of economic power, military and diplomatic capacities, and "national power resources" of each country and government's macro-control capacity to give an overall score for each nation (*China Daily*, 6 January 2006, p. 1).
9. China's high savings rate is a consequence of the insecurity of her people about their future. Chinese save their income for their worries about high medical expenses, education for children, job insecurity in a fast changing business environment and retirement.
10. Figures published on China's General Administration of Customs' website (*China Daily*, 11 November 2005, p. 12).
11. *China Daily*, 7 December 2005, p. 1.
12. *China Daily*, 10-11 December 2005, p. 1.
13. Figures from Zhang (2004: 55-56), and also *http://www.stats.gov.cn/tjgb/ndtjgb/qgndtjgb/t20040226_402131958.htm*
14. China President, Hu Jintao's address to the Republic of Korea National Assembly (*China Daily*, 18 November 2005, p. 1).
15. Report published by United Nations Conference on Trade and Development (*China Daily*, 15 November 2005, p. 9).
16. Disputes related to hospital charges over medical treatment are often and widely reported in the Chinese media. For pneumonia treatment in the hospital for one week costs around 2,000 yuan.
17. The US, a key player in the talks, promised not to make military attack on the DPRK and agreed to join ROK, China, Japan and Russia in providing energy supplies to DPRK. In exchange, DPRK agreed to scrap all her nuclear weapons-

related programs, rejoin the nuclear Non-Proliferation Treaty and allow outside nuclear inspections.

18. *China Daily*, 20 October 2005, p. 2.

19. When Indonesian President Susilo Bambang Yudhoyono visited China in July 2005, more than 10 Chinese and Indonesian businesses signed co-operation agreements worth over US$4 billion involving finance, oil, gas, engineering and information technology projects (*China Daily*, 22-23 October 2005, p. 12).

20. *China Daily*, 20 October 2005, p. 13, special supplement.

21. During Chinese President Hu Jintao's visit to ASEAN in April 2005, Hu set a target to increase China-ASEAN trade volume to US$200 billion by the year 2010. *China Daily*, 20 October 2005, p. 9.

22. The Luoyang-Zhanjiang Railway connecting Guangxi province to Henan province has kicked off and scheduled to be completed in 2008. In 2004, Guangxi has signed an agreement with the Ministry of Railways to begin construction on the Guangxi section of the Luoyang-Zhanjiang Railway. (*China Daily*, 20 October 2005, p. 13, special supplement.)

References

Banning, Garrett (2005), "US-China Relations In The Era Of Globalization – A Framework For Analysis", paper presented at the Beijing Forum, November 16-18, 2005, Beijing.

Cai, Jianguo 蔡建国 (ed.) (2004), *21 Shiji de Dongya: Jiyu, Tiaozhan yu Chuangxin* 21 世纪的东亚: 机遇, 挑战与创新 (21st Century East Asia: Opportunities, Challenges and Construction), Shanghai: Shanghai Shehuikexue Yuan Chubanshe.

Chen, Xiangyang 陈向阳 (2004), *Zhongguo Mulin Waijiao – Sixiang, Shijian, Qianzhan* 中国睦邻外交– 思想, 实践, 前瞻 (China's Good-neighbour Diplomacy: Thought, Practice, Prospect), Beijing: Shishi Chubanshe.

Jiang, Zemin 江泽民 (2002), *Quanmian Jianshe Xiaokang Shehui, Kaichuang Zhongguo Tese Shehuizhuyi Shiye Xin Jumian – zai Zhongguo Gongchandang Di Shiliu Ci Quanguo Daibiaodahui shang de Baogao* 全面建设小康社会, 开创中国特色社会主义事业新局面 – 在中国共产党第 16 次全国代表大会上的报告 (Full-Scale Developing Middle-Class Society, Turning Over a New Leaf to Chinese Socialism – Report on the 16th China Communist Party Congress), Beijing: Renmin Chubanshe.

Liang, Zhiming 梁志明, Zhang Xizhen 张锡镇 and Zhao Jing 赵敬 (eds) (2002), *Huigu yu Zhanwang: Mianxiang Xin Shiji de Zhongguo Dongnanyaxue Yanjiu* 回顾与展望: 面向新世纪的中国东南亚学研究 (Reflections and Prospects: Towards China's Research on Southeast Asian Studies in the New Century), Hong Kong: Hong Kong Press for Social Sciences Ltd (Conference papers of the 6th Annual Meeting of China Symposium on Southeast Asian Studies CSSAS).

Liu, Wanyuan 刘婉媛 (2005), "Meiguo Chongxin Dingwei Zhongguo: Liyi Xiangguan

Zhe 美国重新定位中国: 利益相关者" (US Restates China's Position: An Interest Party), *China Newsweek*, November 28, 2005, pp. 40-41.

Mauzy, Diane K. (1984), *Politics in the ASEAN States*, Kuala Lumpur: Marican & Sons (Malaysia) Sdn Bhd.

Sun, Fusheng 孙福生 (2002), "Dongnanya Diqu de Daguo Guanxi: Zhongguo yu Meiguo 东南亚地区的大国关系: 中国与美国" (Big Nations Relations in Southeast Asia Region: China and USA), in Liang Zhiming 梁志明, Zhang Xizhen 张锡镇 and Zhao Jing 赵敬 (eds), *Huigu yu Zhanwang: Mianxiang Xin Shiji de Zhongguo Dongnanyaxue Yanjiu* 回顾与展望: 面向新世纪的中国东南亚学研究" (Reflections and Prospects: Towards China's Research on Southeast Asian Studies in the New Century), Hong Kong: Hong Kong Press For Social Sciences Ltd (Conference papers of the 6th Annual Meeting of China Symposium on Southeast Asian Studies CSSAS), pp. 22-32.

Wang, Shilu 王士录 (2002), "Dongmeng yu Dongyaqu Hezuo 东盟与东亚区合作" (ASEAN and East Asian Cooperation), in Liang Zhiming 梁志明, Zhang Xizhen 张锡镇 and Zhao Jing 赵敬 (eds), *Huigu yu Zhanwang: Mianxiang Xin Shiji de Zhongguo Dongnanyaxue Yanjiu* 回顾与展望: 面向新世纪的中国东南亚学研究" (Reflections and Prospects: Towards China's Research on Southeast Asian Studies in the New Century), Hong Kong: Hong Kong Press For Social Sciences Ltd (Conference papers of the 6th Annual Meeting of China Symposium on Southeast Asian Studies CSSAS), pp. 118-129.

Wang, Yiming (2006), "Five-Year Plan Sets Stage For Solving Problems", *China Daily*, 4th January 2006, p. 4.

Yang, Guiyan 杨贵言 (2004), *Dangdai Dongya Wenti Yanjiu Jianlun* 当代东亚问题研究简论 (Discourse On Contemporary East Asian Study), Beijing: Renmin Chubanshe.

Yu, Xiangdong 于向东 (2002), "Yuenan yu Daguo Guanxi de Ruogan Dongxiang 越南与大国关系的若干动向" (Vietnam and Big Nations Relations: Several Directions), in Liang Zhiming 梁志明, Zhang Xizhen 张锡镇 and Zhao Jing 赵敬 (eds), *Huigu yu Zhanwang: Mianxiang Xin Shiji de Zhongguo Dongnanyaxue Yanjiu* 回顾与展望: 面向新世纪的中国东南亚学研究" (Reflections and Prospects: Towards China's Research on Southeast Asian Studies in the New Century), Hong Kong: Hong Kong Press For Social Sciences Ltd (Conference papers of the 6th Annual Meeting of China Symposium on Southeast Asian Studies CSSAS), pp. 48-61.

Yu, Xintian 俞新天 (2005), *Zai Heping, Fazhan, Hezuo de Qizhi xia – Zhongguo Zhanlüe Jiyu Qi de Duiwai Zhanlüe Zonglun* 在和平, 发展, 合作的旗帜下 – 中国战略机遇期的对外战略纵论 (Under the Banner of Peace, Development, Cooperation – Discussion of China's External Strategies during Strategic Opportunities), Beijing: Zhonggong Zhongyang Dangxiao Chubanshe.

Zhang, Liangmin 张良民 (2002), in Liang Zhiming 梁志明, Zhang Xizhen 张锡镇 and Zhao Jing 赵敬 (eds), *Huigu yu Zhanwang: Mianxiang Xin Shiji de Zhongguo Dongnanyaxue Yanjiu* 回顾与展望: 面向新世纪的中国东南亚学研究" (Re-

During the 1990s the bilateral trade has accelerated in the second stage. Except for a low ebb in 1998 due to the financial crisis, Sino-Malaysian trade value grew at 21.5 per cent annually from 1991 to 1997, reflecting the mutual efforts of the governments and the intrinsic increasing domestic needs due to the rapid economic development of both countries.

Since 1998, Sino-Malaysian trade has undergone a breakthrough, not only in terms of the expansion of aggregate trade (see Table 9.1) but also the improvement of commodity composition.

Table 9.1 Trade between China and Malaysia, 1998-2005
(unit: US$100 million)

Year	Export	Import	Total of Sino-Malaysia	Total China-ASEAN Trade
1998	15.96	26.68	42.64	235
1999	16.74	36.06	52.8	270
2000	25.65	54.8	80.45	395
2001	32.2	62.05	94.25	416
2002	49.75	92.96	142.71	548
2003	61.41	139.87	201.3	783
2004	80.87	181.74	262.6	1058
2005	106.07	200.96	307.03	1304

Source: *Yearbook of China's Foreign Trade and External Economic Cooperation*, 1998-2005, China Foreign Economic Relations and Trade Publishing House.
Note: The statistics refer to the trade from China to Malaysia.

From Table 9.1, it is obvious that Sino-Malaysian trade surged much faster in the post-crisis period than that in the previous phase. The bilateral trade increased by 33.3 per cent from 1999 to 2005 annually, even exceeding the average growth rate of 28.5 per cent in the trade between China and ASEAN over the same period.

The remarkable performance of Sino-Malaysian trade can be seen not only through the gross value, but through the gradual progress of trade commodity structure as well (see Table 9.2). At the beginning of the 1990s, Malaysian exports to China concentrated on agricultural products, such as palm oil, wood products as well as rubber, etc. But the share of these products dropped drastically after 1995 while the share of capital-intensive goods rose quickly. For example, the exports of electrical machinery & apparatus accounted for

Table 9.2   Commodity Composition of Exports to China from Malaysia
(per cent)

Year	Agriculture-intensive	Mineral-intensive	Labour-intensive	Capital-intensive
1990	78.7	7.5	1.4	12.5
1995	66.3	6.2	4.3	23.2
2000	21.5	9.5	2.4	66.7
2003	14.4	7.7	1.3	76.7

Source: Calculation from UN Comtrade database.

48 per cent of Malaysia's export to China in 2005. Likewise, Malaysia used to be an import market of primary bulky goods for China, such as foodstuff, vegetable oil, fruits, livestock, textile yarn and fabrics, but now the products of electrical and electronic (E.E.) equipment & parts plus machinery appliances occupied 65 per cent of Malaysia's import value from China. From 2000 on, the structure of trade goods remains stable relatively, the top four exports of China to Malaysia are: E.E. products, machinery & mechanical parts, chemical products, textile product; the top four import from Malaysia are: E.E. products, palm oil & products, chemical products, mineral oil. Specifically, automatic data processing equipment is the leading export goods of China to Malaysia, with integrated circuit and micro-electronics parts being the largest part of import from Malaysia. In addition, the surging deficit of Sino-Malaysian trade mainly results from China's substantial import from Malaysia in the products of integrated circuit and micro-electronics parts after 2002.

All the indicators mentioned above show that there existed a major shift of Sino-Malaysian trade pattern in the past decade. The increasing source of trade goods mainly attributed to the rapid growth of capital-intensive products, especially electrical machinery and mechanism appliance that is also the largest export category for China and Malaysia respectively. Therefore, it deserves looking into the reason for the shift in bilateral trade pattern which is presented in the following section.

Intra-Industry Trade between China and Malaysia

To explore the present trade pattern between China and Malaysia, the methodology of intra-industry trade (IIT) is introduced here.

In the "New Trade Theory", intra-industry trade provides an explanation why a substantial amount of world trade occurs in similar products[1]. Different from the traditional theories of comparative advantage, ITT theory argues that, given the imperfect competition and scale economies effect in modern market, intra-industry trade in differential products results from the interaction between preferences for variety and scale economies. Empirical studies (Grubel and Lloyd 1975, Brander 1981, Helpman 1987, Leamer 1992) pointed out that IIT mostly occurs in developed countries due to the similar industrial structure and high per capita income level and consumption preference alike, and is usually assumed to be the unique characteristic of north-and-north trade.

However, as regional economic integration progresses rapidly in East Asia that encompasses economies of different types since the mid-1990s, it is found that the share of IIT in overall trade among these economies is growing in importance (Fukao, 2003). Moreover, recent studies divide IIT into two types in a narrower manner – one is the horizontal intra-industry trade (HIIT) which stands for the trade in the similar goods with the same quality but differential function and design, showing preferences variety and scale economy effect; the other one is the vertical intra-industry trade (VIIT) which refers to the exchange of products with different quality in the same category, arising from different factor endowment, comparative advantages as well as various technology level. E.g., though bilateral trade takes place with the sort of IIT, developed country can export more advanced products to developing countries, meanwhile import less advanced goods from developing country. According to the model of Greenaway et al. (1995), if export unit values / import unit values of IIT goods varies from 0.8 to 1.25, we can classify this kind of IIT as the type of HIIT, otherwise it belongs to the sort of VIIT.

This paper uses the conventional Grubel-Lloyd index in analyzing the IIT status in Sino-Malaysian trade. We get from the Grubel-Lloyd measurement model:

$$GL_{ij} = 1 - (X_{ij} - M_{ij}) / (X_{ij} + M_{ij})$$ Eqs. (1)

Here X_{ij} denotes export of commodity J in country I, M_{ij} denotes import of commodity J in country I. To assess the overall level of IIT in country I, the methodology can be described as follow. Generally the higher GL_{ij} index, the higher intensity the intra-industry trade in this sort of commodity has, reflecting the advantage of specialization in international division of labour.

$$GL_i = \sum_{j=1}^{n} GL_{ij} \left[\frac{\left| X_{ij} - M_{ij} \right|}{\sum_{j=1}^{n} \left(X_{ij} + M_{ij} \right)} \right]$$ Eqs. (2)

Considering the unbalanced trade between China and Malaysia in recent years, using the GL adjusted IIT model, we can get the following figure, which shows that the benchmark of IIT index was relatively low (less than 30 per cent) until the mid-1990s. However the share of IIT index in Sino-Malaysian trade increased steadily during 1998-2001, reaching the high point of 50 per cent or so.[2] This phenomenon is consistent with rapid growth of gross bilateral trade in the corresponding period. Compared with other ASEAN countries, the IIT index of Sino-Malaysia still lags behind that of Singapore, ahead of the Philippines and Indonesia, roughly parallel to Thailand after 2002.

Figure 9.1 IIT Index between China and Malaysia in 1994-2003

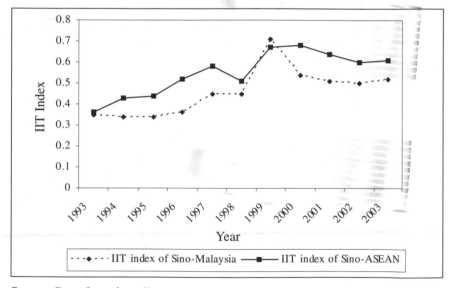

Source: Data from *http://www.aseansec.org*

Being the largest source of Sino-Malaysian trade products, the IIT index of trade goods at HS (i.e., Harmonized Commodity Description And Coding System) 84 & 85 has representative significance. From Eq. (1), in 2004[3], it is calculated that IIT index of commodity at HS 84-digit code, which occupied 15 per cent of overall trade value, reached 0.89, belonging to highly horizontal IIT group. While HS 85 goods accounted for 46 per cent of Sino-Malaysian trade value, the IIT index was only 0.37, indicating that there exists a low level of specialization division in this group.[4]

All these indicators highlight that the international division in Sino-Malaysian trade used to be confined to the dependence on natural resources and endowments. However, though inter-industry division based on traditional endowments could partly explain the performance of the Sino-Malaysian trade expansion, the growing part of the present trade largely reflects their comparative advantage in different technology-intensive manufactured goods (especially niche products in E.E. apparatus & parts as well as machinery appliances, given the rapid industrialization in both countries concerned, particularly for China in recent years), showing the ongoing complementarities in heterogeneous intermediate products in a broad spectrum of E.E. apparatus & parts which benefit each other.

Remarks on Bilateral Trade Pattern

There are several dimensions to observe in the Sino-Malaysian trade expansion as well as the shift of trade pattern over the last decade.

First, the healthy political relations between China and Malaysia have been contributing a great deal to the rapid and comprehensive economic ties. Since the 1990s, the frequent visits of two countries' leaders not only have strengthened the political trusts but also encouraged the business circles to cooperate closely in the field of trade, investment as well as construction contract, etc.

Second, as far as the growing intra-industry trade is concerned, two factors can be used to interpret this trend. A very important role was played by the inward FDI in China and Malaysia. The industry of E.E. apparatus & parts is the common industry with concentrated inflowing FDI for the two countries. The production of this industry can be readily decomposed to many working procedure with different intermediate input goods at diverse technology level, which combines labour-intensive procedure with low-tech and high-tech procedure. In the case of East Asia, an empirical study (Fukao, 2003) shows that the IIT index of all industries in the East Asian region reached 20.5 per cent, and the share of IIT also increased rapidly among these developing economies concerned. In particular, it is worth noting that the IIT shares are exceptionally high in the trade in electrical machinery and general and precision machinery, reaching 30.5 per cent and 19.2 per cent respectively, in accordance with active export-oriented FDI in the production of these goods in this region. Therefore, from the supply side, it is manifest to explain the motivation from MNCs to distribute the inner production along the value chain in various countries so as to create growing intra-industry trade between China and Malaysia.

Meanwhile, from the perspective of domestic demand, with the rapid economic development in China and Malaysia, per capita GDP is upward with PPP GDP per capita in China and Malaysia being US$4990 and US$8940 respectively in 2005[5]. According to previous studies, such as Linder (1961), Balassa (1986), the higher the income per capita, the greater the need is for differentiated attribute of finished products and various intermediate goods. Thus, the rising income provides the favourable conditions for intra-industry trade between China and Malaysia.

Third, in contrast to the worry of the surging China's impacts on regional economies, empirical evidences demonstrate that China has brought about positive effects on economic growth of ASEAN countries through trade links since the 1990s. As for Malaysia, econometric measurement revealed that the multiplier effects on GDP growth created by a 1 per cent positive shock to China arrived at 0.43 in 1986 and 0.96 in 2000 respectively (Abeysinghe, 2003), showing an upward trend for China to become a new growth engine for its neighbours. Considering that China has overtaken Japan to become the largest import market in Asia as well as the world's third largest trading country after the U.S. and Germany since 2004, China's import is growing faster relative to its exports, providing enormous opportunities for its neighbours. As Chirathivat (2002) pointed out, China would increasingly regard ASEAN as an alternative source of inputs of natural resource-based and intermediate products. This also provides the basis to explain why China has a large deficit consecutively in Sino-Malaysian trade.

Prospects for Trade

As for the future of Sino-Malaysian trade in the coming years, there are significant signs to notice:

From the side of China, through increasing public spending and encouraging domestic consumption, the Beijing government exerts many efforts on the shift from an overly export-oriented growth strategy toward an internal-demand-driven growth model in recent years. The new 11th Five-year Economic and Social Development Plan of China (2006-2010) highlights the importance of the economic growth pattern switch from the extensive type to the intensive one, and also vows to establish the independent innovation capability so as to maintain sustainable economic development and create a balance with the outside world. This long-term strategic adjustment implies that China will take initiatives to accelerate industrial upgrading, thus it can contribute to forming the horizontal international division of labour at a more advanced technology level, especially in intra-industry manufacturing trade with high elasticity of demand between China and Malaysia, so as to avoid overly competition in the low-tech products such as some labour-intensive industries in the third market.

In the context of China-ASEAN Free Trade Area (CAFTA), China has committed a comprehensive package of market liberalization reforms, which are more preferential than its commitments toward WTO. To push this agreement, an early harvest programme has been launched since July 2005, covering 7000 items. Given a small share of trade between China and Malaysia in these coverages, this plan will not affect the bilateral trade greatly. However, with the implementation of CAFTA, some of Malaysia's export products to China such as palm oil, rubber products and wood products etc. will benefit more from the lower tariff level and the elimination of trade barriers. Today 70 per cent of the palm oil import of China comes from Malaysia; China is also the largest export destination for Malaysia's rubber. Besides the merchandise trade, service trade has been progressing, including the field of tourism, finance, transportation, accounting, etc. In the framework of CAFTA, decreasing barriers will make the flow of capital, commodities, and information more convenient in this region and hence enhance the market appeal to MNCs outside the region as well as intra-region enterprises. Mutual investment generally incurs more bilateral trade, especially intra-industry trade.

Facing the process of globalization as well as regionalism, we cannot ignore the competition pressure. Being a big market, China has established comprehensive industries varied from low-technology to high-technology, and depended on the large economic scale and abundant human capital to own its comparative advantage in the field of iron & steel, petrochemical industry and textile industry relative to Malaysia. On the contrary, as an early comer in the E.E. industry, Malaysia has accumulated its comparative advantage of production capability in niche products. Therefore, the export structure of both countries has not overlapped severely in the third market up to now. However, given that China is catching up quickly in many fields, competition seems to be inevitable. Thus, both countries should make use of the enlarged market to share the spillover effects and upgrade industrial technology so as to get a win-win situation in the future.

Conclusion

In this paper, we discuss the present trade relationship between China and Malaysia, showing that there exists a dramatic switch in terms of growth rate as well as trade pattern. It is found that intra-industry trade has been growing in its significance, indicating more advanced intra-industry specialization to link the countries concerned closely. As the World Bank pointed out that Malaysia would gain most from China's accession to WTO in the ASEAN region, the evidence of Sino-Malaysian trade expansion shows a win-win situation on both sides. Moreover, both sides also face the challenges resulting from increased competition in the future.

Notes

1. In general, the trade products within the same division, the same section as well as the same group can be seen as intra-industry products according to the Standard International Trade Classification (SITC).
2. The average level of the IIT index among developed countries is approximately close to 0.6.
3. The source is the *China Customs Statistics Yearbook, 2004.*
4. The broader items the classification standard includes, the higher the index of IIT will be. So, the result of the IIT index is related to the classification standard.
5. The data are from the World Bank online database (*http://www.worldbank.org*).

References

Abeysinghe, Tilak and Ding Lu (2003), "China as an Economic Powerhouse: Implications on Its Neighbors," *China Economic Review*, Elsevier, Vol. 14(2), pp. 164-185.

ASEAN Annual Report 2004-2005.

Balassa, B. (1986), "Intra-industry Trade Specialization: A Cross-Country Analysis", *European Economic Review*, 30(1), pp. 27-41.

Brander, James A. (1981), "Intra-industry Trade in Identical Commodities", *Journal of International Economics*, 11 (February), 1-14.

Chirathivat, Suthiphand (2002), "ASEAN-China Free Trade Area: Background, Implications and Future Development", *Journal of Asian Economics*, 13, pp. 671-686.

Dai, Feng 戴枫 (2005), "Zhongguo yu Dongmeng Chanye Nei Maoyi Tanxi 中国与东盟产业内贸易探析", *Shijie Jingji yu Zhengzhi Luntan* 世界经济与政治论坛, 5.

Ding, Jie 丁杰 (2005), "Woguo yu Malaixiya Jingmao Guanxi de Xianzhuang, Wenti yu Duice 我国与马来西亚经贸关系的现状, 问题与对策", *Guoji Maoyi Wenti* 国际贸易问题, 5.

Fukao, Kyoji (2003), "Vertical Intra-industry Trade and Foreign Direct Investment in East Asia", *Journal of the Japanese and International Economies*, 17, pp. 468-506.

Greenaway, D., R. Hine and C. Milner (1995), "Vertical and Horizontal Intra-industry Trade: A Cross Industry Analysis for the United Kingdom", *Economic Journal*, 105, pp. 1505-1518.

Grubel, Herbert G. and P.J. Lloyd (1975), *Intra-Industry Trade: The Theory and Measurement of International Trade in Differentiated Products*, London: The Macmillan Press Ltd.

Guoji Shangbao 国际商报, various issues (2004-2006).

Helpman, E. (1981), "International Trade in the Presence of Product Differentiation, Economies of Scale and Monopolistic Competition: A Chamberlin-Heckscher-Ohlin Approach", *Journal of International Economics*, 11, pp. 305-340.

Leamer, E.E. (1984), *Sources of International Comparative Advantage*, Cambridge, MA: MIT Press.

Liao, Shaolian (2005), "Sino-Malaysian Economic Relations", paper presented at international conference on Malaysia, Xiamen University.

Linder, S.B. (1961), *An Essay on Trade and Transformation*, New York: Wiley and Sons.

Wang, Juan 王娟 (2005), "Zhongguo-Dongmeng Chanye Nei Maoyi de Qushi, Dongyin yu Duice 中国-东盟产业内贸易的趋势, 动因与对策", *Shijie Jingji Yanjiu* 世界经济研究, 7.

Wang, Lanfen 王兰芬 (2004), "Zhongguo yu Dongmeng de Jingzheng yu Hezuo Guanxi Fenxi 中国与东盟的竞争与合作关系分析", *Dangdai Caijing* 当代财经, 12.

Yamazawa, I. (2001), *China Enters WTO: Pursuing the Symbiosis with the Global Economy*, Tokyo: Institute of Developing Economies.

Zhao, H. (1997), "Foreign Trade in the People's Republic of China: Past Performance and Future Challenges", *Asian Development Bank Review*, 15, pp. 88-110

Zhongguo Haiguan Tongji Nianjian 中国海关统计年鉴, various years (1992-2005).

10

The Impacts of China's WTO Entry on Southeast Asian Economic Growth and Development: A Case Study on the Philippine Economy

Shen Hongfang

Introduction

China's WTO membership acceptance is recognized as a grand event for the global economy in the beginning of the 21st century. China's WTO entry means that China could enjoy the most-favoured-nation clause and country treatment endowed that will benefit a great deal its economic growth. At the same time, China has to assume its corresponding obligations as a member of WTO to further open up its market, and to increase the transparency of trade policies and other related codes and to abide by the international rules, which make a contribution undoubtedly to the expanding of global investment and trade, and to the stimulating of global economic growth with a potential market of 13 hundred million population. The Chinese government as well as many countries in the world consider that the outcome for China's WTO entry will be a "win-win" situation for both China and its trade and investment partners.

Nevertheless, China's accession to WTO brings also more severe clamor of China's "economic threat" on its neighbouring countries, particularly on the aspects of "job depriving" caused by massive Chinese exports to Southeast Asian domestic and international markets, and large amount of foreign investment going into China instead of Southeast Asia resulting in the dwindling of foreign investment of the later, as well as the rivals of Chinese cheap labourers on Southeast Asian overseas workers.

This paper probes into the impacts of China's WTO entry on Philippine economic growth and development within the framework or, rather limited on Sino-Philippine bilateral trade, investment and service. The competitions of trade, investment and personal of the countries brought forth probably by China's WTO entry in global markets will be less talked about here due to

The perceptions held by the Philippine government and the public with regard to China's "economic threat" that would be even more severe after China's accession to WTO are under the following discussion:

- Whether deficits existed from the Philippine side in Sino-Philippine trade intercourse should be considered as "job depriving" of Filipinos by the Chinese.
- Whether certain amount of direct investments of Chinese Filipinos flow into their ancestral home, Fujian province and other advanced areas of China should be regarded as complex of "Chineseness", or "loyal to their native place", or "improper way of the Chinese government in absorbing foreign investment".
- Whether competitions of all kinds of "China-made commodities" in international market are the main reason for the shrinking of the Philippines' traditional and non-traditional markets abroad for Philippine-made goods.
- Whether the large amount of foreign investment pulling into China in the years running is one of the important causes for the dwindling of Philippine foreign investment.
- Whether the Chinese cheap labourers are the rivals of overseas Filipino workers.

Engulfing myself in conducting the study of Sino-Philippine economic relations for quite a long period of time, I have found profoundly the coexistence of complementarity and competition in the course of economic cooperation of the two countries. The reality of diversification and expansion of the two country's economic exchange since 2000, whereas, proved that there are more opportunities than challenges to the two countries' economic relations after China won the membership of WTO.

China's WTO Accession is in Favour of the Expansion of Bilateral Trade

As a member of WTO now, the Chinese government has to strictly abide by WTO rules and earnestly fulfill its pledges. The Chinese merchants must follow the international routines and regulations in conducting international trade and commerce. Therefore, while further opening to the outside world the Chinese domestic market for foreign commodities, the Chinese government has to strengthen its transparency on market information and to provide a predicable environment for trade. A massive dismantling of trade protection is taking place according to the schedule set by China's pledges.

The Chinese government's commitments with regard to China's import and export include:

a) Its average tariff of farm products drops from 21 per cent in 2001 to 15 per cent below five years later in 2006. There is a period of protection for implementing quota system of tariff due to the weak rivalrousness of China's agriculture products following the WTO regulation. However, the implementation of the concrete quota system depends on the negotiation between China and the relevant countries.

b) Its average tariff of industrial goods drops from 24 per cent in 2001 to 8.9 per cent below five years later in 2006. Two thirds of the items must be in place in 2003, and the rest have to be in place in 2005. China's tariff for some specific products such as CMOS chip, semiconductor in consent by the Chinese government have been lowered to zero, and China's average tariff for automobile is lowered from 80 per cent in 2001 to 25 per cent in July of 2006. The Chinese government has pledged and implemented to lower the tariffs for various kinds of goods including paper pulp, leather, transformer, textile, etc.

It can be seen that commitments made by the Chinese government of lowering the level of China's market admittance of many farm products and industrial products are actually in accord with those Philippine exports, which cannot but benefit the Philippine export products. Those manufacturers are covering farm products, processed food, metal manufactures, furniture, jewel, toy, lumber, paper pulp, plastic products, electronics etc. As a matter of fact, many of the Philippine exports to China have already got substantial tariff reduction including marine products, plant oil, coconut products, garments, electric computer, calculator, tape record, diskette, paper and paper products, electronic input and output fittings.[4]

China's WTO Entry Brings about Opportunity for Chinese Private Entrepreneurs to Invest in the Philippines

There are approximately more than one million Chinese Filipinos – more than one per cent of the total population of the Philippines are of Chinese origin, mostly from Southern China (the provinces of Fujian and Guangdong). While playing an important role in the country's creation of wealth and jobs, they have very close relationship with their ancestral home since China's opening to the outside world in the 1980s. Most of the Chinese Filipino merchants have gained benefits while doing business with China. Benefiting from favourable policies, the economic development in Southern China has that were not in accord with the products prescribed in the customs declaration. Such behaviour not only shatters the image of the People's Republic of China, but also damnifies the benefit of the Philippines' local tradesman.

c) The relatives or family dependants of Filipino Chinese are leaving for Manila, the capital of the Philippines, to identify their kinfolk since the setting up of official relations of the two countries, among whom are those who do not want to go back to China, and become illegal migrants. They are doing vender's stand illegally in Binado, Manila and some- where else, shaping competition with the Filipino small businesses and infusing adverse impact on the manufactures of the Filipino small and middle manufacturers, which also arouse the extreme antipathy of the Filipino vendors.

d) Used by the gangland of Hong Kong and Taiwan, quite a few illegal stayers from Mainland China are conducting illegal drug trafficking under the disguise of doing business. Such behaviours offend the law of the Philippines, and leave terrible impression to the Philippine people.

WTO regulations related to relaxing goods, capitals and personnel of the member countries no doubt strengthen the flow of goods, capitals and personnel of the two countries, not only because these two countries are geographically close, but also because many people of the countries have consanguinity on the other side. Because of the limitation of the Philippine market's capacity and scarcity of job opportunities, the implications of Chinese medium and small capital as well as personnel moving to the Philippines are not always positive and the disputes related possibly in- creased. For instance, 145 Chinese accused of selling illegal cheap China- made Christmas adornments in the Philippine market in December of 2005 were arrested and fined for some 50 thousand Peso each, and were repatriated by the Philippine immigration.[8] The Philippine government vows to use efficiently the mechanism of dispute settlement and procedures of WTO to protect the interests of Filipino merchants.

Empirical Studies of the Impacts of China's WTO Entry on the Philippine Economic Growth and Development

This section shows the Sino-Philippine economic interchanges in the four years since the year of 2000 reaching its peak and within the framework of bilateral ties that have been mainly driven by China's commitments to WTO upon its accession to the organization. The facts showed that an open China not only does no harm but is a boost to the Philippine economy.

The Total Value of Bilateral Trade Is Greatly Increased and Trade Surplus Is on the Philippine Side

According to records from China's customs, the significant growth of Philippine exports to China from 2000 to 2002 helped to expand the trade turnover from US$3.365 billion in 2000 to US$5.259 billion in 2002 reaching an annual increase of 33 per cent. Total trade value of both sides increased even faster in 2003 and 2004, reaching US$9.4 billion and US$ 13.33, an increase of 78 per cent and 42 per cent respectively. Moreover, the Philippines has enjoyed favourable trade balance of US$1.175 billion in 2002, US$3.212 billion in 2003 and US$4.09billion in 2004, a complete reversal in the history of their bilateral trade (Table 10.1).

Table 10.1   China-Philippine Bilateral Trade, 1985-2004
(in hundred million US dollars)

Year	Total Value	Percentage Change	Exports to Philippines	Imports from Philippines	Balance of Trade
1985	4.05	–	3.11	0.94	2.17
1986	2.94	-0.27	1.57	1.37	0.20
1987	3.85	0.31	2.45	1.40	1.05
1988	4.04	0.05	2.69	1.35	1.34
1989	3.39	-0.16	2.56	0.83	1.73
1990	2.95	-0.13	2.10	0.85	1.25
1991	3.83	0.30	2.53	1.30	1.23
1992	3.64	-0.05	2.09	1.55	0.54
1993	4.95	0.36	2.81	2.14	0.67
1994	7.48	0.51	4.76	2.72	2.04
1995	13.06	0.75	10.30	2.76	7.54
1996	13.87	0.06	10.15	3.72	6.43
1997	16.67	0.20	13.39	3.28	10.11
1998	20.00	0.20	15.00	5.00	10.00
1999	22.87	0.13	13.79	9.08	4.71
2000	31.42	0.37	14.64	16.77	-2.13
2001	35.63	0.14	16.20	19.45	-3.25
2002	52.60	0.47	20.43	32.17	-11.75
2003	94.00	0.78	30.94	63.06	-32.12
2004	133.3	0.42	42.70	90.60	-40.90

Source: China Customhouse, quoted from Economic and Commercial Consular of Embassy of P.R.C. in R.P. web site *http://ph.moftec.gov.cn*

Since 2002, China has been listed as one of the Philippines' top ten export markets. Philippine official data shows that China ranked as the 9th largest trading partner of the country in 2002, 6th in 2003, and 4th in 2004, accounting for about 6 per cent of total Philippine trade with the world.

With the characteristics of low price and high quality of Chinese export commodities to the Philippines, the Chinese exports, as a matter of fact, are mostly welcome by the Philippine lower and middle class, and have brought about the effects of poverty alleviation in the Philippines. The fast expansion of China's imports from the Philippines, on the other hand, has in fact provided job opportunities for the Philippine workers.

Sino-Philippine Cross Investments Are Expanding

Chinese Investment in the Philippines Small but Expanding

According to China's Ministry of Commerce, about 40 Chinese companies and corporations are investing in the Philippines in the form of "joint ventures" with local counterparts. The total contracted amount reached US$39.5974 million, US$16.4104 million of which came from the Chinese. Chinese investment in 12 service or trading corporations reached US$2.5324 million; in 24 manufacturing or processing corporations, US$10.083 million; in one agribusiness corporation, US$0.7 million; in two resource-based corporations, US$2.115 million; and in one investment corporation; US$7 million.[9] According to the Philippine source, Chinese investment is still small when compared with other foreign investors. Total China investment in the Philippines in 2000 and 2001 accounted for only 0.2 per cent of Philippine's total foreign investment. In 2002, the percentage increased to 2.0 per cent (Table 10.2). In 2003, major investors from China were in IT-enabled

Table 10.2 China's Investment in the Philippines (value in US$ million)

Year	China's Investments in the Philippines	Total Foreign Investment in the Philippines	Per cent of China's Investment to Total Foreign Investment
1999	3.8	1223.55	0.3
2000	3.9	1818.83	0.2
2001	2.87	1224.48	0.2
2002	16.65	858.80	2.0
2003 (Jan-June)	3.02	244.06	1.2

Sources: Philippine Board of Investment (BOI), CDC, PEZA, SBMA.

Table 10.3 Major BOI Registered Investors from China, 2003

Company	Product/Activity
Phiweb Corp (formerly Philweb Com, Inc.)	IT-Enabled Services
New Phil-China Group Dev. Corp	Hotel & Commercial Complex Operation
Binga Hydroelectric Plant, Inc	Hydroelectric Plant Binga (ROL Scheme)
Salcon Power Corp	Naga Power Plant
Intermedia Solutions, Inc (formerly IMGAME Com., Inc.)	IT Service Firm ASP Platform
Grand Ocean (Phil) Co. Inc.	Transport equipment (evaporating and condenser coils)
United Silicom Mindanao, Inc.	Exporter of silicom crystals and microsillica

Source: Philippine Board of Investment.

services, hotel and commercial complex operation, energy generation, transport equipment and exports of silicon crystals/micro silica (Table 10.3).

However, encourage by the Chinese government's "Go Out" strategy and endeavors of both sides, more and more Chinese enterprises will invest in the Philippines. In her official visit to China during September 1-3, 2004, the Philippine President Gloria Macapagal-Arroyo had not only witnessed some of the agreements being signed between Filipino and Chinese business-men on many trade deals, but also witnessed the signing of agreements on Chinese investment to the Philippines, covering the setting up of a $312-million glass manufacturing facility at Subic Bay, Olongapo City, and a $30-million iron ore processing plant in Camarines Nort that are expected to create at least 30,000 jobs. The Chinese government also agreed to promote Chinese investments in Mindanao, particularly in the Brunei Indonesia Malaysia Philippine-East ASEAN Growth Area (BIMP-EAGA).[10]

Philippine Investors Benefit from China's Open-door Policy and China's WTO Entry

Philippine investments have a good return after China's open-door policy in the 1980s; some Philippine Chinese corporations and companies started to invest in their ancestral home taking advantage of the common language, blood ties, mores and practices. Their businesses grew faster because they stayed clear of the Philippines' domestic politics and were not affected by economic recessions from the mid-1980s to the early 1990s. With China's entry into the WTO, Philippine merchants are also expanding their investment in China. Chinese data show that there are rapid increases in Philippine investment, contracted or utilized, in China since 2002 (Table 10.4).

Table 10.4   Philippine Investments in China under China's various
Investment Incentive Laws, 1986-2004 (in million US dollars)

Year	Number of Projects	Contract Amount	Utilized Amount
1986	9	3.81	1.08
1987	10	30.39	3.80
1988	22	7.30	3.63
1989	12	4.71	1.52
1990	18	10.78	1.67
1991	30	17.44	58.50
1992	153	273.16	16.28
1993	302	630.63	122.50
1994	162	290.69	140.40
1995	125	213.15	105.78
1996	78	165.81	55.51
1997	102	181.13	155.63
1998	86	144.37	179.27
1999	99	184.45	117.28
2000	132	361.53	111.12
2001	**126**	**297.19**	**209.39**
2002	**153**	**325.48**	**186.00**
2003	**326**	**600.98**	**175.64**
2004	**241**	**684.00**	**233.00**

Sources: Compiled by the author; data of 1986 to 2002 from various issues of *The Yearbook of China's External Economic Relations and Trade*, published by the China Foreign Economic Relations and Trade Publishing House; data of 2003 and 2004 from the *China Commerce Yearbook* 2004 and 2005, published by the China Commerce Publishing House, September 2004 and September 2005.

Philippine investments in China are mostly in real estate, including gin shops, resorts, mansions and villas; commerce, such as shopping malls; manufacturing including brewage, glass, and terylene and chemical fiber and so on. In the retail sector, the well-known Philipino-Chinese merchants Mr Henry Sy has promised to open as many "SM" (Philippine-typed shopping mall) as possible in China. He has so far already opened two SM in Fujian Province, South of China, and another four SM are under construction, and will be opened recently in the inland of China (including Shandong, Kunming and Jiangxi) due to China's pledge of opening its retail sector to foreign investment. Mr Henry Sy has promised to open 61 SM in every small- and medium-sized cities of China in the rest of his lifetime.[11] In the financial sector, Lucia Tan has established in Xiamen and Beijing his Commercial Banks and the Philippine Metro Bank has opened branches in Beijing, Shanghai and Xiamen. The Filipino merchants have so far gained a good return in their investment in China, and the rich profit derived is one of the reasons that the living standard of Filipino-Chinese are much better than the local Filipinos.

Other Forms of Economic Cooperation Inspired by China's WTO Entry Increasing

These include contracted projects, labour cooperation and tourism.

According to the Chinese official source, up to the year 2000, China has completed more than 400 construction projects in the Philippines including highway, harbour, hydro-electric power plant, thermal power plant, power transmission line, rural water supply and public market. The contracted projects and labour cooperation between the two countries have gain momentum afterward; 37 joint construction projects with a total value of US$74 million were completed only in a year of 2001. There were 33 newly signed construction agreements in 2002, with a total value of US$184.67 million; the complete turnover in 2002 was US$75.37 million. From January to May 2003, 10 contracts were signed with a total value of US$45.17 million; the accomplished turnover was US$31.78 million in that period.[12]

The two governments had signed a memorandum on September 1, 2003 during the state visit of Mr Wu Bangguo, Chairman of China People's Congress, to the Philippines. China's Import and Export Bank loan to the Philippines totals US$400 million in the form of purchaser credit based on the preferential condition of modernizing and extending railroad project in north Luzon and improving fishing ports in Mindanao.[13] The initial segment of the railroad construction started on April 5, 2004 with maximum credit extended by China to the Philippines in construction.[14] With the expansion of financial cooperation, the two countries' importers and exporters were able to settle commercial transactions without transiting through the banks. The two governments have also signed bilateral currency exchange agreement in which China's People's Bank will provide credit of US$1 billion to the

Philippine Central Bank in case of emergency under the framework of the 10+3 Chiang Mai Initiative.[15]

In recognition of China's potential as a big tourist country since a part of the Chinese people has been getting rich, the Philippine government has adopted various measures in attracting Chinese tourists to boost the Philippine tourism. The Philippine Department of Tourism has targeted China as one of the priority markets; in 2003, there were 32 thousand Mainland Chinese tourists in the Philippines. In order to attract more Chinese tourists to the Philippines, the Philippine Department of Tourism has opened the first Philippine tourism office within the Philippine embassy in Beijing on July 18, 2004. The tourism attaché of the Philippine embassy in Beijing deals with tourism and travel-related services including the promotion of Philippine tourist destinations to an expanding Chinese tourist market. The Philippine tourism office in Beijing is aiming at raising the number of Chinese tourists to more than 60,000 or a 100 per cent growth in near future.[16]

Notes

1. "Philippines: We Need to Get Our Act Together", *http://www.inquirer.net*, October 16, 2001.
2. "China's entry to WTO seen as threat to RP", *http://www.inquirer.net*, November 25, 2001.
3. Shen, Hongfang, "China and Philippine Political and Economic Relations in the Context of China's WTO Entry and the Framework of '10+1'", *Contemporary Asia-Pacific Studies*, Beijing, No. 11, 2004; "Philippine Reversal Response to China's Entry to WTO and CAFTA", *Southeast Asian Studies*, Guangdong, No. 4, 2004; "China and Philippine Economic Relations", in Wang Qin (ed.), *New Pattern of China-ASEAN Economic Relations*, Xiamen University Press, 2003, pp. 189-217; "Inquiry Into the Impacts of China's WTO Entry on Sino-Philippine Economic Relations and Philippine Economy", *Southeast Asian Affairs*, Fujian, No. 1, 2002.
4. Palanca, Ellen, "China's WTO Entry and Trade between the Philippines and China", *Around Southeast Asia*, No. 11, 2001.
5. In Filipino language, Pinoy means "Philippine-made" goods.
6. "'Buy Pinoy' – A covenant for National Economic Survival and Prosperity", *http://www.phionline.comph/dti/buypinoy.htm*, Feb. 26, 2003.
7. Huang Xinyi, "Buy Pinoy Movement", *www.worldnews.com*, December 13, 2001.
8. According to the Philippine law, a foreigner is prohibited to deal in retail trade while living in the Philippines. See Editorial: "Be Back Safely", from Philippine Chinese Newspaper *World News*, December 17, 2005; Zhuang Ming-ding, "145 Chinese who were arrested in China town released", Singapore Chinese newspaper *Zaobao*, December 17, 2005.

9. Data from the China Ministry of Commerce, October 2003. *http://www. mofcom.gov.cn*

10. Philippine English newspaper *Business World*, September 1, 2004. *http:// www.bworld.com.ph*

11. Hong, Jun, "SM must be overwhelmed among the malls in China", *Xiamen Daily*, November 25, 2005.

12. Data provided by the China Ministry of Commerce, quoted from the Economic and Commercial Consular of Embassy of P.R.C. in R.P. web site *http://www. chinatrade.org.ph./cn*

13. Philippine Chinese newspaper *Business Daily*, p. 1, September 1, 2003.

14. Philippine Chinese newspaper *World News*, April 5, 2004. *http://www.worldnews. com.ph*

15. In May 2000, ASEAN+3 finance ministers discussed the content and form of the organization in their financial cooperation, and later signed the Chiang Mai Initiative. The agreement was designed to create a regional facility to cope with volatile capital flows and speculative attacks and to economize on foreign reserve holding. According to the initiative, the original currency exchange arrangement among the ASEAN members should extend to China, Japan and ROK, capital involved to be expanded to $1 billion, and a series of bilateral exchange agreements should be reached among ASEAN members, China, Japan and ROK.

16. Compared to other countries in Southeast Asia, the Philippines is still largely unexplored. Only 32,000 Chinese tourists visited the Philippines last year, compared to the approximately 700,000 who visited Vietnam, the 600,000 who visited Thailand, the 500,000 who visited Singapore and the 350,000 who visited Malaysia. Philippine's English newspaper *Business World*, July 22, 2004. *http: //www.bworld.com.ph*; Philippine Chinese newspaper *World News*, July 18, 2003. *http://www.worldnews.com.ph*

References

Almanac of China's Foreign Economic Relations and Trade (2001), published by China Foreign Economic Relations and Trade Publishing House, September.

Baltazar, Eric (1995), "Chinese Investment in the Philippines", in *China Current*, Vol. 6, No. 2.

China Commerce Yearbook 2004, and 2005, published by China Commerce Publishing House, September 2004, and September 2005.

de Dios, Emmanuel S. and Paul D. Hutchcroft (2003), "Political Economy", in A. Balisacan and H. Hill (eds), *The Philippine Economy: Development, Policies, and Challenges*, Ateneo De Manila University Press.

Economic and Commercial Consular of Embassy of P.R.C. in Republic of the Philippines, web site *http://www.chinatrade.org.ph./cn*

Fabella, Raul V. (1999), "The Great Dragon Effect: Whose Lunch is Mainland China Eating?", PASCN Discussion Paper No. 99-05.

Framework Agreement on Comprehensive Economic Co-operation between the Association of South East Asian Nations and the People's Republic of China, *http://www.aseansec.org*

Hall, Hil (2003), "Industry", in A. Balisacan and H. Hill (eds), *The Philippine Economy: Development, Policies, and Challenges*, Ateneo De Manila University Press.

Little, Frank M. (2000), "Technological Change, Structural Change and Economic Development: A Case Study of the Philippines", unpublished paper.

MOFTEC, *Almanac of China's Foreign Economic Relations and Trade 2001*, China Foreign Economic Relations and Trade Publishing House, September 2001.

MOFTEC, *Yearbook of China's Foreign Economic Cooperation and Trade*, various issues between 1987 and 2000, China Social Publishing House.

Palanca, Ellen (2001), "China's WTO Entry and Trade between the Philippines and China", *Around Southeast Asia*, No. 11.

PCDRC, Forum: "Philippine-China Relations", in *China Currents*, Vol. 6, No. 2, April-June 1995.

PHILEXPORT, *Philippine Export Development Plan 1999-2000*.

Philippine Business Report (1999), "President Signs Anti-Dumping Act", published by the Department of Trade and Industry, Vol. 10, No. 9, September.

Philippine: "President Joseph Ejercito Estrada's One and a Half Year Report to the Filipino Nation", *http://www.bworld.com.ph*, 2000-01-09.

Philippine Department of Trade and Industry, *http://www.dti.gov.ph*

Philippine English Newspaper *Business World*, <*http://www.bworld.com.ph*>

Philippine English Newspaper *Manila Bulletin*, <*http://www.mb.com.ph*>

Philippine English Newspaper *Inquirer*, <*http://www.inquirer.net*>

Philippine Chinese Newspaper *Overseas Chinese Business*, <*http://www.siongpo.com.ph*>

Philippine Chinese Newspaper *World News*, <*http://www.worldnews.com.ph*>

Shen, Hongfang (1991), "China-Philippine Relations: History, Present Situation and Prospects", in *Prospects for the China-Southeast Asian Relations Around 2000*, Zhongshan University Press.

Shen, Hongfang (1997), "Sino-Philippine Bilateral Trade: Status Quo and Prediction", in *China Currents*, Vol. 8, No. 3, July-September, published by Philippine-Chinese Resource Center, the Philippines.

Shen, Hongfang (2002), "Inquiry Into the Impacts of China's WTO Entry on Sino-Philippine Economic Relations and Philippine Economy", *Southeast Asian Affairs*, No. 1.

Shen, Hongfang (2003), "ASEAN China Free Tree Area: An Arduous Journey", *Southeast Asian Affair*, No. 3.

Shen, Hongfang (2003), "China and Philippine Economic Relations", in Wang Qin (ed.), *The New Pattern of China-ASEAN Economic Relations*, Xiamen University Press.

Vanzi, Sol Jose (2001), "RP Not Ready for China-ASEAN Free Trade Concept", *Philippine Headline News Online*, November, 10.

11

India's Economic Relations with ASEAN: Implications for China

Zhao Hong

Introduction

Regionalism[1] has become a truly fashionable construct in the world today. One of the facets of regionalism has been a trend towards increasing economic and political linkages between neighbouring countries and between close regions, while the other was the strategic security in a post-Cold War world. Yet, India's involvement, as a big power in South Asia, in the South Asian Association for Regional Cooperation (SAARC) has neither resulted in greater trade, nor greater security. The level of intra-regional trade among SAARC was low mainly because of the lack of comparative advantages in their economies. Moreover, the small economies feared that Indian capital and lower-priced goods might flood their markets if they were to liberalize their economies. SAARC countries have resorted to non-tariff policy barriers such as anti-dumping measures to limit trade with India.[2] Contrary to the principles and goals of SAARC, bilateral disputes between India and Pakistan such as over the disputed territory of Kashmir and nuclear weapon tests had also impeded the development of regionalism in SAARC. India has become increasingly concerned and worried that it will be marginalized in the trend of regionalism and globalization[3]. While disappointed at SAARC's lack of economic progress, India has been impressed at the economic progress made by ASEAN and its objective of achieving economic integration for all its members (Green p, 1994). India is fascinated and drawn to the dynamic of economic regionalism in ASEAN, and has been making great efforts to be getting involved in the process of regionalism in East Asia.

India's involvement has aroused different reflections from East Asian countries. For example, on the issue of regionalism in East Asia, China and Malaysia prefer to use the "10+3" as a vehicle to take this region to a desired community. They seem to be favouring a regional cooperation in East Asia excluding the US, India and other powers. Malaysia once opposed the proposal to have a separate India-ASEAN summit despite the strong support that this proposal had received among the other ASEAN members[4] – some ASEAN countries and Japan need India and other non-East Asian countries to balance China's increasingly influence in Southeast Asia and check China's possible leading role in East Asia. Moreover, most of the prevailing explanations believe that under the framework of ASEAN+3, the centre of East Asian cooperation is on Northeast Asia. As India's involvement in ASEAN grows stronger, this centre might move to ASEAN. This leads us to ponder whether ASEAN's leading role in institutional building in East Asia will be enhanced; whether the India factor would add to the momentum of open regionalism[5] there and turn East Asia into a community – geopolitically rather than geographically defined and more or less modeled on the European Union.

The other objective of this article is to examine the challenges of India's involvement in East Asia facing China and its responses to these challenges. From the Indian perspective it needs to diversify its trade and economic ties away from its traditional trade partners, such as the European Union and the United States, and counter China's growing influence in Southeast Asia. From the perspective of the ASEAN members, India has the potential to be an alternative market, a source of capital, professionals, and technology to rival China. In this context, India is likely to be a potential opponent and competitor of China in the Southeast Asian market.

India's Relations with ASEAN: From Initial Cooperation to Antagonism

As the biggest country in the South Asian sub-continent which is neighbouring to South East Asia, India attached great importance to developing relations with ASEAN countries after the Second World War. In the 1950s and 60s, India actively expanded its influence in Southeast Asia, fully supporting Indonesia's struggle for national independence and taking part in solving the political issues in Indochina. During this period, Jawaharlal Nehru visited Southeast Asian countries respectively, signing treaties of friendship with Indonesia, Myanmar and the Philippines, thus consolidating the bilateral political and diplomatic relations. This friendly relationship reached its high tide at the Bandung conference in 1955. "The Conference revealed that most of Southeast Asian countries acknowledged the positive role India played in Asian and international affairs" (Lei, 2000: 400). Under this background, India's economic relations with Southeast Asian countries witnessed a significant development, with cooperation in trade, investment, technology and cultural sectors being promoted to a new level. India was one of the earliest countries which established joint ventures in Southeast Asia and provided general economic assistance to them. For example, during the initial post-independence period, Myanmar faced a lot of difficulties, such as low rice price in the world market and lack of capital. India initiatively imported a large amount of rice from Myanmar at a favourable price and provided low interest loans of 200 million rupee for its domestic economic construction in 1957.

When ASEAN was founded in 1967, the UK was withdrawing its military forces from Southeast Asia and the US had not yet formed a definite attitude towards Southeast Asia, thus leaving a security vacuum there. Under this background, India and ASEAN formed common concerns and interests: India did not want to see China expanding its influence in Southeast Asia, while ASEAN worried about the "China threat" and did not want to see the communist parties pursuing powers in three Indochina countries. So India initially and actively sought to cooperate with ASEAN militarily. Indian Prim Minister Indira Gandhi visited Singapore and Malaysia in 1968 to make breakthrough in this respect. However, because of some different under-standings on regional cooperation, India's efforts did not create expected results. India emphasized cooperation with ASEAN mainly for regional security, while the newly established ASEAN emphasized the concept of a geographical Southeast Asia, aiming at resolving contradictions and conflicts among member countries, and promoting economic, social and cultural integration in this region. So ASEAN firmly opposed India's proposal that "powers jointly guaranteed" Southeast Asia's security and channeled ASEAN into the track of a Pan-Asian cooperation led by India (Han, 2002: 240).

In the 1970s, India drew closer to Soviet Union gradually. In August 1971, India signed "India-Soviet Peace and Friendship Cooperation Treaty" which was of obvious military implications, indicating that India had formed strategic alliance with Soviet Union. In the end of 1978, Vietnam invaded Cambodia and intruded to the boundaries between Thailand and Cambodia. India adopted the strategy of adhering to Soviet Union and officially recognized the People's Republic of Kampuchea regime under Heng Samrin propped up by Vietnam in July 1980, thus leading to direct conflicts with ASEAN (Han, 2000: 242). In the 1980s, with the support of Soviet Union, India expanded its military forces continuously and built solid political and military relation with Vietnam. In order to counterbalance India's threat, ASEAN chose to unite with the US and China, and supported the Coalition Government of Democratic Kampuchea. As a result, the relations between

ASEAN and India fell to the lowest point in history. The Indian leadership viewed ASEAN as an American "imperialist surrogate" while ASEAN dubbed India as "the surrogate of the Soviet Union". "India was notorious in Thailand, Singapore, Malaysia and other Southeast Asian countries, and was considered to be a country which could not face its own problems and economic reform, but wanted to play a dominant role in the world" (Lei, 2000: 405).

In sum, India and ASEAN had experienced a short period of political exchanges and economic cooperation in the early days of the post-Second World War. But due to some inevitable estrangement and barriers existed between India and most ASEAN countries, the two sides could not establish solid political relations and cooperation mechanism all along, hence hindering the development of economic relations between the two sides. It is evident that under the environment of Cold War, India's economic relations with ASEAN could not shake off the influence of political factors. On the contrary, it became a derivative of geopolitics and bilateral political relations. Neither could this kind of economic relations play a role to improve political and diplomatic relations between India and ASEAN. As the Cold War ended in the early 1990s and regionalism emerged globally, India re-realized ASEAN's importance in terms of politics, economy and diplomacy, and put forward its "Look East" policy to be actively engaged in Southeast Asian affairs. Thereafter, India's economic relations with ASEAN entered a new development era.

New Strategies towards ASEAN: India's "Look East" Policy

India's Look East policy was initiated in 1991 after the Cold War when India faced a number of successive strategic and economic challenges which threatened its political survival (Rao, 1996: 763). The breakup of the Soviet Union deprived India of its main trading partner and source of cheap imported oil. India was forced to purchase oil at market prices which were inflated because of the First Gulf War in 1990. India had to realign its foreign policies and implement "towards big power strategy", with the characteristics of an all-direction foreign policy. Look East policy is an important component of this development strategy. Diluting the strategic antagonism between India and ASEAN, enhancing ties with the Southeast Asian region represented India's intention to join the Asia Pacific Economic Cooperation (APEC) grouping and Asia Europe Meeting (ASEM) for its eventual leap into the global market. At this phase, India's Look East policy was implemented to recover its economic relations with Southeast Asia so as to diversify trade away from its main trading partners in North America and Europe, reducing its economic vulnerability.

ASEAN, realizing India's potential and importance as the third largest economy in Asia, responded positively to India's initiatives and advances. In 1992, India was accepted as a sectoral dialogue partner of ASEAN in the fields of trade, investment and tourism. In 1995, India became a full dialogue partner of ASEAN, making its relations with ASEAN reach high tide. In 1996, India formally became a member of the ASEAN Regional Forum. This was the first time in fifty years for India to attend the dialogue on politics and security in Asia-Pacific region, indicating India's Look East policy had made an important achievement.

However, the Look East policy also faced a number of impediments that hindered its progress. Internally, from India's perspective, frequent changes in its federal government created political instability indicating that foreign economic policy took a lower priority. Externally, India's nuclear test in May 1998 followed by those in Pakistan brought swift retaliation from developed countries such as the United States and Japan in the form of economic sanctions. ASEAN abided by the imposed sanction. Thereby, trade and investment relations between India and ASEAN suffered greatly. Moreover, India's armed skirmish with Pakistan at the Kargil region in 1999 also took India's attention away from its Look East policy (Faizal, 2005: 477).

The end of 1990s and early 2000 marked the second phase of India's Look East policy. In 1998, Vajpayee assumed his power as Indian prime minister and intended to hasten Look East policy. The second phase of India's Look East policy saw greater efforts to forge links with CLMV states (Cambodia, Lao, Myanmar and Vietnam) and gain support for India to have a summit level meeting with the ASEAN. In June 1997, led by India, three South Asian countries (India, Bangladesh and Sri Lanka) and two Southeast Asian countries (Thailand and Myanmar) jointly established an economic cooperation organization, aiming at creating a free trade zone among member countries before 2017. In 2000, sponsored by India, the " Mekong-Ganges River Cooperation Project" between India and ASEAN 5 (Vietnam, Lao, Cambodia, Myanmar and Thailand) was initiated in 2000, aiming at promoting cooperation on tourism, culture and education in this sub-region. India is clearly aware that economic cooperation with ASEAN will depend very much on how fast the new ASEAN countries are able to catch up with the rest of ASEAN. So India proposed to provide economic and technical assistance to those new members, including setting up centres for English language training in Cambodia, Laos, Myanmar and Vietnam, and providing unilateral tariff concessions to the goods from these countries. After intensive efforts

Table 11.2 FDI Inflows into ASEAN by Source Country, 1995-2003 (US$ million)

Source Countries	1995	1996	1997	1998	1999	2000	2001	2002	2003	1995-03
EU-15	5049.6	7362	6333.6	5553.5	9806	8386.9	9179	3790.7	7083.3	62544.6
Other EU	1171.7	2121.1	1992.9	1307.9	2242	1099.5	-46.2	679.4	1604.3	12172.5
USA	4318.4	5177.2	4950.1	3222.3	5931.7	5334.7	4881.4	-1018.1	2919.6	35717.3
Canada	609.2	204.7	1110.9	-207	-14.2	61.2	-482.9	280.8	-372	1190.7
Japan	5949.3	5283.3	5229.5	3937.6	1688.2	943.6	1422	1758.7	2060.6	27972.9
South Korea	660.2	504.2	721.8	90.8	528.9	-31.4	-268.5	67.8	282.3	2556.1
Hong Kong	1271.1	927.5	1884.8	1162.2	697.7	1296.8	-294.3	-352.8	481.9	7074.8
Taiwan	914	810.3	914	677.5	402.5	565.5	632.3	388.4	227.2	5531.6
China	136.7	117.9	62.1	291.3	62.5	44	60.8	-156.9	12.8	631.4
India	**108.1**	**68.8**	**90.2**	**92.6**	**41.7**	**57.9**	**-5.8**	**130.6**	**83.2**	**667.3**
ASEAN	4654.4	4271.8	5235.7	2730.8	1789.3	1194.9	2391.7	3556.9	2068.9	27894.4
Australia	534.9	325.1	245.6	-302.2	-935	-42.2	-391.3	745.7	46.3	226.9
New Zealand	35.4	31.2	29.1	25.3	80.2	22.6	4	106.3	89.6	423.8
All Others	2966.8	2709.8	5130.1	3581.1	4929.2	4471.1	2268.5	3490.3	2757.9	32304.7
Total	28079.9	29914.9	33930.5	22163.6	27250.5	23404.9	19350.8	13468.1	19346	216909.1

Source: ASEAN Secretariat (2004c), *ASEAN Statistics Yearbook 2004*, p. 142, *http://www.aseansec.org/statistics%202004/06-fdi.pdf*

on telecommunication, petroleum and heavy industrial sectors, with main source countries being Singapore, Malaysia and Thailand. At present, Singapore has been the third largest foreign investor in India, with its investment of US$1.5 billion in telecommunication sector and, U3$2 billion in technology, finance service sectors and astronavigation industry.[7] Malaysia is the tenth largest investor in India, having completed 21 projects worth an estimated US$1.2 billion. In contrast, as of December 2004, India had invested in 144 projects worth approximately US$420 million in Malaysia, mainly in the manufacturing sector (Faizal, 2005: 481). According to Table 11.2, between 1995-2003, the accumulation of India's FDI in ASEAN reached US$0.667 billion, accounting for 0.4 per cent of total FDI inflows into ASEAN during this period. ASEAN's FDI in India mainly focuses on high-technology and capital-intensive sectors.

Free Trade Agreement

As the bilateral economic relations developed significantly, the then Indian Finance Minister Yashwant Singha was concerned that India' s bilateral trade with ASEAN were mainly limited on a narrow range of commodities in only a few economic sectors and countries, and the balance of trade was in ASEAN's favour. The first ASEAN-India Summit was held in Cambodia in November 2002, and the issue of bilateral trade was mainly discussed. At the 5th ASEAN-India Senior Officials Meeting in New Delhi in May 2003, Malaysia, being a co-chair of the meeting emphasized the importance of moving ASEAN-India trade linkages towards a Framework Agreement on Economic Cooperation. This idea was discussed further at the Second India-ASEAN Summit in Bali, Indonesia in October 2003, and the establishment of India-ASEAN FTA was put on the agenda. But negotiations ran into difficulties as India insisted on excluding 1,414 items (including textiles, agricultural products) from FTA. As Malaysian Prime Minister Abdullah Badawi said: "ASEAN is concerned on the proposal by India to exclude a substantial portion of trade from the FTA through exclusion of a large number of products from tariff concessions" (Siddharth, 2005). India's import duties and sectoral FDI caps in telecommunications and aviation are also impeding investments from ASEAN countries. After several rounds of negotiations, the Framework Agreement on Comprehensive Economic Cooperation between ASEAN and India was eventually signed on 8 October 2003 to establish an ASEAN-India Regional Trade and Investment Area, which includes an FTA in goods, services and investment. Establishing the FTA in goods is targeted for completion by 31 December 2011 for Brunei, Indonesia,

Malaysia, Singapore and Thailand, and India. For the Philippines and the CLMV, the target is 31 December 2016. In order to promote this process, India has been negotiating with individual ASEAN countries. India signed bilateral FTA with Thailand in July 2003, a Comprehensive Economic Cooperation Agreement (CECA) with Singapore in June 2005, and is negotiating another CECA type FTA with Malaysia.

Factors for India's New Policies towards ASEAN

Strategic Adjustments and Domestic Reform

In the early 1990s, as the Soviet Union collapsed and the Cold War ended, the world entered a transitional period to a new international order, accompanying the development trend of regionalism and globalization. Under this background, big powers competed to adjust and change their national strategies so as to occupy a more advantageous position in a new international political and economical order. In East Asia, both Japan and China spared no efforts to adjust, develop and promote their international relations with the ASEAN countries. Japan, especially China's "Look South" policy raised concerns and worries from India. From the perspective of an Indian senior diplomat, China's Southeast Asian policies had become a main factor affecting India's approaches to Southeast Asia (J.N. Dixit, 2001, p. 331). On the other hand, the 9/11 terrorist attack was a significant turning point of US's relations with South Asia. In order to make use of India's bases for counter-terrorism operations, US waived sanctions and provided assistance to India. On September 22, 2001, Bush lifted the sanctions that were imposed under the terms of the 1994 *Nuclear Proliferation Prevention Act* following India's nuclear tests in May 1998. President Bush and Prime Minister Vajpyee held their first summit in November 2001 and presented a vision for the rapid transformation of the relationship between the two countries. This provided more space and flexibility for India to carry out its "Look East" policy. Apart from this, India's efforts to strengthen its political and economic relations with ASEAN are based on the following considerations:

During the Cold War period, relying on its role of a leadership in non-alliance movement and in the third world, India played a balancing act between two superpowers, and created a somewhat significant influence on regional and international affairs. After the Cold War, as the Soviet Union collapsed, India lost a strong ally, hence military and financial assistance. Thus its international space was squeezed, and its international position and influence decreased dramatically. India must readjust and change its foreign strategy, and create new international space. But from the angle of geopolitics,

Pakistan is on the west of India, and it becomes a big geographic obstacle to India's efforts to create and develop relations with West Asia. Moreover, the political situation in Middle East is unstable in the long term, Central Asia and Afghanistan located on the north of India are backward and lack potential for cooperation. As an immediate neighbourhood of India, ASEAN countries share much commence with India in terms of regional interests and traditional cultures. India realized that if it wanted to maintain a profile of a big country, complete its design from "South Asian big power" to "Asian big power" and eventually become a "World big power", it must develop political and economic relations with ASEAN, making ASEAN as a bridge connecting itself to East Asia.

Before 1990s, India was a Socialistic Planned Economy with government's overdue protection over its state-own enterprises. Furthermore, India was faced with domestic political turmoil and frequent government changes, resulting in long-term economic recession and large financial and trade deficits. When Prime Minister P.V. Narasimha Rao assumed his power in June 1991, India was experiencing the most serious economic crisis since independence. The percentage of India's imports and exports in the world trade had decreased from 2.4 per cent in 1951-1952 to 0.4 per cent in 1990-1991 (Sun, 2001: 135). In 1991, faced with dwindling foreign reserves of only around US$240 million, which was only sufficient for approximately two weeks' worth of imports, India had to realign its foreign trade and economic policies. Narasimha Rao government began to carry out a large-scaled economic reform, relaxing government's intervention on economic sectors, promoting exports and introducing foreign capitals. In order to maintain rapid economic development and carry out domestic reform, India not only needs ASEAN's market, but also needs Singapore and Malaysia's technology and investment to ramp up its infrastructure such as airports, roads and power. The current Prime Minister Manmohan Singh was committed to carry on this reform when he took office in November 2004 and needs new forces to deepen the reform. "His economic reform plans have been repeatedly stymied by crucial coalition partners and the left parties, and he hoped to introduce momentum and stimulus from outside to push ahead with his reform policies." (Siddharth)

Competition from China

The emergence of China as an economic dynamo and its increasing trade linkages and cooperation with ASEAN has been another motivating factor for India to enhance its own linkages with the ASEAN countries. At the

ASEAN Summit meeting in Cambodia in November 2002, the Chinese and ASEAN leaders had signed an agreement to establish a China-ASEAN Free Trade Area (CAFTA) by 2010. The CAFTA would cover 1.8 billion consumers and two-way annual trades of US$1.2 trillion. CAFTA will not only symbolize China's economic ascendancy in East Asia but will also foster its closer economic integration with the Southeast Asian states. It will spur intra-regional investments, increase the access of ASEAN imports to the huge Chinese market, and lead to a massive influx of Chinese products to the Southeast Asian market. While the CAFTA will promote smooth movement of goods, products and services, it also provided safeguards for the less-developed ASEAN member countries. For example, the CLMV (Cambodia, Laos, Myanmar and Vietnam) were given deferred deadlines for FTA implementation and provisions for foreign aid. China also decided to assist Cambodia by writing off its debt of around US$200 million.[8] On October 8, 2003, China signed the Treaty of Amity and Cooperation of Southeast Asian Countries, further easing worries that China's rise could constitute a threat to ASEAN countries.

China's actions and CAFTA created a " chain reaction": Japan reacted to CAFTA by fostering the development of the framework for Comprehensive Economic Partnership (CEP) with ASEAN in October 2003. The CEP is the most integrative concept to figure out the future economic relationship between Japan and ASEAN. The United States followed suit by negotiating and establishing FTAs with individual ASEAN countries. In 2005, during his visit to Southeast Asia, the former Deputy Secretary of State Robert Zoelick stressed the Bush Administration's determination to negotiate more FTAs in the region. He also offered economic assistance and strategic initiatives to the Southeast Asian states, reminding them that the United States still retains greater capacity than China to contribute to regional economic development and security.[9] While ASEAN reacted by accelerating its internal economic integration through ASEAN Free Trade Area, "ASEAN Economic Community", and "ASEAN Security Community", aiming at building ASEAN Community by 2020.

The case of India's efforts to enhance its economic linkages with ASEAN countries is part of overall efforts of New Delhi to work with the ASEAN to balance increasing influence that China might wield in its FTA within ASEAN. From the perspective of the Ministry of External Affairs, engagement with the Southeast Asian region was in line with India's strategic policy to meet the growing threat of China in the region (Kuppuswamy, 2002). To curb China's growing influence in Southeast Asia, India and selected ASEAN countries began holding joint military exercises. For instance, Indian navy has conducted joint exercises with Singaporean, Vietnamese, Japanese, and South Korean navies to ensure the safety of strategic waterways in the region such as the Strait of Malacca (Faizal, 2005, p. 479). The Indian navy also alternated with their US counterparts to conduct naval patrols along the Strait of Malacca.

Although from the ASEAN and Japan's perspectives, India was seen as a possible counterweight against China in Southeast Asia, India has at least publicly avoided being drawn into such a role. India's former Prime Minister Vajpayee once said that India's competition with China in Southeast Asia would be a kind of healthy and complimentary one. Nonetheless, what India has been doing and saying reflects its concerns and worries about China's competition. When India exploded a nuclear device in 1998, then Indian Defense Minister George Fernandes said that India needed a nuclear deterrent not because of Pakistan's nuclear ambitions but for the long-term threat from China. India was also concerned that China has persisted in transferring nuclear and missile technology to Pakistan even after China joined the Nuclear Non-Proliferation Treaty in 1992 and agreed to abide by several Missile Technology Control Regime norms (Nayar, 2003: 227). At the bilateral level, Vietnam was once India's "close ally" during the Cold War. India takes the opportunities of developing relations with ASEAN to further enhance its influence in Vietnam in the form of foreign aid, military equipment sales, and other cooperation. For India, another neighbour of Myanmar, the implications were direct and no less important (Sudhir: 2006: 182). For a long time, Myanmar seemed to maintain an equidistance from both China and India. These years, Myanmar has been becoming a strategic battleground for influence between China and India. China managed to build a maritime reconnaissance and electronic intelligence system on Myanmar's Coco Islands to monitor Indian naval activities, especially in the Bay of Bengal[10], and China is blamed of supplying conventional weapons from Pakistan to Myanmar (Sudhir: 2006: 188). India has changed its previous hostile attitude toward Myanmar's military government and initiated cooperation measures such as assistance to convert the Myanmar port of Dawei into a deep-sea facility (Faizal, 2005). At the sub-regional level, sponsored by India, the "Mekong-Ganges River Cooperation Project" between India and ASEAN 5 (Vietnam, Lao, Cambodia, Myanmar and Thailand) was initiated in 2000. This organization underlines cooperation on tourism, culture and education, emphasizes links between Indian traditional culture and ASEAN's culture, indicating its intention to elbow out China's influence from this area. Involvement in infrastructure projects in ASEAN also aided India in countering the influence of China in this sector. During

Prime Minister Vajpayee's visit to Malaysia in May 2001, India signed several agreements related to the expansion and improvement of roads in India and railway lines in northern Malaysia. India's railway operates the third largest rail network in the world and employs over a million people. In September 2004, Vajpayee declared in New Delhi that India would cooperate with ASEAN to build a railway from New Delhi to Hanoi, cutting through Myanmar, Thailand, Lao and Cambodia. Some analysts considered this as India's response to China's proposal to build "Pan-Asian Railway". India's intention is to open up a new trade corridor in Mekong sub-region, changing its backward situation in Mekong sub-regional economic cooperation and competition.

Implications for China

India Factor in East Asian Integration

Regional integration in East Asia was basically encouraged and stimulated by increasing regionalism in other parts of the world. Since the establishment of the North American Free Trade Area (NAFTA) and successful launch of the Euro, the regional economic integration has got new momentum in the global arena. NAFTA is going to expand its boundary to include more Latin American countries and a new American FTA is being under discussion. The EU's eastward expansion is also on its accelerating pace. However, in East Asia, regionalism has lagged far behind those in other regions. The slow regional integration in East Asia might be ascribed to several factors, such as profound diversity in many fields, great power rivalry and lack of trust. Governments in this region seemed conservative and little enthusiastic in taking steps towards pan East Asian regionalism. Although the ASEAN+3 framework is paving its way to promote the integration process in East Asia, it has is own weak-points as it is dependent on ASEAN and is more a forum than an institution. It needs to embrace an East Asian framework beyond its double structures so as to explore the full potential of East Asian regional integration. It is believed that for East Asia, the costs of using regional integration as a form of "Fortress", that is, to maximize trade diversion, are consequently much higher than they were in the past. As a South Korean expert pointed out:

> The heavy reliance on extra-regional markets, capital and technology would not enable East Asia to set up a buttress against outsiders. For its part, East Asian states should not pursue what extra-regional states think constitutes an exclusive

regionalism. The avenue for extra-regional powers to have access to East Asian dynamism should be sought within a broader framework than East Asian regionalism.[11]

India, as an outsider of East Asia, seems to have brought some heat and new ideas for pushing through pan East Asian integration. Indian Prime Minister Manmohan Singh put forward the proposal to establish "Asian Economic Community" at November 2004 and it gained positive response from East Asian Countries promptly. At the Fourth Summit international conference on "Asian Economic Community" held in New Delhi, India raised up some concrete suggestions and proposals on East Asian FTA, Asian Financial System, establishing Asian energy forum and promoting regional cooperation on science and technology. At the East Asian Summit held in December 2005 in Kuala Lumpur, leaders from India, together with China, Japan and the ROK reaffirmed that the establishment of an East Asian Community was a long-term objective, and "the EAS inauguration has led to the development of a new framework for co-operation in the region by taking an open, inclusive approach."[12]

India's involvement in East Asia has also stimulated and promoted Sino-India economic relations. Since the early 1990s when India adopted East Look policy, China-India bilateral trade has moved up from US$0.26 billion in 1991 to US$13.6 billion in 2004, and reached US$20 billion in the year 2005.[13] China has been India's second largest trading partner. The two sides agreed to a target of US$30 billion by 2008 and US$40 billion by 2010. India's sustained rise and closer involvement with East Asia since 1990s have greatly contributed to this transformation and have opened new avenues for expanding China-India economic cooperation.

In June 2003, India and China agreed to set up a Joint Study Group (JSG) to expand trade and economic cooperation between the two countries. On 21 March 2005, the report of the India-China JSG on Comprehensive Trade and Economic Cooperation was finalized. It recommended a China-India Regional Trading Arrangement, covering trade in goods and services, investments, identified common ground for trade and investment promotion and facilitation, and proposed measures for the promotion of economic cooperation in identified sectors.

According to a comment in the *Indian Express*: "even if an East-Asian super state seems an impossibility, the future creation of a free trade zone with 16 participants is a distinct target. The movement towards that goal has already begun". China has become Japan's largest trading partner, and FTA between ASEAN and China will be working by 2010, the Indo-ASEAN FTA individual Southeast Asia countries encourage China's participation in multilateral organizations, international dialogue and economic cooperation. On the other hand, Southeast Asia would not passively accept China's domination that appeared to challenge important national interests. Establishing links with other large outside powers is an important means to counterweight China' s influence. At the regional level for ASEAN, India does provide an alternative market and strategic partner to ASEAN countries.

In this regard, China would have to invest more time and resources into building bilateral relations with both India and ASEAN, and work hard to transform its foreign relationships accordingly.

Notes

1. The process of Regionalism is demonstrated through institutionalized cooperation among groups of states to give mutual trade benefits that may or may not extend to third parties (from Faizal Yahya, 2005).
2. *Financial Express*, 2005.
3. The term "globalization" here is defined as the process of transition towards a global community with common norms and institutional framework to facilitate cooperation. The progress towards the free flow of people, capital, technology, and information is often impeded as growing interdependence tends to trigger protective nationalist sentiments which are manifested in the form of tariff and non-tariff barriers (from Faizal Yahya, 2005).
4. Baruah, A. 2001. "PM May Stress Need for India-ASEAN Summit". *Hindu*, 13 May.
5. Open regionalism is defined as sustained cooperation among contiguous countries "that would strengthen rather than weaken the members' extra-regional linkages". (Athukorala, Prema-Chandra and Jayant Menon (1997), "AFTA and the Investment-Trade Nexus in ASEAN.", in *World Economy* 20, no. 2: 159-74).
6. IMF, *Direction of Trade Statistics Yearbook*, 2005.
7. *http://zaobao.com/yl/yl.html*, 8 January 2005.
8. *Asia Times*, 6 November 2002.
9. Goh, Evelyn (2005), "Renewed American Diplomacy: Keeping Southeast Asia on the U.S. Radar". *PacNet* (Pacific Forum CSIS), no. 22, 26 May, 2005, p. 3, *http://www.csis.org/media/csis/pubs/pac0522.pdf*
10. *Asia Times*, 8 October 2004.
11. Kak Soo Shin (2006), "East Asia needs genuine regional integration", *http:// www.adb.org/regionalcooperation/index.asp*
12. *China Daily*, 15 December 2005.
13. M.K. Venu. "India, China may join hands at WTO ministerial", *The Economic Times* (New Delhi), 19 September 2005.

14. Pandit, Rajat. "India to 'Arm' itself for Strategic Interests," *The Times of India*, 27 October 2004.
15. Zhang Guihong, "US-India Strategic Cooperation: Implications for China", paper submitted to "The ASIA Fellow China Alumni Conference", 13-14 November 2005, Beijing University, China.
16. Hong Kong, *South China Morning Daily*, 8 October 2004.
17. World Bank, *World Development Indicators 2005*.

References

Devare, Sudhir (2006), *India & Southeast Asia: Towards Security Convergence*, Singapore: Institute of Southeast Asian Studies.
Dixit, J.N. (2001), *India's Foreign Policy and its Neighbors*, New Delhi: Gyan Publishing House.
Faizal Yahya (2005), "Challenges of Globalization: Malaysia and India Engagement", *Contemporary Southeast Asia*, Volume 27, Number 3, December.
Goh, Evelyn (2005), "Renewed American Diplomacy: Keeping Southeast Asia on the U.S. Radar", *PacNet* (Pacific Forum CSIS), No. 22, 26 May.
Green p, D.J. (1994), "Convergence and Cohesion within the ASEAN-4", *Journal of Asian Economics*, 5, No. 1, pp. 119-45.
Haacke, Jurgen (2005), *ASEAN's Diplomatic and Security Culture: Origins, Development and Prospects*, Routledge.
Han, Feng (2002), "ASEAN's Relations With Big Powers", in Samuel C.Y. Ku, *Southeast Asia in New Century: An Asian Perspective*, Seng Lee Press Pte. Ltd.
Kuppuswamy, C.S. (2002), "India's Policy: Looking Eastward", South Asia Analysis Group, India, Note no. 151, 29.4.2002.
Lei, Qizhun 雷启准 (2000), *Dangdai Yindu* 当代印度 (Contemporary India), 四川人民出版社 Sichuan People's Press.
Nayar, B.R. and T.V. Paul (2003), *India in the World Order: Searching for Major-Power Status*, U.K.: Cambridge University Press.
Rao, B. (1996), "Indian Economic Reforms and ASEAN-India Economic Relations", *Journal of Asian Economics*, 7, No. 4, pp. 759-68.
Srivastava, Siddharth (2005), "India's Flexible Approach at ASEAN", *The Jakarta Post*, 19 December 2005.
Sun, Peijun 孙培钧 (2001), *Yindu Guoqing yu Zonghe Guoli* 印度国情与综合国力 (India's National Conditions and Comprehensive Power), 中国城市出版社 China City Press.
Terada, Takashi (2004), "Creating an East Asian Regionalism: The Institutionalization of ASEAN + 3 and China-Japan Directional Leadership", *The Japanese Economy*, Vol. 32, No. 2, Summer, M.E. Sharpe, Inc.

Domestic Challenges

12

A Study on Indonesian Migrant Workers in Malaysia

Lin Mei

Introduction

Malaysia is now a major receiving country with estimated over 2 million migrant workers. Such large inflow was caused by the scarcity of jobs in plantation, construction and domestic growth. Migrant workers come mostly from Indonesia, Bangladesh and the Philippines. A large number of them are in irregular situation. A Malaysian official report released by the Ministry of Finance in 1997 stated that there were at least 1.7 million foreign workers in the country, counting about 1 million unregistered workers. This number accounted for 20-25 per cent the total number of labour force in Malaysia and are largely unskilled and semi-skilled workers. The number of registered foreign unskilled and semi-skilled workers increased dramatically at the start of the 1990s and reached 532,000 in 1993 and 1,472,000 in 1997 (Table 12.1).

As labour demand in the economy stagnated due to the Asian economic crisis and the management policy for foreign workers was changed accordingly, the number of registered foreign workers declined thereafter to 769,000 in early 2002. According to 2000 Population Census of Malaysia, non-Malaysian citizens had increased to 1,384,774 and raised their percentage in total population to 5.7 per cent. Government and research institutions have estimated the existence of a considerably greater number of foreign workers in reality than is shown in the population census. However, somewhere between 500,000 and 1,000,000 illegal workers allegedly exist in the country in addition to registered workers. In any event, there is no doubt that Malaysia is one of the countries with a large number of foreign workers and that her economy is highly dependent on foreign workers (Watanabe, 2003). At the same time, its neighbour country, Indonesia, has become one of the world's major sources of unskilled labour migrants. The

Table 12.1 Estimates of Legal Migrant Workers in Malaysia:
Semi-skilled and Unskilled Workers

	Malaysia	Peninsula	Sabah	Sarawak
1993.7-12	532,732	414,336,	100,000	18,387
1994	642,057	515,983	100,000	26,074
1995	726,689	576,441	120,719	29,529
1996	745,239	586,796	121,144	37,299
1997	1,471,652	1,190,437	226,565	54,643
1998	1,127,652	789,684	283,968	54,000
1999	897,705	680,846	162,269	54,590
2000	799,685	632,720	75,232	91,733
2001.7	807,984	618,946	99,281	88,120
2002.1	769,566	–	–	–

Source: Kassim (2002) for 1993-2001; and Malaysia, Department of Immigration
for 2002.

bulk of Indonesian migrant workers regard Malaysia as major destination of
migration from 1990s. It is estimated that 83 per cent of total migrant
workers in Malaysia are Indonesian (Kaur, 2004). It is not possible to give
accurate figures of migrant worker from Indonesia to Malaysia because of:
(1) Malaysia does not make public data on migration; (2) the bulk of illegal
migrants exist; (3) estimates of the numbers involved in the movement vary
considerably.

Labour migration has been the trend of globalization and has made multidimensional influences on economy, society and politics as well as on
receiving and sending countries of labour migrants and bilateral or regional
relations. This paper will focus on analyzing the features, reasons of Indonesian migrant workers in Malaysia and its impact on bilateral relations.

Brief Review of Indonesian Labour Migration to Malaysia

Indonesian labour migration to Malaysia has been an historical and on-going
process. The second half of the nineteenth century was marked by trade
liberalization in Europe and Southeast Asian states became colonies, pro-
tectorates or part of the informal empire of European powers. After 1870
the British assumed control over the whole of the Malay peninsula by
bringing the Malay States under formal protectorate status between 1874 and
1914. At the same time, the Dutch took control over most of the island realm

of the Malay Archipelago (Kaur, 2004). Malaysia was integrated into world commodity and capital markets, became the provider of resources for its colonizer (suzerain) and began to be shortage of labour workers. The Malay administration thus sourced labour from outside countries including India and China. Javanese was the third migrant labour stream which reflected the historical links in the Malay world. This was the first time that Malaysia was confronted with the problem of multi-ethnicity (Mantra, 1998). During the colonial period, a liberal immigration policy was adopted, but the British viewed and treated Javanese migrants different from the other migrants from India and China since they were regarded as origination from the same racial stock as the Malays. A pattern of differential treatment for migrants based on ethnicity was thus established, which was to have major implications for labour migration into Malaya after independence in 1957. The flow of Indonesian migrant workers to the Malaysian Peninsula experienced a sharp increase in the 1930s. The results of the 1950 Malaysian population census indicated that there were 189,450 people born in the Island of Java, 62,200 people originated from South Kalimantan, 26,300 people from Sumatra, 24,000 people from the Island of Bawean (East Java), and 7,000 people from Sulawesi (Hugo, 1993).

Movement of Indonesian migrant workers to Malaysia declined during the War and also during the period of the confrontation between Indonesia and Malaysia. However, it increased again after the relationship between the Indonesian government and Malaysian Kingdom normalized (Mantra, 1998). From 1970s, Indonesian labour migration to Malaysia took place again, following the implementation of the New Economic Policy. The New Economic Policy, emphasizing public sector expansion and export-oriented industrialization, fostered the rural-urban migration and urban job-orientation of many Malays, thus creating labour shortage in certain sectors such as construction industry, low-paid service and rural area. The Malaysian government thus pursued a proactive policy to recruit foreign migrant workers, mainly from Indonesia but also from Bangladesh, Myanmar and the Philippines. Besides official recruitment, much migration to Malaysia is clandestine. Mid-1980 estimates of Indonesians in Peninsular Malaysia ranged between 200,000 and 700,000 (ESCAP, 1985; Hugo, 1988). This inflow was relatively unrestricted by the Malaysian government before the Asian financial crisis because of its importance for Malaysia's economic development, as advocated by the Federal Land Development Authority and Malaysian employers association. Indonesian labour migrants were also considered less threatening to the volatile ethnic and political balance than Chinese and Indians (Spaan, Naerssen and Kohl, 2002). Therefore, large-scale labour migration from Indonesia to Malaysia has continued up to the present and has been an ongoing process, following increasing clandestine migrants.

Indonesian Migrant Workers in Malaysia: General Features

The mobility of people from Indonesia to other countries constitutes the important part of international migration in past several decades. Indonesia characterized as a sending country of labour migrants and the number of labour migrants has been increasing as time goes by. The Indonesian government have perceived labour export as a valuable means of earning foreign exchange and solved domestic unemployment. Based on a report issued by the Department of Manpower (Depnaker RI 1994), prior to the early program of Indonesian development, Indonesia had actively sent its workers to various countries. In the beginning, the number was relatively small in comparison with other countries such as the Philippines, Pakistan, India and Sri Lanka, but later, the figure increased rapidly. Table 12.2 shows that by the third repelita the number of Indonesian migrant workers working abroad was 96, 410. At the end of Repelita IV the figure had reached 292,262 workers. In other words during 2 Repelitas the number of Indonesian migrant workers working abroad had doubled. During Repelita V the figure had reached 652,272. This figure actually was far smaller than it appears because it did not include workers who migrated illegally (Nasution, 2000).

Countries like Saudi Arabia, Malaysia, Singapore, Hong Kong, Brunei Darussalam, Taiwan and South Korea constitute the main destination areas of most Indonesian migrants, with Malaysia and Saudi Arabia attracting the

Table 12.2 Overseas Indonesian Workers, Repelita I – Repelita VI

Repelita	Period	(N)
Repelita I	1969-1974	5,624
Repelita II	1974-1979	17,042
Repelita III	1979-1984	96,410
Repelita IV	1984-1989	292,262
Repelita V	1989-1994	652,272
Repelita VI	1994-1999	1461,236
Total		2524,846

Source: Indonesian Manpower Department, Directorate General of Overseas Labour, *The Development of Export Labour Program in Repelita IV and V*, 1994.

largest number (Tables 12.3 and 12.4). According to Kompas figures, up to 1997/1998, about 900,000 Indonesian migrant workers were recorded (Table 12.3). A thorough examination reveals that men dominated migration to Malaysia, whereas women were more numerous among those going to Saudi Arabia. This aspect is closely related to the unique characteristics of the demand for labour or the type of labour demanded in each of those countries (Keban, 2000).

Table 12.3 Settlement of Indonesian Workers Abroad by Country up to 1997/1998

Country	Male	Female	Total
Saudi Arabia	24,406	295,038	319,444
Malaysia	220,993	187,218	408,211
Singapore	20,853	65,355	86,208
United Arab Emirates	626	19,044	19,630
Hong Kong	443	10,513	10,956
Brunei Darussalam	1,134	5,205	6,339
Taiwan	17,598	4,958	22,556
South Korea	22,266	4,012	26,278
Total	308,319	591,303	899,442

Source: *Kompas*, Monday, 5 January 1998.

Table 12.4 Overseas Indonesian Workers by Destination Country, Repelita IV – Repelita V (Nasution, 2000)

Destination Countries	Repelita IV (1984-89)		Repelita V (1989-94)	
	(N)	(%)	(N)	(%)
Australia	7	0.0024	213	0.0326
Holland	4,357	1.4902	5,515	0.8445
Belgium	3	0.0010	38	0.0058
Brunei Darussalam	920	0.3147	10,205	1.5626
Cyprus	1	0.0003	34	0.0052
United Arab Emirate	1,109	0.3793	2,323	0.3557
Hong Kong	1,735	0.5934	5,304	0.8122
India	–	–	11	0.0017
United Kingdom	77	0.0263	310	0.0475
Iraq	303	0.1036	–	–
Italy	25	0.0086	114	0.0175

Most of the Indonesia migrant workers who were sent by the government are the semi-skilled and unskilled workers, which are characterized by low education, limited knowledge and skills, occupy mostly by men and are aged between 15 and 40. Most Indonesian migrant workers are only capable of competing in less skilled jobs, which require manual labour. Based on the level of education, Indonesian migrant workers abroad have, on average, attained a maximum level of education of junior secondary school while some do not even have any educational background at all. One research on education attainment of the returnee migrants originated three areas in Indonesia from Malaysia revealed this fact (Table 12.6), which conducted by Mantra. They are limited to three sectors: plantations, domestic services, and construction. But since 1993, their employment has been extended to other sectors like manufacturing, attendants at filling stations, and as cleaners (Suko Bandiyono and Fadjri Alihar, 2000; Sukamdi and Abdul Haris, 2000). Therefore, approximately 36 per cent of Indonesian migrant workers in Malaysia were employed in manufacturing; 26 per cent in agriculture; 23 per cent in domestic work and 8 per cent in construction in 2002 (Kaur, 2004). Many of them come from Sumatra, Java, Bawean, Sulawesi and Nusa Tenggara.

As Sukamdi and Haris (2000) noted: the entire process of international labour migration can be generally categorized into two forms, based on the status of migration itself. First, is the formal labour migration, which is a process whereby the migrant leaving the country is forced to go through a

Table 12.6 Educational Attainment of Returnee Migrants from Malaysia

Education Level	NTT		NTB		Bawean Island	
	Total	%	Total	%	Total	%
Never Completed Elementary School	27	15.3	63	38.7	39	20.9
Completed Elementary School	110	62.5	57	35.0	86	46.0
Completed Intermediate School	29	16.5	24	14.6	38	20.3
Completed High School	10	5.7	19	11.7	24	12.8
Total	176	100	163	100	187	100

Source: Mantra (1998). NTT refers to East Nusa Tenggara; NTB refers to West Nusa Tenggara.

number of procedures in order to acquire a clear legal legitimacy and warranty. This formal international labour migration is therefore the kind of migration that is carried out formally, through the channels that have government approval. Workers who migrate through this formal procedure are usually provided with various documents that legitimize their migrant status in the country of destination. Second, is the informal process. This is the kind of migration that takes place informally and that in most cases is carried out without documentation. At a macro level, these kinds of migration activities are normally known as illegal migration, undocumented migration, and clandestine migration. Thus, whatever the form of international labour migration that takes place, it is evident that either of the two forms of processes is involved, depending on the development or growth of regional inequality. The pattern of Indonesian migrant workers to Malaysia includes two forms above mentioned. In any way, Indonesian migrant workers in Malaysia constitute majority of overall migrant worker in Malaysia either in terms of legal migrants or illegal migrant. Indonesian migrant workers in Malaysia constitutes majority of total foreign workers in Malaysia. According to the 1991 Population Census of Malaysia, there were 751,100 foreign nationals in Malaysia, accounting for 4.3 per cent the country's total population of 17.56 million. As for nationality, Indonesians accounted for 54 per cent of all foreign nationals, followed by 27 per cent Filipinos. Table 12.7 shows that registered foreign workers as of January 2002 were 769,566, of which Indonesians were the largest in number (73 per cent), followed by Bangladeshis (13.7 per cent), Nepalese (6.3 per cent) and Filipinos (2.2 per cent) (Machiko WATANABE, 2003).

Table 12.7   Foreign Workers in Malaysia by Country of Origin
(January 1, 2002)

	Number (persons)	*Share (%)*
Indonesia	566,983	73.7
Bangladesh	105,744	13.7
Nepal	48,257	6.3
Philippines	17,287	2.2
Myanmar	6,539	0.8
Thailand	2,440	0.3
Pakistan	2,218	0.3
Others	20,098	2.6

Source: Malaysia, Department of Immigration.

Based on the report issued by the Malaysian Bureau of Emigration, by June 30 1992, the number of illegal Indonesian workers who had registered with the Malaysian government reached almost half a million people, which was 83 per cent of total illegal migrants in Malaysia. This figures ranked highest among illegal workers registering themselves voluntarily with the Malaysian government (Nasution, 2000). Hugo (2000) and Kassin (2001) estimated the number of illegal Indonesian migrant workers in Malaysia alone in the 2000 at about 1 million. Department of Manpower and Transmigration (2004) estimated the illegal Indonesia labour migrants were at about 3.5 million between 1999 and 2001. This number has been increasing due to the increasing number of unemployed workers in Indonesia since 1999 (Firdausy, 2005). In addition, many experts estimate that the number of illegal Indonesian workers is larger than the number of legal ones, which constitutes important migration stream. (Amjad, 1996; Prijono Tjiptoherijanto, 2000; Hugo, 2001). Over the last 10 years, migration flow to Malaysia, which has had a tendency to increase in volume, is a very real phenomenon. It is extremely difficult to obtain accurate statistics on Indonesian migrant workers to Malaysia because most of the migrants get there illegally. Basing on a study conducted by Kasim (1993), an anthropologist at Malaya University, it was estimated that there are between 600-700 thousand illegal migrant workers in Western Malaysia and between 200-400 thousand of them in Eastern Malaysia (Sabah and Sarawak). Indeed, labour mobility from Indonesia to Malaysia constitutes the largest illegal labour migration flow in Asia (Prijono Tjiptoherijanto, 2000).

In terms of sex distribution, male migrant workers have been twice female migrant workers in formal sectors. For the informal sector, female migrant workers (mostly domestic helpers) have been more numerous than the male migrant workers (Table 12.8). Female workers tend to migrate to countries to work as domestic helpers and entertainment jobs, while the large number of male workers tends to migrate to countries to work in construction, transportation, agricultural and estate sectors.

The feminization of new migrant workers starts to be trend. This feminization of the migrant labour force may be attributed to two factors related to change of Malaysian industrial structure and labour market. The first is linked to changes in the production niches (mass-customization products such as electronics, textiles and garments). The new international division of labour, which facilitated the increased labour force participation of the agricultural sector and rural-urban migration, principally of women. The second factor is related to the maturing of the labour market in Malaysia, which is relatively high labour force participation rates of women, and general

Table 12.8 Placement of Indonesian Migrant Workers in
Formal and Informal Sectors by Sex, 2003

	Formal sectors			Informal sectors		
	Male	*Female*	*Total*	*Male*	*Female*	*Total*
Malaysia	27,148	13,543	40,691	1,615	6,622	8,237
Taiwan	1,054	246	1,300	39	287	326
South Korea	5,075	929	6,004	92	23	115
Japan	61	0	61	0	0	0
Saudi Arabia	534	224	758	9,931	94,009	103,940

Source: Department of Manpower and Transmigration (2004), in Firdausy (2005); Ford (2005).

labour shortages. This in turn has created an increased demand for domestic work and childcare services, which has been met by principally by Indonesian women. According to the Minister of Human Resources of Malaysia, there were about 155,000 foreign domestic workers (FDWs) in Malaysia in 2002, 70 per cent of whom were Indonesians. These statistics refer to documented workers (Piper, 2005). Another source provided by Human Rights Watch (2004) revealed that more than 90 per cent of domestic workers in Malaysia are Indonesian (Kaur, 2004).

The Reasons Why Indonesians Emigrate to Malaysia (Including Illegally)

We know from the second part above that Indonesia is one of major migrant source countries and Malaysia became the largest receiving country of Indonesian migrant workers in 1990s. Why so many Indonesians prefer to emigrate to Malaysia?

1. Malaysia has been facing labour shortage and Indonesia has been facing surplus of unskilled and semi-skilled labour, so Malaysian government attract foreign workers into Malaysia and Indonesian government encourage Indonesians go abroad for working. On the one hand, Malaysian economy has experienced sustained growth though indus-trialization since the 1970s and put it into "labour shortage" situation. With rapid growth and structural changes of the economy, the structure of the labour market has also changed significantly. The increase in total number of employed persons had exceeded the increase in labour force since the 1970s. The total number of employed persons increased at an

annual average of 3.7 per cent during the decade from 1987 to 1997 when the annual average growth rate reached 8.5 per cent while the increase in labour force remained at 3.1 per cent. A large number of workers shifted to the manufacturing and services from rural plantation sector that had relatively inferior working conditions and lower wages compared with these urban industries. As a result, labour shortage became first in the agriculture, especially in the rural plantation, and then in the construction, manufacturing, service sectors. So, the Malaysian government pursued a proactive policy to recruit foreign migrant workers. On the other hand, Indonesia has been facing surplus of unskilled and semi-skilled labour and poverty problem. Indonesia has been backward behind its neighbour country, Malaysia, in terms of economic development, but has bigger population than that of Malaysia (Table 12.9). In terms of the incidence of poverty, the Indonesian Central Board of Statistics (2005) using the official poverty line of per capita income per month at an average Rp.110,000 (equivalent to US$12.50), estimated the number of the poor in 2004 was about 19.6 per cent, much higher the 11.3 per cent in the pre-crisis year of 1996. In order to solve domestic unemployment and get more foreign exchange, Indonesia government encourage Indonesians to work abroad and put emigrants into the Five Year Plan. Department of Labour office, particularly Directorate of Overseas Workers Services (AKAN), is in charge of planning and implementation of the migration program. The government of Indonesia through the office of AKAN has tried to maximize the profits and minimize the costs of the overseas migration through formal recruiters coordinated by an organization called the Indonesian Manpower Suppliers Association (IMSA). In one word,

Table 12.9 Indonesia and Malaysia: Key Indicators

	Indonesia	Malaysia
Population (millions)	216 (2004)	25.6 (2004)
Total working age population (millions)	113.0 (1997)	13.0 (1997)
Unemployment Rate and number of unemployment	9.5% 9.5 million (2003)	3.6% 0.3 million (2003)
Per Capita GDP (US$)	728 (2000)	3881 (2000)
$1-a-day Poverty Index	6.5 (2003)	0.2 (2003)
$2-a-day-Poverty Index	50.5 (2003)	9.0 (2003)

Source: Selected from *Key Indicators 2005*, published by ADB.

labour shortage in Malaysia and labour surplus in Indonesia is one of pull-push factors for migration from Indonesia into Malaysia and the two governments act as facilitator in the process of this migration.

2. With the Malaysia experienced more rapid economic development and labour shortage comparing to Indonesia, wage and salary in Malaysia has been higher than that of Indonesia. This constitutes another pull-push factor for migration from Indonesia to Malaysia. Table 12.10 and Table 12.11 show wage differences paid in Indonesia and Malaysia for a similar job (Mantra, 1999). In Malaysia, the wage is several times higher than that of similar job in Indonesia. Moreover, it is also true that the demand for labour in Malaysia especially for manual work in the agricultural, mining, plantation and construction sectors is indeed needed. This situation is made even worse by the fact that Malaysians, especially those who have

Table 12.10 Wage Differences between Indonesia and Malaysia

Year	Area of Origin	Local Wage Rate (Indonesia)	Wage Rate in Malaysia
1990	Lombok	Rp.500 – Rp.1000/ Day	Rp. 7000 – Rp. 8000/ Day (Plantations)
1982	Bawean	Rp. 500/Day	Rp. 9000/Day
1991	Semarang	Rp. 2500/Day	Rp. 10,800/Day (Sarawak)
1990	Indonesia	Rp. 1000/Day	Rp. 10,000/Day
1984	East Java	Rp. 3000/Day	Rp. 9000/Day

Source: Hugo (1993).

Table 12.11 Labour Costs per Worker in Manufacturing by Selected Country

	US$ per year		Indonesia = 1.0 (Index of wages)	
	1980-84	*1990-94*	*1980-84*	*1990-94*
Indonesia	898	1008	1.0	1.0
Philippines	1240	2459	1.38	2.44
Malaysia	2519	3429	2.81	3.40
Thailand	2305	2705	2.57	2.68
Singapore	5576	21534	6.21	21.36

Source: World Bank (2000), *World Development Indicators 1999*, cited from Manning (2002).

attained some intermediate or higher education, are no longer willing to take up some manual jobs in these sectors. They usually go to large cities to look for better working condition, higher pay and industrial jobs. In contrast, many Indonesians face the pressure of unemployment and poor living life, and intend to emigrate for getting high wages and improving their family living condition.

3. Geographic, historical and cultural links are also the reasons why Indonesian migrants choose Malaysia as a destination country of migration. From geographic perspective, Malaysia as a neighbour of Indonesia share very long costal and land boundary. Indonesian migrants, especially those illegal migrants, are easy to enter into Malaysia either by sea or cross-border. From historical perspective, mobility of Indonesian migrant workers to Malaysia has taken place in colonized time or even earlier. Pioneering migrants still maintain relationships with their origin area. They not only provide information for new migrants about job availability but also help them to find job. In one word, the new migrants are initially settled by the old migrants, mostly of their relatives and friends. From cultural perspective, Malaysia shares the same religion, same racial stock with Indonesia. Therefore, Indonesian migrant workers were ever more welcomed by Malaysia to extent because of similar culture background comparing migrants from other countries. Even Indonesian migration into Malaysia was also encouraged by the Malayan government for political reasons as their easy integration into the Malay community allowed Malays to maintain a numerical edge in population over the Chinese and Indians (Liow, 2003).

4. Intermediaries (called Tekong) play a crucial role in migration process including legal and illegal. Sometimes their role is limited to taking the prospective migrant to a recruiting agent, sometimes it involves financing the cost of migration (which is then repaid twice as much), and sometimes it covers the whole process (Battistella, 2002). A whole network of middlemen and recruitment agents has over the years "institutionalized" the movement and contributed to the growth of what has been called the "immigration industry". These agents operate both within and outside the legal ambit, in both Malaysia and Indonesia. They organized most of the illegal migration into Malaysia, including recruiting workers, arranging the move, and obtaining and settling them into jobs (Pillai, 1996).

5. Irregular Migrants is caused by the factors mentioned above besides, especially caused by the high administrative costs of migration (including payments to labour agencies in Indonesia and Malaysia), bureaucratic procedures and restrictive immigration policies in Malaysia. Potential

migrants who want to work abroad by formal channel have to apply for overseas work permits, take skill training, obtain clearance from Labour Department and then get all compulsory travel documents. The entire process is slow, cumbersome and costly, and most of times bureaucratic delays in processing applications. The costs incurred by migrant workers include: fees charged by recruitment agents and middlemen; registration fees, visa fees, exit permit fees, travel and transport expenses before departure, air ticket, repatriation cost and various government levies and legal costs (Piyasiri Wickramasekera, 2002, and Firdausy, 2005). The costs and delays on both sides are therefore major factors encouraging illegal migration, which is cheaper and faster. Indonesian official migration system is also a significant factor in the growth of such a huge level of irregular migration from Indonesia on one hand. On the other hand, Malaysian restrictive immigration policies also facilitate the irregular migration from Indonesia into Malaysia. Rigid immigration laws in receiving countries and the continued tendency on the part of labour shortage countries to refuse admission to unskilled workers are a major cause of irregular and disorderly migration (Piyasiri Wickramasekera, 2002).

In general, the disparities of labour market and economy with close borders and well-established migration networks between these two countries, combined with improved transportation and information flows, are the major determinants that cause the flow and pattern of labour migration from Indonesia to Malaysia.

Terms and Routes Used by Irregular Migrant Workers from Indonesia into Malaysia

According to Piyasiri Wickramasekera (2002), typical examples of irregular migrant workers are: overstays on tourist visa and engaged in work; students engaged in employment; trainees overstaying their visas; regular migrants continuing beyond the contract period; regular migrants running away from their designated employer before expiry of contract; and persons trafficked into the sex industry. Indonesian irregular migrant workers in Malaysia include all of terms above. As well, clandestine movement across borders (undocumented labour migration or illegal movement) is also an important form.

Mantra described clearly the routes taken by illegal Indonesian migrant workers into Malaysia. Illegal Indonesian migrant workers usually enter Malaysia through two directions or routes, that is, the eastern route and the western route. The western route which is popularly known as the "Peninsular Malaysian System" is usually taken by the illegal Indonesian migrant workers going to the Malaysian peninsula (western part of Malaysia). Illegal migrants following this route usually originate from East Java including Bawean island, North Sumatra, Aceh, West Sumatra (Minangkabau), Central Java, West Nusa Tenggara (mainly from the districts of East and Central Lombok). There are various routes to enter the Melaka Strait through the west:

- Through the ports in the islands of Riau like Bengkalis, Dumai, Rupat and Bagan Siapiapi, entering the western coast of Johor and then docking at Pontian and Batu Pahat. A journey through this route takes almost one night to reach.
- Through Tanjung Pinang and Tanjung Uban in the islands of Riau or Batam near Singapore, then through Johor Sea (Pangerang, Guntung, Johor Lama, and Langisati Gulf). This journey requires approximately three hours to complete.
- For the Indonesian migrant workers particularly from East Java, they first of all travel to Bawean Island. It is from this island that middlemen from Malaysia then meet them and then illegally maneuver them into the country.

The eastern route also called the "Eastern Malaysian System" is usually followed by illegal Indonesian migrant workers from South Sulawesi and East Flores district. These intending migrants usually first go to Ujung Pandang, then to Pare-Pare where they join other migrant workers and move on to Nunukan island in East Kalimantan. It is from here that they then cross to Tawau (Sabah in East Malaysia). This route is more dangerous compared to the western route and takes up to four days to reach. There are also other Indonesian migrant workers from East Flores who go directly to Balik Papan from where they then go to Tarakan, Nunukan, and to the border at Tawau in Sabah (see Figure 12.1) (Mantra, 1998, 1999).

The Impacts of Indonesian Migrant Workers in Malaysia on Relationship between the Two Countries

Malaysian immigration policy has evolved from laissez-faire to a policy established on economic need, and more recently on based on social and security concerns (Pillai, 1999). Malaysia government carried out a laissez-faire immigration policy until mid-1980s. After that, it began to take restrictive immigration policy with the objectives of transforming the economy to a knowledge-based industrial structure and lowering dependence

Figure 12.1 Main Migration Routes of Illegal Migrants from Indonesia to Malaysia

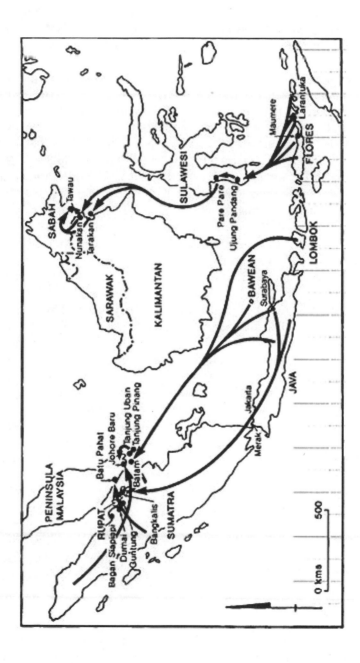

Source: Cited from Hugo (2002).

on foreign workers in the long term. The first measure to control the inflow of illegal foreign workers was taken in 1982 and in 1984 in order to legalize the recruitment of foreign workers. A Committee for the Recruitment of Foreign Workers was established in 1982. The first bilateral agreement on migrant workers with Indonesia was signed in May 1984 (the Medan Agreement), followed by signing similar agreements with Thailand, Bangladesh and the Philippines. From 1984 onwards, several measures have been taken to control illegal migrants such as: the Foreign Worker Regularization Programme in 1989, 1992 (Ops Nyah I) and 1996 (Ops Nyah II) to register illegal workers; Amended Immigration Act in 1997; Ban on new recruitment of foreign workers and renewal of work permits during crisis between 1997-1998; Ban on new recruitment of Indonesians for all sectors except domestic maids in February 2002; More rigid new immigration law in August 2002; Amnesty for illegal foreign workers in 2002, 2004 and 2005; etc. All these measures were intended to promote legal employment and restrict (stop) illegal entry. However, these efforts taken by Malaysian government to curb the rise of illegal migrants did not yield any spectacular changes.

As mentioned above, Indonesian migration to Malaysia has long history extending back to colonial times, but almost halted during the World War Two and the years of confrontation of the two countries. From 1970, migration flow from Indonesia into Malaysia picked up again and continued to increase up to now. Finally, Malaysia became the largest destination of Indonesian migrant workers from 1990s instead of Saudi Arabia (see Table 12.5). Malaysia immigration policy toward Indonesian migrants has changed from welcome to rigid restrictive with the increase number of illegal migrant workers from Indonesia as the time goes by. Malaysia's tough new immigration laws went into effect August 1, 2002. The Immigration Act (Amended) 2002 calls for illegal foreigners to be fined up to M$10,000 ($2,631), imprisoned for five years, and to receive six strokes of the cane. There is going on cracking down illegal migrants in recent years. Illustrative of the government's changing stance towards irregular immigrants are the phrases used in political rhetoric. In general, the language used has toughened: a shift is notable from the use of the term "irregular migrants" in the 1970s to "illegal immigrants" in the early 1980s, gradually shifting to the common usage of "illegals" and "aliens" in the 1990s (Spaan, Van Naerssen and Kohl, 2002).

Indonesia migrant worker became more conspicuous, controversial and politicized in Malaysia with increasingly associated with crimes and worry about the spread of HIV and terrorism, following the increase inflow of illegal migrants. Some issues relating to Indonesian migrant workers, especially illegal migrants, were seriously concerned by Malaysians including media, citizens and government (Spaan, Van Naerssen and Kohl, 2002): (1) Crimes. One report indicated that the majority of recorded cases of burglary, rape and murder involved Indonesians (*New Straits Times*, July 1 2001); (2) Health hazard. The spread of HIV, malaria and leprosy through immigrants was feared; (3) Fraudulent marriage. Fraudulent marriage between Indonesian men and Malaysian women were considered socially unacceptable and deemed as immoral; (4) Immigrants are regarded to replace Malaysian workers and there has been rising resentment among Malaysians towards immigrants; (5) Chinese-dominated Democratic Action Party is suspicious that Indonesian immigrants will numerically increase the Malay population because the Indonesian immigrants will eventually assimilate to Malay society; (6) Stability and security. Stability and security caused by immigrants became widely debated after rioting by Indonesian immigrants at Malaysian immigration depots (i.e. Semenyih) in 1998. The phenomenon of illegal Indonesian migrant workers was fast becoming a "threat" to "national security" and had a potential rupturing effect on the fabric of Malaysia society (Liow, 2003).

Even more, illegal migrant workers from Indonesia to Malaysia caused conflicts and tension of relationship between Malaysia and Indonesia even though the two governments try to tone down the issue of illegal Indonesian migrant workers. Mass repatriation of illegal migrant workers taken by Malaysian government resulted in many problems because of under-estimation of number, a lack of communication and co-operation between Malaysian and Indonesian governments. For example, Malaysian parliament passed legislation in October 2001 that capped work permits foreign workers from 6 years to 3 years. Thus, Kuala Lumpur changed the official status of many Indonesian from "legal" to "illegal" almost overnight. In response to the sudden changes, many Indonesian migrant workers detained at the Machap Umboo detention centre in Alor Gajah rioted and made a Malaysian policeman injured. Later in November at the same year, 2,000 illegal workers who detained at the Pekan Nenas detention centre in Johor also rioted. On 17 January 2002 in the state of Negri Sembilan, some 400 Indonesian workers at a textile factory in the Nilai industrial estate rioted and torched building after police tried to detain sixteen of their co-workers for alleged drug abuses. Three days later, another riot involving 70 Indonesian workers in Cyberjaya took place. Following these incidents, Malaysian government announced a "Hire Indonesians Last" policy and banned on new recruitment of Indonesians for all sectors except domestic maids in February 2002. In response to

Malaysian policy toward Indonesian workers, there were protests outside the Malaysian embassy in Jakarta to criticize Malaysian treatment of Indonesian workers. Members of the Laskar Merah Putih burned the Malaysian flag outside the Malaysian embassy in Jakarta. Former National Assembly Speaker Amien Rias criticized Malaysia in Parliament and called for Jakarta to take action against its neighbouring country. In turn, Malaysia responded with a stout diplomatic defense, and later warned its citizens against traveling to Indonesia, and calling for the Indonesian government to take action against those who threatened to jeopardize bilateral relations with their protests.

In addition, Malaysia's decision to embark on a "Hire Indonesians Last" policy was undertaken without prior consultation or negotiation with Indonesia, and such unilateral action was not satisfied with the latter. Indonesian authorities were poorly prepared to deal with the chaotic situation that developed along parts of the country's border with Malaysia. Before new immigration law took effect on 1 August 2002, in Kalimantan, the Indonesian province which borders Malaysian's Sabah state, a transit town, Nunakan, turned into a heaving mass of human misery. Some 350,000 migrant workers and their families entered the town and camped in squalid condition. It was reported that as many as 85 people, including young children, died in Nunakan camps. On August 9, 2002, four Indonesians were sentenced to be fined, caned and jailed under the new law, which had mixed reactions in Indonesia. At the same time, the respective government finger-pointed each other that the other has not been doing its part in the joint attempt to eradicate the problem of illegal immigration. Malaysian government has continually highlighted Jakarta's apparent unwillingness to render maximum co-operation in repatriating Indonesian illegal immigrants. In its parts, Indonesia has argued that Malaysia has been insensitive and un-co-operative by demanding the immediate repatriation of undocumented Indonesian labour, knowing that Jakarta itself was undergoing an even greater economic meltdown and could barely provide adequate holding and transportation facilities for returning workers.

The period from the second half of 2004 through to the beginning of 2005 was another vulnerable time for Indonesian migrant workers in Malaysia because the Malaysian government had again carried out mass deportations of undocumented migrant workers in Malaysia based on its Immigration Act of 2002. Despite the Malaysian government's early warning in July 2004, no significant response came from the Indonesian government to anticipate the implementation of this policy. A May 2004 Malaysia-Indonesia MOU sets out procedures for Indonesians to work in Malaysia; it allows Malaysian employers to hold workers' passports and other documents for "safekeeping."

Law No.39/2004 on overseas placement and protection of Indonesian migrant workers has not made a significant impact on labour placement management. Either Malaysia-Indonesia MOU or Law No 39/2004 did not cover the issues of illegal Indonesian migrant workers. Critics noted that the Indonesian government did little to assist returning unauthorized migrants. For the governments of Malaysia and Indonesia have assumed that deportation is the only way to settle the issue of illegal (undocumented) migrant worker. In its reality, however, deportation leaves many issues unresolved. Instead, every time a deportation takes place, tension increases in Indonesia-Malaysia diplomatic relations. There is also great potential for violence and human rights violations, especially when civilian vigilante groups are mobilized. Massive accumulations of deportees at transit points also leads to many serious problems, as was the case in Nunukan.

Until now, both of governments have not succeeded in co-operation over the issue of repatriation of Indonesian illegal immigrants. Inability to find a solution of illegal Indonesian migrant worker remains a thorn in both sides and shadows the relationship between them in long run.

Conclusion

The labour flow between Indonesia and Malaysia has been the important part of labour migration in Asia-pacific region and catch more and more attention. Indonesia has been the labour sending country and Malaysia has been the labour receiving country. Malaysia has been the largest destination of Indonesian migrant workers and Indonesian migrant workers have constituted majority of foreign migrant workers at the same time. Indonesian emigrant workers dominated by semi-skilled and unskilled workers with low education in oversea countries, including in Malaysia. Many experts estimate that the number of illegal Indonesian workers in Malaysia is larger than the number of legal ones, which constitutes important migration stream. There are complex factors caused labour migration from Indonesia into Malaysia. In general, the disparities of labour market and economy with close borders and well-established migration networks between these two countries, combined with improved transportation and information flows, are the major determinants that cause the flow and pattern of labour migration from Indonesia to Malaysia. In addition, Irregular Migrants is especially caused by the high administrative costs of migration (including payments to labour agencies in Indonesia and Malaysia), bureaucratic procedures and restrictive immigration policies in Malaysia. As we know, labour flow, unlike commodity export and import, will make multi-dimensional impacts on migrant workers themselves, the labour sending country, the labour receiving country, the relationship between labour sending and receiving countries, even region. Illegal migrant workers from Indonesia to Malaysia caused conflicts and tension of relationship between Malaysia and Indonesia. Until now, both of governments have not succeeded in co-operation over the issue of repatriation of Indonesian illegal immigrants. Inability to find a solution of illegal Indonesian migrant worker remains a thorn in both sides and shadows the relationship between them in long run.

Semi-skilled and unskilled labour migration from Indonesia will still be dominant in the near future. There is a must for the governments in both Indonesia and Malaysia to facilitate international labour migration, particularly to unskilled and semi-skilled labour migrants. On both sides, greater cooperation between the two countries is needed. These aims to ensure a smooth flow of labour supply to meet labour demand, minimize the problem of illegal migration and its negative political, economic and social effects, and provide adequate protection for migrants. The approaches to solve the issues of labour migration, especially illegal migration, are not included in this paper.

References

Amjad, R. (1996), "Philippines and Indonesia: on the way to a migration transition?", paper presented at The Nihon University International Symposium on the Dynamics of Labor Migration in Asia, March 6-8, 1996, Tokyo, Japan.

Battistella, Graziano (2002), "Unauthorized Migrants as Global Workers in ASEAN", paper presented at the IUSSP Regional Population Conference on Southeast Asia's Population in Changing Asian Context held at Chulalongkorn University, Bangkok, Thailand, 10-12 June 2002.

ESCAP (1985), "The Return of International Labor Migrants in the ESCAP Region", *International Migration*, 25 (1): 129-147.

Firdausy, Carunia Mulya (2005), "Trends, issues and policies towards international labor migration: an Indonesian case study", paper presented in United Nations Expert Group Meeting On International Migration and Development, New York, 6-8 July 2005.

Ford, Michele (2005) "Migrant Labor in Southeast Asia: Case Study of Indonesia", paper presented in Workshop on Migrant Labor in Southeast Asia, jointly organized by the Friedrich-Ebert-Stiftung (FES) Philippine Office and the Asia Research Institute of the National University of Singapore (NUS), in Singapore, on 25-27 August 2005.

Hugo, Graeme (1993), "Indonesian Labor Migration to Malaysia: Trends and Policy Implications", *Southeast Asian Journal of Social Science*, 21 (1): 36-72.

Hugo, Graeme (1988), "Population Movement in Indonesia since 1971", *Tijdschrift voor Economische en Sociale Geografie*, 79 (1): 242-256.

Hugo, Graeme (1995), "International Labour Migration and the Family: Some Observations from Indonesia , *Asian and Pacific Migration Journal*, 4 (2-3). 273 301.

Hugo, Graeme (2001), "Patterns and levels of international migration in Indonesia", in Graeme Hugo (ed.), *Population Mobility and HIV/AIDS in Indonesia*.

Hugo, Graeme (2002) "Indonesia's Labor Looks Abroad", *http://www.migration information.org/Profiles/display.cfm?ID=53*

Kaban, Yeremias T. (2000), "International Migration, The Strategy for National Development and Globalization", in Sukamdi and Abdul Haris (eds), *Labor Migration in Indonesia: Policies and Practices*, Population Studies Center, Gadjah Mada University, Indonesia.

Kaur, Amarjit (2004), "Mobility, Labor Mobility and Border Controls: Indonesian Labor Migration to Malaysia since 1900", paper presented at the 15th Biennial Conference of the Asian Studies Association of Australia in Canberra, 29 June – 2 July 2004.

Liow, Joseph (2003) "Malaysia's Illegal Indonesian Migrant Labor Problem: In Search of Solutions", *Contemporary Southeast Asia*, Vol. 25, No. 1, April 2003, pp. 44-64.

Mantra, Ida Bagoes (1998), "Indonesian Labor Mobility to Malaysia (A Case Study: East Flores, West Lombok, and The Island of Bawean)", paper presented at the National Workshop on International Migration at Yogyakarta, 9-11 March 1998, by the Population Studies Center, Gadjah Mada University, Indonesia.

Mantra, Ida Bagoes (1999), "Illegal Indonesian Labor Movement from Lombok to Malaysia", *Asia Pacific Viewpoint*, Vol. 40, No. 1, pp. 59-68.

Nasution, M.A. (2000), "International Migration in Southeast Asia: A Case Study of Indonesian Workers in the Malaysian Peninsula", in Sukamdi and Abdul Haris (eds), *Labor Migration in Indonesia: Policies and Practices*, Population Studies Center, Gadjah Mada University, Indonesia.

Manning, Chris (2002), *Structural Change, Economic Crisis and International Labor Migration in East Asia*, Blackwell Publishers Ltd.

Pillai, Patrick (1996), "Labor Market Developments and International Migration in Malaysia", *Migration and the Labor Market in Asia: Prospects to the Year 2000*, OECD Documents, OECD.

Pillai, Patrick (1999), "The Malaysian State's Response to Migration", *Sojourn*, 14 (1), pp. 178-197.

Piper, Nicola (2005), "Migrant labor in Southeast Asia: Case Study of Malaysia", paper presented in Workshop on Migrant Labor in Southeast Asia, jointly organized by the Friedrich-Ebert-Stiftung (FES) Philippine Office and the Asia Research Institute of the National University of Singapore (NUS), in Singapore, on 25-27 August 2005.

Piyasiri Wickramasekera (2002), "Asian Labor Migration: Issues and Challenges in an Era of Globalization", International Migration Programme, International Labor

Office, Geneva. *http://www.oit.org/public/English/protection/migrant/download/ imp/imp57e.pdf*

Prijono Tjiptoherijanto (2000), "International Migration: Process, System and Policy Issues", in Sukamdi and Abdul Haris (eds), *Labor Migration in Indonesia: Policies and Practices*, Population Studies Center, Gadjah Mada University, Indonesia.

Spaan, Ernst, Ton Van Naerssen and Gerard Kohl (2002), "Re-imaging Borders: Malay Identity and Indonesian Migrants in Malaysia", *Tijdschrift Voor Economische en Sociale Geograpfie*, 93 (2): 160-172.

Suko Bandiyono and Fadjri Alihar (2000), " A Review of Research Work on International migration in Indonesia", in Sukamdi and Abdul Haris (eds), *Labor Migration in Indonesia: Policies and Practices*, Population Studies Center, Gadjah Mada University, Indonesia.

Sukamdi and Abdul Haris (2000), "A Brief overview of International Migration", in Sukamdi and Abdul Haris (eds), *Labor Migration in Indonesia: Policies and Practices*, Population Studies Center, Gadjah Mada University, Indonesia.

Watanabe, Machiko (2003), "Economic Development and International Labor Migration in Malaysia", in Yasuko Hayase (ed.), *International Migration in APEC Member Economies: Its Relations with Trade, Investment and Economic Development*, APEC Study Center, Institute of Developing Economies, JETRO, Japan, March 2003.

13

Ningxia Khufiyyah Akhung Culture Training Plan: An Action Anthropology Perspective

Sun Zhenyu

The Background under Which the Plan Is Conducted

Islam is one of the major religions in China and Islamic education being popular among the Hui and Uyghur peoples is, too, one of the various nongovernmental educations of Chinese minority nationalities, which contributes greatly to the advancement of Chinese Islamic culture. The Hui Islamic education being called historically "Preaching-Hall Education" (*jingtang jiaoyu* 经堂教育) was founded by a Muslim scholar named Hu Dengzhou 胡澄洲 (c. 1522–1597) from today's Shaanxi province and continued till nowadays for more than 400 years. The Huis are people who attach great importance to their culture and education, and in the past there were some enlightened scholars, who being trained by Islamic education and having mastered Confucianism, developed the Chinese Islamic philosophy (*Huihui lixue* 回回理学) by absorbing the quintessence of the Confucian philosophy into their Islamic writings. These scholars also made their best effort in reforming Islamic education and called on their compatriots to learn secular as well as scientific knowledge. It was these scholars, too, who have established a system of folk education which includes both religious and secular education (Arabic education and Schools for Girls) at the beginning of the 20th century and especially during the period of China's reform and opening out. However, there are still problems need to be solved in the Hui Islamic education such as the knowledge it taught was outmoded and the scholars it trained know only religious knowledge while almost never learned systematically about secular and scientific knowledge, so it is difficult for them to meet the urgent demands of the modernization of the Hui society.

Nowadays, China is just in a great period of the four modernizations. However, there still exist serious problems that the minority nationalities of

China have to cope with if they want to keep pace with the times, and one of which is how to explore resources needed for their modernization. This is especially urgent for the minorities who are short of the means of development and demands that they would be of greater initiative and more wisdom.

Akhungs are one kind of very important human resources, which cannot be replaced for the modernization of the Hui society. Unfortunately this was not paid enough attention to before. Akhungs indeed play a very important role in strengthening Islamic belief, conducting Islamic education, maintaining cultural customs, and bringing about democratic self-government in the Hui society. However, the questions we have to ask here is that could they play the same role in the modernization of the Hui people as they play in religious affairs? Could they change their conservative image in the eyes of other people? Could they become the talents being of modern personality?

As for the Chinese governments at various levels, the question is without doubt how to guide religions which includes Islam, Daoism, Buddhism, and Christianity, etc. to adapt to the socialist system of China. In doing so another question which has to be raised is how the governments change their passive ways in the past in managing the affairs concerning akhungs?

Very fortunately all the questions asked above are already considered by some Chinese Muslims. They even took actions in solving them. Hong Yang 洪洋, the leader of the Khufiyyah *Menhuan* 门宦 (a Chinese name for the Islamic Sufi order), is one of those Muslims. Before succeeding his father, Hong Weizong 洪维宗, as the leader of the *Menhuan* he had already finished Islamic education abroad, and then got the master degree in ethnology from the Central University for Minority Nationalities (Zhongyang Minzu Daxue 中央民族大学) domestically. Having mastered both the religious and secular knowledge himself, Hong Yang also sent and sponsored more than 30 Muslim youths of the *Menhuan* to universities in Beijing and Yinchuan to study such subjects as modern Arabic, Chinese language and history, etc. And what is important is that he before long had a new idea, that is, he wanted akhungs to learn systematically secular and scientific knowledge, too. That the initiative like this made by the leader of the Khufiyyah *Menhuan* is not without enough reason. For the *Menhuan* has a very good tradition in keeping pace with the times. As earlier as the time when Hong Shoulin 洪寿林, the founder of the *Menhuan*, was in his lifetime, he established a good relationship with the Red Army of the Chinese Communist Party, by supporting the revolutionary struggle of CCP and especially by protecting a soldier of the Red Army, who was at that time in danger of being arrested by the Guomindang Army.

The above tells the background under which the Ningxia Khufiyyah Akhung Culture Training Plan was to be conducted. As for the reason why I also take an active part in the plan and play a role of designer of the program, this is because I think that it is the responsibility of the researcher of social science such as anthropology to discover any new development of Islam (or Islamic education) and to try his/her best to help it develop healthily.

What Relevance Does the Plan Have?

In a general view, the conducting of the Ningxia Khufiyyah Akhung Culture Training Plan will be beneficial to lead Islam to adapt to the socialist system of China, to build a harmonious society in a multi-nationality country like China, and to meet the demands of the modernization of the Hui society. Practically, the followings would be involved. First, by conducting the plan we can know the new development of Islam under changed conditions as soon as possible. I noticed that the new development of Islam in China, showed by the Khufiyyah *Menhuan*, is of great importance not only in China but also internationally, and not only in religious fields but also in secular areas. Second, by carrying out the plan we can train more religious talents of modern quality for Islam, can successfully put into effect the free-belief policy, and guarantee the normal development of religions in China. Third, by implementing the plan it would be advantageous for Chinese governments to lead the Hui Muslims to take their active part in the development of culture and civilization, to maintain social order, and to realize the great goal of constructing a united, prosperous and strong society of China. Lastly, it would be useful in creating new conditions for the development and reformation of Islamic education, which has existed for several hundred years in China, in order that it can make new contributions to the progress of the Hui nationality in modern times. Furthermore, through the plan, we can academically explore the new ways in combining anthropological research with the modernization of the minority nationalities, accumulating new knowledge from experience, and promoting the development of ethnology or anthropology in China.

Principles or Norms for Training

The basic ideas of the Training Plan come from action anthropology. According to the international popular theories of anthropology and related disciplines and by considering the conditions under which the plan was conducted, the following principles or norms are made for the plan: It will pay full attention to the living conditions of the Hui people (akhungs), who will be studied and participate in the research process; their values, beliefs, and the right of self-policy-deciding will be respected; the interaction of the Hui people (akhungs) and the researches will be laid stress on; the problem-finding and changing what are changeable in the research process will be focused on; and goal-guiding, practical effectiveness, and gradual develop-ment will be pursued in the research process.

Aims of the Training Plan

The goal of "Preaching-Hall Education" is to strengthen and purify akhungs' Islamic belief, cultivate their good personality, and build their sound Islamic knowledge, etc., upon which the Training Plan will make its best effort to turn them again into a new type of religious talents by teaching them secular and scientific knowledge, introducing them with the spirit of reason and the consciousness of progress, cultivating them with a sense of social responsi-bility, the purpose of which is to make them not only love their religion (Islam, which is taught by Islamic education) but also be loyal to their country – China, and to guarantee that they will play a leading role in the develop-ment of modern culture and civilization of the Hui nationality.

How Was the Plan Conducted?

An anthropological research group was established, which is responsible for making and carrying out the plan, monitoring research process, making improvements if any problem be found, building knowledge from the experience of training, and at the same time working out new theories and methods in response to any newly changed conditions and situations. The group is led by this author, assisted by Hong Yang, the leader of Khufiyyah *Menhuan*. A teaching group was also established, too, which is responsible for all teaching works.

Curricula

The principles of cause-planning of the research are as the followings: Because akhungs have received systematic Islamic education through the "Preaching-Hall Education", the curricula of which includes *Kalam* (Islamic teaching), *Sheri'ah* (Islamic law), Arabic, Persian, Islamic literature, etc., the course-planning of the plan thus will lay stress mainly on introducing akhungs secular and scientific knowledge and cultivating them with modern way of thinking and knowing.

1. The module of anthropology and the study of religion: the theories and policies of nation and religion, Chinese national history, the history and culture of the Hui nationality, the history of Arabs, a brief introduction of the science of religion, and a brief introduction of Judaism and Christianity.
2. The module of politics and law: the political system of modern China, the political system of modern West, an outline of the policies of China, the system of civic law in China, and the system of penal law in China.
3. The module of traditional cultures: an outline of Chinese traditional culture, history of Western philosophy, history of Islamic philosophy, history of Chinese literature, and selected readings of *Huihui lixue* (the Huihui philosophy).
4. The module of professional quality training as akhungs: ancient Chinese, modern Chinese, Arabic, English, Chinese writing, lecture and eloquence, and the knowledge of computer.

(With total of 23 courses and 1530 hours)

The Process of Training

According to the Training Plan the first class would be opened on the September of 2004 but postponed to the beginning of October that year because of not getting fully prepared. The first class has 23 akhung-students, all of them are already akhungs (that means they graduated from Islamic education and got the title of akhung), that is, they already take charge of one community locating around a mosque after graduated from Islamic education. These akhungs, having solid Islamic knowledge and rich practical experience of akhung-profession, desire very much to become modern religious talents through learning systematically secular and scientific knowledge provided by the curricula. The first class was planed to continue for two years and now is in its last half of the second year.

The details about the akhung-students are as followings:

Name	Gender	Age	Secular education	Home place	GIE	OIS
Zhou Jinfu	M	42	Middle school	Tongxin	1988	1991
Yang Maoping	M	32	Middle school	Guyuan	1996	1996
Ma Guolin	M	36	Middle school	Tongxin	1993	1993

Name	Gender	Age	Secular education	Home place	GIE	OIS
Ma Chenglong	M	38	Middle school	Haiyuan	1988	1988
Ding Puhong	M	42	High school	Guyuan	1988	1998
Ma Yanli	M	41	Middle school	Tongxin	1990	1991
Ma Yingping	M	32	Middle school	Tongxin	2002	2002
Jin Zhengzhong	M	29	Middle school	Tongxin	2004	
Zhao Minggui	M	28	Middle school	Haiyuan	2002	2003
Yang Hucheng	M	34	Middle school	Haiyuan	2002	
Tian Zhongfu	M	28	Middle school	Haiyuan	2004	
Ma Xiaohui	M	30	Middle school	Tongxin	2004	
Ma Xiaoyue	M	30	Middle school	Tongxin	2004	
Bai Xiaojun	M	29	Middle school	Tongxin	2004	
Ma Zizhen	M	30	Middle school	Tongxin	2004	
Ma Haibo	M	25	Middle school	Tongxin	2005	
Ma Hailin	M	25	Middle school	Zhongning	2005	
Ma Tiancai	M	24	Middle school	Zhongning	2005	
Jin Yugui	M	24	Middle school	Zhongning	2005	
Ma Long	M	22	Middle school	Haiyuan	2005	
Tian Yuguo	M	26	Middle school	Haiyuan	2005	
Ma Guangzong	M	24	Middle school		2005	
Ma Ruizong	M	24	Middle school	Zhongning	2005	

Notes: The GIE stands for Graduation from Islamic education; The OIS stands for that after graduating from Islamic education, these akhungs began to take charge of the religious affairs in a Hui community located around a mosque and teach Islamic knowledge there (in the mosque).

What Was Learned from the Training Plan?

The first class will continue to the end of June 2006. The akhung-students of the class all felt that it was very lucky for them to get the opportunity of study and so cherished it very much and studied very hard, which left a very deep impression on the researchers (teachers), and which also proves that the Training Plan is indeed what they need urgently. What we learned from the research process is as the following.

First, the action research like the Ningxia Khufiyyah Akhung Training Plan represents surely a correct development in the anthropological research of Chinese Islamic study, which try to intervene the old-style education of akhungs. We are convinced that the research, by choosing akhungs as the object of study and letting them participate in the research process themselves, will be of relatively great values to the Hui society. This is because, as everyone knows, akhungs indeed occupy an important position and play a key role in the Hui society.

Second, the Training Plan proves that it is worth trying to cultivate the new type religious talents for the modernization of minority nationalities such as the Hui nationality by making full use of the educational resources of both secular high education and religious (Islamic) education, and allowing the former give its beneficial affects to the later.

Third, as anthropologists, we should pay high attention to the urgent desire of the minority nationalities for modernization and appreciate their hard effort already made in it not only in China but also in other countries everywhere. It is our responsibility to discover in time and to make research on the new development of the minority nationalities. We should intervene in their modernization so as to make their good hope to be realized and their effort to result in best achievements by making use of our academic resources.

Fourth, it should not be neglected that the traditional folk educations, popular in some minority nationalities like the Huis and including both of religious and secular ones and having a very long history, indeed perform very important roles in the cultural development and talent training even in the era of modernization. And there are still new tasks we have to implement, that is, to try to overcome the old and conservative elements exited in the religious (Islamic) education and make the education to serve the modernization, too.

Lastly, of course there are some problems found in the research process, such as the secular education of the akhung students is relatively low (besides the two akhungs who finished high school, the rest of them only finished middle school), and their old methods of Islamic knowledge study are relatively conservative, which does not fit them to the new study in the training class. Furthermore, as everyone knows, Northwestern China is a region where serious religious disputes in Islam between various sects have taken place not only in history but, in a less degree, nowadays, so the plan will have to try to avoid causing any new trouble to Islam and the security of the region, especially under a condition that we are not sure enough about how the governments at various levels and the Hui people would view it.

14

Demographic Diversity and Economic Reform in a Globalizing World: Regional Development and the State in China

Émile Kok-Kheng **Yeoh**

Introduction: China – Threat or Opportunity in a Globalizing World?

The highly remarkable economic performance of the once low-income, xenophobic and inward-looking state of China over the past three decades has attracted increasing interest from the academics and policy-makers all over the world to the "China miracle" and the impact of such impressive achievement of the world's most populous country on regional and world economies. Flassbeck, Dullen and Geiger (2005) argued that the ability of China to both master the challenges of globalization and modernize the domestic economy at the same time has depended upon the strategy of unilaterally fixing the exchange rate since 1974 that was accompanied by a reform of the wage-setting regime in the mid-1990s, a heterodox macro-economic demand management and a rather closed capital account. China's performance over the past three decades was no mean feat – whether in terms of the fivefold increase in income per capita and average private consumption since the beginning of the reform phase in 1979, or her ability to lift over 200 million people out of absolute poverty (*ibid.*).

The phenomenal rise of China as an economic power, as well as her heightened political and military clout that has been growing in tandem with this, inevitably brought forth, both regionally or globally, increasing concern over whether she is posing a threat to regional stability and prosperity, and if so, in what way. For instance, In terms of changes in market share for China and regional exporting economies, Lall and Albaladejo (2004, cited in Weiss, 2005: 55) listed five possibilities of "China threat" for any given market or the world economy as a whole:

1. *Partial threat* – where China and the economy concerned gain market share, but China gains more.

2. *No threat* – where both China and the other economy both gain market share, but with China growing slower.
3. *Direct threat* – where China gains market share and the other economy loses it.
4. *China under threat (or reverse threat)* – where China loses market share and the other economy gains.
5. *Mutual withdrawal* – where both China and the other economy lose market share.

Using these groupings Lall and Albaladejo found that all East Asian NIEs except the Philippines (which is also close to this) have a majority of their exports under some form of "threat", as shown in Figure 14.1.

However, despite being a threat, China is more often regarded also as an opportunity for her trade partners. Unlike the earlier economic "miracles" of East Asia, China has been following a liberal foreign investment regime in the last two decades (McGregor, 2005), opening its domestic markets and

Figure 14.1   China's Threat to NIEs in the World Market, 2000
(percentage of total exports)

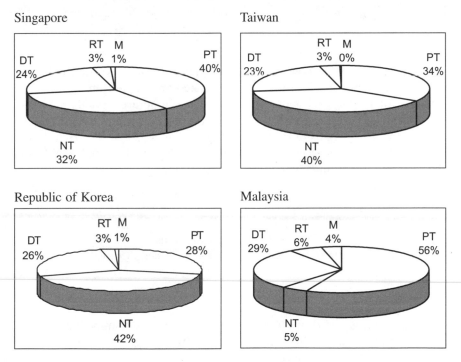

Figure 14.1   (continued)

Thailand   Indonesia

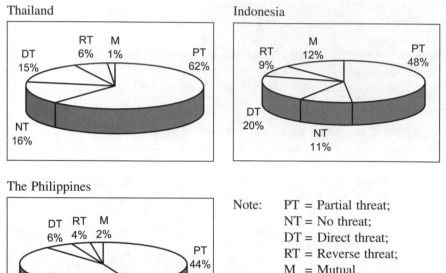

The Philippines

Note: PT = Partial threat;
          NT = No threat;
          DT = Direct threat;
          RT = Reverse threat;
          M = Mutual.
Source: Data from Lall and Albala-
          dejo (2004), Table 6, cited in
          Weiss (2005: 56).

"not building an export powerhouse behind a wall of protective tariffs"[1]. The country's rapid economic growth has generated great opportunities for large volumes of imports of both primary and manufactured goods from her regional trade partners. This has served to compensate the latter for their losses of market share in the U.S. and Japan (Weiss, 2005: 72). Hence, to a world that is watching her rise with a mix of curiosity, hope and trepidation, the rapidly transforming China remains an enigma:

> Is China a threat to the region, a potential hegemon busy establishing an economic power base on which to build an invincible military force? Or is she a large yet insecure country with painful memories of various colonial predators, fearfully aware of the immense technological superiority of the United States military, but intent on international and regional cooperation? Then there is the question of China's economy, and whether the Middle Kingdom will ever be anything more than a middle power.
>
> (Arnott, 2001: 70-71)

Against this general backdrop, this paper attempts to examine the so-called "China threat" from a different perspective, by asking whether the threat to

China herself in the post-Cold War world and the oft-cited potential threat posed by China to her neighbours and to the world at large could in fact come from within China herself, engendered by her increasingly volatile interethnic relations owing to her breakneck economic transformation and the accompanying income and wealth disparities. The resultant intensified resource contest may see groups coalesce along ethnolinguistic and ethnoreligious lines and thus further polarized by such divides, aggravated by transnational influences brought about by the selfsame globalization that has ironically contributed to her very economic "miracle" in the first place. The potential threat to China's economic growth and political stability due to any mismanagement in her internal intergroup relations would also pose a threat to the world, in particular the country's Southeast Asian neighbours in her backyard since their economic well-being is now very much tied to China's rise as an economic power and the engine of growth in the region.[2]

Ethnic Politics and the Politics of Ethnicity

It is a growing consensus today that the study of public policy determination in the developing countries should take into consideration their specific, often peculiar, socio-economic milieu. This is because most of the obstacles they are facing now are very different from those experienced by today's affluent, industrialized countries when they were at the similar stage of development in earlier days – a central fact that is sometimes ignored by development economics. One of the issues that deserve more in-depth research is the possible impact of these countries' ethnic diversity upon public policy planning and implementation, the size of the public sector, and the State's fiscal functions of allocation, distribution, stabilization and growth. For instance, in Malaysia, the impact of ethnic diversity has been inseparable from public policy planning and implementation, and it has left an indelible mark upon the remarkable growth of the public sector, particularly since the promulgation of the New Economic Policy in 1970.

Taking into consideration the two major dimensions of ethnopolitics – ethnic politics and the politics of ethnicity[3] – the objective of this paper is to look at the role of the State[4] in ethnically diverse societies, with special reference to the case of the People's Republic of China. More specifically, it aims to find out whether a relationship exists between ethnic diversity of a country and the development of its public policy, and if it does, in what form.

Despite the highly remarkable economic achievement over the past two decades, China is facing acute problems on various fronts, not least of which being her expanding interregional and urban-rural disparities. Agriculture accounted for only about 14.6 per cent of China's GDP in 2003 but 49.5 per cent of her labour force, while up to 59.5 per cent of the country's total population is rural. This is in addition to the fact that only 13 per cent of China consists of arable land and the country has 40 per cent less arable land per capita than anywhere else in the world. Thus, with more people and less arable land in rural areas, the country has a lower comparative advantage in agriculture, and hence investments have been concentrated in the cities and industries and this has led to increasing rural-urban disparities in socioeconomic development and income distribution (Bi, 2005: 114), as well as the increasingly alarming socioeconomic disparity between the country's eastern, coastal regions and the inland, especially western, regions.

Figure 14.2 China: Eastern and Western Regions

Notes: Officially designated Western Regions in bold italics.
　　　　———— East-West Boundary.

Many different factors have led to the disparity between China's eastern and western regions. In the modern history of the country, the coastal belt has been the focus of foreign influence and the site of foreign concessions and open cities, with business and production bases established there to take advantage of the convenience of import and export facilities. Hence, ironically, it was the foreign powers who first stimulated China's industrial development, mainly in the coastal cities – and Shanghai in particular. This imbalance in favour of the coastal belt was accentuated further in the 1930s by the Japanese take-over of Manchuria where the puppet state of "Manchukuo 满洲国" was established as an industrial centre, concentrating on heavy industry and mining (in contrast with the other foreign treaty ports and concessions that concentrated more upon the light industries), to feed Japan's industrial and military needs.

Besides such historical factors, geographical location also contributed to the east-west disparity. The eastern coastal regions have benefited from the availability of widespread, interconnected water and land freight lines – such as the Yangzi River (Chang Jiang) 扬子江/长江, the Beijing-Guangzhou and Beijing-Shanghai railway lines – that have greatly facilitated the transportation of people and merchandize. The western regions generally lack connexions to major domestic and foreign markets, except some cities that are located along the main east-west railway lines and the Yangzi River. The high population density and bigger urban sector of the eastern coastal regions also give them an advantage over the inland regions. Even their rural areas resemble large urban centres. Their residents thus have better access to regional, provincial or national commercial markets around them. The large and extensive consumer markets represent a boon to more production and sales[5] (Zhou, 2006: 251). Furthermore, under the Dengist market-oriented reforms and open-door policy, the eastern regions – the open economic zones like Shenzhen in particular – were the first to benefit from all sorts of investments – from government-funded infrastructure to the injection of foreign capital, including those from overseas Chinese, who in their first business foray back to the land of their ancestors, often prefer to begin with investing in their ancestral province, village or county where, for many, their relatives still live. Despite guidelines for more balanced investment strategies, in a scenario akin to the flypaper hypothesis, increasing economic prosperity in eastern China was creating more and more business opportunities, better projects and higher returns, compared with the inland regions, and hence attracting more and more State funding and private investment even from the other parts of the country. As projects in the eastern, coastal regions are more likely to be approved due to the better prospects, they tend to attract surplus and unused funds from the other regions. All these had resulted in the ever-growing disparity between the eastern and western regions during the 1990s. Furthermore, preferential treatments – in taxation, tariffs, approval of joint ventures with overseas companies, etc. – during the three decades of reform contributed greatly to the prosperity of the eastern, coastal regions, in addition to the leeway they were given in experimenting with new economic measures.

Inequality and Poverty: The Regional Dimension

While China's reforms have been successful in giving many people higher incomes and producing more goods and services, they also led to increasingly acute inequality in income and wealth among the populace. From one of the most egalitarian societies in the 1970s, China has turned into one of the most unequal countries in the region and even among developing countries in general. The unusually rapid rise in inequality had led to the Gini coefficient of household income rising by 7 percentage points (18 per cent), or by 1.0 percentage point per year, between 1988 and 1995. Inequality of rural household income per capita increased by about 23 per cent over the period, and that of the urban household income per capita by 42 per cent (Riskin, Zhao and Li, 2001:3). As Bert Hoffman of the World Bank recently noted, China's Gini rose from 0.25 – equal to that of Germany – in 1980 to about 0.45 today, as the country becomes less equal than Russia or the United States of America. In the 1980s the richest 10 per cent of the people of China earned 7 times the income of the poorest 10 per cent, today they earn more than 18 times as much.[6] Or as another observer put it, "Ever since the early years of reforms, the divide between the rich and the poor had been emerging, and it is now getting to the stage of ripping the entire society apart." (Zhou, 2006: 286).

With official poverty line set at an annual income of 625 yuan per capita, the rural population living in poverty in 2002 numbered 28.2 million. If the line were raised to 825 yuan, as it has been in more recent years, the number would be 90 million. If the United Nations' definition of the poverty line at US$1 income per day (i.e. about 3,000 yuan per year) is used, the number in poverty, both rural and urban, would be greatly increased (*ibid.*: 288).

According to Ohara (2001), by the yardstick of China's government, with a poverty line of (annual) 100 yuan per capita in 1978, the country had a poverty population of 250000000 and an incidence of poverty of 30.7 per cent. The figures for the subsequent years are 206 (poverty line), 125000000 (poverty population), 14.8 (incidence of poverty) in 1985; 300, 85000000, 10.1 in 1990; 317, 80000000, 9.4 in 1992; 440, 70000000, 8.2 in 1994; 580,

58000000, 7.6 in 1996; and 635, 42100000, 5.8 in 1998. With a poverty line of 625 yuan in 1999, the poverty population was 34000000. The poverty population declined to 26000000 in 2000, with an incidence of poverty of less than 3. However, if the international yardstick were to be employed, with the poverty line set at (daily) 1 dollar per capita, the poverty population would have been 263 million in 1990, i.e. an incidence of poverty of 31.3 per cent. With the same poverty line of 1 dollar per capita per day, the figures for subsequent years were 255 million (poverty population), 30.1 (incidence of poverty) in 1992; 222 million, 25.9 in 1994; 130 million, 15.0 in 1996; and 106 million, 11.1 in 1998. (Ohara 2001: 54, Table 1).

In line with the now well-known fear of instability (*luan* 乱) on the part of China's ruling Communist Party, the main objective of the country's poverty alleviation policy is to prevent income and wealth inequality from growing out of political control, by attempting to improve the economic position of the poorest through considerably limited administrative intervention. Furthermore, discontent brewing in the areas resided by ethnic minorities is taken seriously because these areas are also places that show a relative concentration of poor people. Just how the western regions populated by the non-Han peoples have been left behind China's economic development is clearly indicated by the poverty problem. Any political or social instability especially in these ethnic minority areas could have grave ramifications throughout the economy that threaten the development efforts of the central government especially in regard to the development of the regional cores.

Table 14.1 China: Interregional Income Disparity
(income index: 1 for the eastern regions)

Year	Eastern Regions	Central Regions	Western Regions
1978	1	0.67	0.55
1980	1	0.68	0.56
1985	1	0.67	0.55
1990	1	0.64	0.55
1993	1	0.53	0.45
1995	1	0.54	0.43
1997	1	0.56	0.43
1999	1	0.54	0.41
2000	1	0.51	0.39
2001	1	0.50	0.39
2002	1	0.49	0.39
2003	1	0.48	0.38
2004	1	0.48	0.38

Source: Computed with data from the *China Statistical Yearbook*, various years.

Table 14.2 China: Incidence of Poverty by Province (*sheng* 省),
Zizhiqu 自治区 + and Zhixiashi 直辖市 ++ (%), at end of 1996
(within category by alphabetical order)

<5%	*10–20%*
Beijing 北京 (Zhixiashi)	***Chongqing*** 重庆* (Zhixiashi)
Fujian 福建	***Guangxi*** 广西* (Zhuang Zizhiqu)
Guangdong 广东	***Guizhou*** 贵州*
Hainan 海南	Hebei 河北
Jiangsu 江苏	Heilongjiang 黑龙江
Shanghai 上海 (Zhixiashi)	Henan 河南
Tianjin 天津 (Zhixiashi)	Jilin 吉林
Zhejiang 浙江	***Ningxia*** 宁夏* (Hui Zizhiqu)
	Shaanxi 陕西*
5–10%	Shanxi 山西
	Sichuan 四川*
Anhui 安徽	***Xinjiang*** 新疆* (Uygur Zizhiqu)
Hubei 湖北	***Xizang/Tibet*** 西藏* (Tibetan Zizhiqu)
Hunan 湖南	***Yunnan*** 云南*
Jiangxi 江西	*>20%*
Liaoning 辽宁	
Shandong 山东	***Gansu*** 甘肃*
	Inner Mongolia 内蒙古* (Mongol Zizhiqu)
	Qinghai 青海*

Notes: + "autonomous region"
          ++ "direct-ruled/independent municipality", i.e. municipality under the
             central government.
          * ***provinces, zizhiqu, and zhixiashi now classified as the "western
            regions"***.
Source: Tabulated with data from Ohara (2001: 56).

When the poverty counties (331 in total) were first designated in 1986,
about 70 per cent of the country's poor lived in these counties. In 1993, 73
per cent of the poor population of 80 million resided in these counties. The
majority – about two-thirds – of China's poor are found in the inland (central
and western) regions, especially the western regions. Indeed the designated
poverty counties are relatively concentrated in the western regions – Yunnan
(73), Shaanxi (50), Sichuan (43), Gansu (41) and Guizhou (40), according
to Ohara (2001: 64) who also showed that there had been improvement
(reduction in regional percentage of poor counties) in the eastern regions,

thanks to the economic growth, but not in the central and western regions. The priority targets of the State's poverty relief measures are the south-western populous regions of Yunnan, Guizhou, Sichuan and Shaanxi that have relatively high incidence of poverty, as well as the ethnic Zhuang zizhiqu of Guangxi. Poverty alleviation faces more problems in the more sparsely populated regions like Inner Mongolia, Gansu and Qinghai that have the highest incidence of poverty (more than 20 per cent) as well as Tibet and Xinjiang (10-20 per cent) – regions all characterized by deserts, heights and mountainous areas. Ohara's figures indicate that poverty counties totaled 21,770,000 in 1998, with 10.6 per cent (2,040,000) of which found in the eastern regions, 33.1 per cent (7,500,000) in the central regions, and 56.4 per cent (12,230,000) in the western regions. In 1999, poverty counties totaled 18,000,000, of which 9.4 per cent (1,900,000) were in the eastern regions, 34.5 per cent (6,950,000) in the central regions, and 56.2 per cent (10,150,000) in the western regions (Ohara 2001: 55, Table 2).[7]

Such disparities also gave the richer provinces a significant advantage in terms of revenue collections since these are determined by income level and tax effort, as can be observed in Table 14.3.

Table 14.3 China: Fiscal and Economic Concentration in Rich[#] and Poor[#] Provinces (*sheng*), Zizhiqu[+] and Zhixiashi[++] (%)

	Year	2003	2004
Five richest provinces, zizhiqu and zhixiashi*			
Percentage of GDP		26.10	25.70
Percentage of population		13.10	13.35
Percentage of government revenue		37.62	36.96
Percentage of government expenditure		27.44	27.06
Five poorest provinces, zizhiqu and zhixiashi**			
Percentage of GDP		8.73	8.73
Percentage of population		17.23	17.22
Percentage of government revenue		8.79	8.80
Percentage of government expenditure		12.60	12.37

Notes: [#] by GDP per capita
        [+] "autonomous region"
        [++] "direct-ruled/independent municipality", i.e. municipality under the central government.
        * Beijing, Zhejiang, Tianjin, Shanghai, and Guangdong.
        ** Guizhou, Gansu, Guangxi, Yunnan, and Anhui.
Source: Computed with data from the *China Statistical Yearbook*, various years.

The Rural Social Economy Survey Group of China's State Statistical Bureau published in 2000 the results of an analysis of the different characteristics of poor and not-so-poor rural families sampled in four regions of the country[8]:

Region 1 – the coastal provinces/zhixiashi of Beijing, Fujian, Guangdong, Jiangsu, Shanghai, Tianjin and Zhejiang. Consisting of the richest regions in China, Region 1 has only 2.9 per cent of the country's total poor. The incidence of poverty is 1.6 per cent or less in the provinces and no higher than 0.5 per cent in Jiangsu, Shanghai and Tianjin. With the poor sparsely scattered and poverty mainly reflects family or individual differences but not regional characteristics, rural poverty problem no longer appears to be a regional issue here.

Region 2 – the provinces/zizhiqu/zhixiashi of Anhui, Chongqing, Guangxi, Hainan, Hebei, Henan, Hubei, Hunan, Jiangxi, Liaoning, Shandong, Shanxi and Sichuan. Though the incidence of poverty is moderate at about 2-7 per cent, Region 2 accounts for 55 per cent of the country's total poor partly due to the large regional population. Concentrations of the poor exist in the mountainous areas in Hubei, Sichuan and Chongqing, but in general, the poor are thinly scattered across Region 2.

Region 3 – the southwestern and northwestern remote provinces/zizhiqu of Gansu, Guizhou, Ningxia, Shaanxi, Qinghai, Xinjiang and Yunnan. Among the four Regions, this one faces the most severe poverty problems, with an incidence of poverty above 9 per cent and accounts for 35 per cent of the country's extreme poor.

Region 4 – the cold, northern provinces/zizhiqu of Heilongjiang, Inner Mongolia and Jilin. Though with only 7 per cent of the country's total poor population, this Region suffers from the relatively high poverty incidence of 6-8 per cent.

Such regional classification by the Survey Group provides, to a certain extent, some idea about the causes of poverty that vary from region to region, for instance, geographical terrain that may have implications for market competitive advantage. Table 14.4 provides a more detailed description of the regions.

Table 14.4 shows that the inland regions' GDP in 2003 and 2004 only accounts for 41-42 per cent of the national total, although these regions hold 62 per cent of the country's total population. Of the inland regions, the western (including Guangxi and Inner Mongolia) have a combined GDP of

Table 14.4 China: Population, Output and Income Indicators by Region, 2003 and 2004

Region Item	National		Eastern (Coastal)*		Inland#		Inland			
							Central**		Western#	
	2003	2004	2003	2004	2003	2004	2003	2004	2003	2004
Population (1000 persons)	1283733	1294150	486212.5	492510	797520.5	801640	428287.2	430370	369233.3	371270
Share (%)	100	100	37.87	38.06	62.13	61.94	33.36	33.26	28.76	28.69
GDP (100 million yuan)	135539.14	163240.43	79283.40	95305.75	56255.74	67934.68	33301.08	40349.51	22954.66	27585.17
Share (%)	100	100	58.49	58.38	41.51	41.62	24.57	24.72	16.94	16.90
GDP per capita (yuan)	10558.20	12613.72	16306.33	19351.03	7053.83	8474.46	7775.41	9375.54	6216.85	7429.95
Ratio to national average	1	1	1.54	1.53	0.67	0.67	0.74	0.74	0.59	0.59
Urban disposable income per capita (yuan)	8472.20	9421.61	10365.80	11522.87	7155.78	7929.17	7036.36	7828.80	7235.39	7996.08
Ratio to national average	1	1	1.22	1.22	0.84	0.84	0.83	0.83	0.85	0.85
Rural net income per capita (yuan)	2622.24	2936.4	4160.42	4564.78	2115.51	2389.54	2407.36	2770.18	1920.95	2135.78
Ratio to national average	1	1	1.59	1.55	0.81	0.81	0.92	0.94	0.73	0.73

Notes: # Including Guangxi and Inner Mongolia.
        * Excluding Guangxi.
       ** Excluding Inner Mongolia.

Source: Computed with data from the *China Statistical Yearbook*, various years.

Table 14.5 China: Industrial and Employment Structures by Region, 2003 and 2004

| | | National Total | | Eastern (Coastal)* | | Inland# | | Inland | | | |
| | | | | | | | | Central** | | Western# | |
Item	Region	2003	2004	2003	2004	2003	2004	2003	2004	2003	2004
Industrial structure (%)	Primary	12.67	12.80	9.21	9.09	17.55	18.02	16.28	17.03	19.39	19.46
	Secondary	49.00	50.50	51.18	52.86	45.93	47.20	48.05	49.16	42.85	44.34
	Tertiary	38.33	36.69	39.60	38.05	36.53	34.79	35.68	33.82	37.76	36.20
Comparison with national industrial structure (% points)	Primary	–	–	-3.46	-3.72	4.87	5.21	3.60	4.22	6.71	6.66
	Secondary	–	–	2.18	2.36	-3.08	-3.31	-0.96	-1.35	-6.15	-6.17
	Tertiary	–	–	1.28	1.36	-1.80	-1.91	-2.65	-2.88	-0.56	-0.49
Employment structure (%)	Primary	49.01	46.91	38.11	35.74	55.83	54.01	53.80	51.76	58.11	56.54
	Secondary	21.60	22.50	29.80	30.93	16.47	17.15	18.76	19.69	13.89	14.28
	Tertiary	29.39	30.59	32.09	33.33	27.71	28.85	27.44	28.55	28.01	29.18
Comparison with national employment structure (% points)	Primary	–	–	-10.9	-11.18	6.82	7.09	4.79	4.85	9.1	9.62
	Secondary	–	–	8.2	8.43	-5.13	-5.35	-2.84	-2.81	-7.71	-8.22
	Tertiary	–	–	2.7	2.74	-1.68	-1.74	-1.95	-2.04	-1.38	-1.41

Notes: # Including Guangxi and Inner Mongolia.
         * Excluding Guangxi.
        ** Excluding Inner Mongolia.

Source: Computed with data from the *China Statistical Yearbook*, various years.

exceeded the national average for primary industry labour force by 7.09 points, whereas the ratios of the labour force in the secondary (17.15 per cent) and the tertiary (28.85 per cent) industries were 5.35 points and 1.74 points respectively below the national average. The disparity was even greater in the case of the western regions, where the ratio of labour force in the primary industry (56.54 per cent) was 9.62 points above the national average. These statistics, on the other hand, also reflect the general widening disparities in urban and rural incomes, with the latter experiencing slower growth rates in the late 1990s and the early 21st century (Table 14.6).

Table 14.6 China: Income Growth Rates in Rural Areas

Year	Growth Rate (%)	Year	Growth Rate (%)
1996	9	2000	2.1
1997	4.6	2001	4.2
1998	4.3	2002	4.5
1999	3.8	2003	4.8

Source: Tabulated with data from Zhou (2006: 288).

A more detailed scrutiny of rural employment and wage at the sub-national unit level is that by Zhang (1998[12], 2001) who found the Gini coefficient (between provinces/zizhiqu/zhixiashi) for rural industrial employment rate to be 0.48 in 1988 and 0.46 in 1995, and that for average monthly wage of township enterprise workers to be 0.12 in 1988 and 0.28 in 1995 [see Zhang (2001: 226), Table 9.7]. Based on the Gini coefficient for wage levels that shows widening interregional disparities, Zhang concludes, in line with a World Bank study of 1997, "China is one of the worst countries in Asia in regards to regional inequality" (Zhang 1998[13]: 10, cited in Cook and Murray 2001: 89).

Inequality, Economic Malaise and the Menace of Socioracial Conflict

One of the most important indicators of economic malaise is rising unemployment. Unemployment in China is officially defined as those unemployed residents in cities and towns, and those who registered at State job centres. Following more closely the international standard, the official definition was clarified from 2003 as those within working age (between 16 and 60 years for males, and 16 to 55 for females), who are capable of working but unable to find employment, and the 2003 official unemployment rate for urban residents was 4.3 per cent, not including workers in the category of *xiagang* 下岗[14]. In 2002, there were about 4.12 million *xiagang* workers at State enterprises. With the exclusion of many categories (such as the *xiagang* workers and surplus farm workers), the accuracy of the official unemployment figure is questionable. Real unemployment rate has been calculated to range from above 11 per cent, according to the World Bank, to as high as 20 per cent (Cook and Murray, 2001:36). Rising unemployment inevitably brings along the threat of labour unrest. Even as early as 1996, the government admitted that there had been 3000 incidents of worker protest, and with as many as thirty million employees planned to be retrenched from the State-owned enterprises, this did not auger well for social stability, as some observers noted in 1999:

> The reaction of the workers has been far from passive. According to the Chinese Academy of Social Science's annual report on social issues, an average of nine explosions rocked the mainland each day in 1998 as part of a growing crime wave. By early March 1999, there had been 13 bomb explosions this year, killing thirty-three people and injuring more than 100. The report blamed rising crime on joblessness, widening income disparity and anger at rampant corruption for this trend.
>
> (Cook and Murray, 1999: 4)

It was reported that in 2005 public order disturbances rose 6.6 per cent to 87,000, or an average of almost 240 a day.[15]

Equally alarming is a series of unrest with an ethnoreligious or ethno-regional content or a mix of the two. A most notable of such incidents is the Han-Hui conflict in October 2004 that occurred in the Nanren village and two other nearby villages in Henan province, that allegedly killed more than 100 people including at least 15 policemen, and injured more than 400 people, and at one point threatened to draw thousands more into the frenzy, thanks to the cellphones and computers that proliferate even in rural China.[16] Though the conflict was probably triggered by a local traffic accident, simmering tensions might have been exacerbated by China's economic success that led to a growing gap between rich and poor, especially in the countryside.

That economic situations play an important role in interethnic conflict seems obvious. Collins (1975: 389-390) believed that the more severe a (political/economic) crisis, the greater the tendency for groups to coalesce along the lines of collective interests and the society to polarize into two-sided conflicts. Van Evera (1994: 9) claimed that the publics become receptive to scapegoat myths (which are more widely believed) when economic conditions deteriorate. Rex (1970) noted that scapegoating is a means to restore social equilibrium, a mechanism whereby resentment may be expressed and the existing power structure maintained. It is "the social process *par excellence* that literally fulfils Parsons' description of one of his functional subsystems as pattern maintenance and tension management" (*ibid.*: 45). Baimbridge, Burkitt and Macey (1994: 432) observed that the deflationary impact of the Maastricht Treaty may intensify nationalism, racism and anti-Semitism "as the economically insecure seek weaker scapegoats to blame for the economic problems confronting them". Hauser and Hauser (1972) stated that scapegoats occur when there is an imbalance between power and citizens' rights and are "often an élite's safeguard in its dealings with a dissatisfied and potentially dangerous majority" (p. 330). In other words, the repressed, negative and hostile feelings of the majority vis-à-vis its own ruling élite are transferred on to the scapegoat. The interethnic hostilities in Malaysia in 1969 (and to a certain extent also the boiling racial tensions in 1987) could in the main be rooted in the resentment of the demographic majority' s lower-class directed at their own ruling élites who were perceived to cooperate with and protecting rich interests of the minority. Similar outbursts could be observed amidst the anti-Suharto campaigns in Indonesia before the regime's collapse in which Chinese commercial institutions were attacked. In the extreme case, the scapegoat may seem to be totally unrelated to the initial cause of the feelings of hostility. The term "free-floating aggression" has been used in this case while the more general concept of "scapegoating" is reserved for the transfer of hostility towards any object (Turner and Killian, 1957: 19). The pattern of ethnic conflict caused by scapegoating may not be solely a racial problem, but may partly result from social class differential and the economic environment. In the case of Malaysia, Mauzy (1993) noted that rapid economic growth could be the most important variable in explaining the absence of ethnic violence (as occurred in Lebanon and Sri Lanka) in response to preferential policies that led to growing ethnic polarization. Every non-Malay she interviewed between October and December 1990 "cited the continued possibilities of making money as the chief reason why there has been no ethnic violence in Malaysia, despite more polarisation, less accommodation and more repression" (*ibid.*: 127).

However, it is interesting to note an opposite view posited by Harris in his study of ethnicity in Latin America (1964: 98) that "the price which the underdeveloped countries or regions… have paid for relative racial tranquillity is economic stagnation". Economic stagnation, he believed, may lead to less ethnic conflict than economic expansion "by virtue of the fact that there has not been too much to fight for" (*ibid.*: 97). While not denying the possibility that ethnic conflict may increase with economic expansion, Hoetink (1973: 111-2) argued that it is not the expanding economy *per se* that disturbs racial tranquillity but rather the presence of poorer members of the dominant ethnic group, "who are not objectively different from the other poor racial groups and hence tend to exploit their ascriptive distinctions *à outrance*". In other words, economic expansion leads to a decline in economic differentiation and therefore results in an emphasis on other dimensions of social distinction, especially racial characteristics, as manifested in the following historical examples:

> In Haiti under President Pétion in the early nineteenth century, land reform, which reduced considerably the differences in economic power and prestige, led precisely to an increased emphasis on the social distinction between Negro and colored, in much the same way in which the poor whites in the U.S. South tended to attach a greater social value to their somatic characteristics vis-à-vis the Negroes than the upper class whites, who could point to so many more socially relevant differences.
>
> *(ibid.: 111)*

As the case of the socioracial conflict in Henan in October 2004 testified, a general increase in unrest in rural areas might also have been fuelled by dissatisfaction over poverty and corruption, perceived inequality in the distribution of resources in favour of the Han, and backlash against certain preferential policies for the minorities.[17] Then there is the long-running, simmering, tension and hostility in Xinjiang and Tibet, where especially in Xinjiang, it has increasingly been taking on a mixed ethnoreligious and ethnoterritorial flavour. While the vast ethnic minority area that covers Shaanxi, Ningxia, Gansu, Qinghai and Xinjiang continues to lag further and further behind the rest of the country since market-oriented economic reforms were introduced in the late 1970s, the realization by the central government in Beijing lately that the region is the treasure trove of mineral wealth has probably helped to change its attitude towards the area:

> Three of China's four largest coal fields are in this area, as well as four of the most important oil fields. Some 140 kinds of mineral ores have been detected along with large reserves of bauxite for processing into aluminium, and gold. The Qaidam Basin in the middle of Qinghai Province, home to a large Tibetan population, for example, is described by local officials as the province's "treasure bowl", containing proven oil reserves of 200 million tons, as well as 4.5 billion tons of mostly high-quality coal with low ash and sulphur content. Under the Kunlun and Qilian mountains are large proven caches of iron, manganese, chromium, vanadium, copper, lead, zinc, nickel, tin, molybdenum, antimony,

mercury, gold, silver, platinum, beryllium and selenium. The iron reserves are estimated at 2.2 billion tons, and the province claims the country's largest lead and zinc mines, and is a primary producer of asbestos. The Hui people in the Ningxia Hui Autonomous Region, meanwhile, are sitting on large proven reserves of oil and natural gas, along with mineral resources such as copper, iron, silver, gold, aluminium and nickel. The growing prosperity of Xinjiang is being built on the back of developments in the vast and inhospitable Tarim Basin, where experts reckon there are reserves of up to 100 billion barrels of oil and 8,300 billion cubic metres of natural gas.

(Cook and Murray, 2001: 126-7)

And all these in the regions with long simmering threat of ethnic separatism. To understand fully China's central State's unwavering position regarding such ethnoregional separatist sentiments, it is not enough to attribute it, as quite often done, to "China's obsession with national security and the integrity of its historical borders" (*ibid.*: 147). Instead, one needs to go back to the fundamental tenets of Marxism-Leninism:

Marxist-Leninist theory on the national question defines a methodology for dealing with specific questions concerning the status of communities called nations or nationalities.... According to Communists, the fundamental cleavages of world society are along class rather than national lines. "Nations" are artificial units which came into being with the rise of capitalism and which are destined to disappear when capitalism is replaced with Communism; nationalism is a club used by capitalists to keep the world proletariat divided and subdued. When the proletariat seizes power throughout the world, then, according to the theory, nations and nationalism will vanish... when one realizes that more than half the population of Russia at the time of the October Revolution consisted of peoples other than the Great Russians, and that more than half the territory of China "liberated" in 1949-1950 was inhabited by peoples other than Han Chinese, it will be appreciated how immensely important the national question was to the success of both revolutions. The national question has been central, not peripheral, to the revolutions in both countries.... In concrete terms, what "Marxist-Leninist theory on the national question" as applied in Russia and China really means is that claims for national independence on the part of minorities in socialist countries is [sic] counter-revolutionary, and only in capitalist and colonial countries are such claims correct. Once the Communist Party, the vanguard of the proletariat, seizes power, then the oppression of one nationality by another is impossible; anyone still demanding independence, therefore, can only be an agent, witting or unwitting, of world imperialism and therefore an enemy of "the people." By similar arguments it is demonstrated that national minorities do not need their own Communist parties, since their interests are abundantly guaranteed by the unique Communist Party of the country.

(Moseley, 1966: 4-7)

The fact remains that with the disintegration of the Russian empire (the "prison of nations"[18], or in its modern form, the Soviet Union) in December 1991, China became the world's only former empire that has not disintegrated as have, besides the Russian empire, all in the 20th century, the Ottoman, Austro-Hungarian and the Western maritime empires. The only ethnic region that managed to break away from China is Outer Mongolia that formed the independent Mongolian People's Republic in 1924, with Russian support, though not recognized by China until 1946. The Uygurs in fact established, with Russian help, a short-lived East Turkestan Republic in 1944, but it collapsed after the 1949 Communist victory in China's civil war, and the region was reincorporated into China as the Xinjiang Uygur Zizhiqu in 1955. Like the de facto independent Taiwan since 1949, with the collapse of the Qing Dynasty that led to the repatriation of the imperial troops from the region, Tibet (today China's Xizang Zizhiqu) was in every respect virtually on her own from 1911 to 1950. Hence, with such recent historical experience of ethnoregional sectionalism and potential separatism, it can be argued that as a political urgency China has no choice but to give due politico-economic consideration to her western regions – regions that are populated by many ethnic minorities and have alarmingly lagged behind during the market-oriented reforms – for the sake of sociopolitical stability that is deemed crucial to the security of the Chinese state.

Ethnic Diversity in China

Before we go further with the issues of ethnoterritoriality and China's regional policy, one question needs to be asked: Just how diverse is China in terms of her ethnic composition?

To provide a preliminary picture of the position of China in the comparative ethnic diversity of countries, a world table[19] of ethnic fractionalization[20] is given here (Table 14.7) where China's position – and Malaysia's in comparison – in the rankings are highlighted. Also highlighted are those of Spain and Belgium to which references will be made in the paper.

A comparison of China's and Malaysia's positions brings out readily the high homogeneity of the former's ethnic composition (0.125) vis-à-vis the latter's heterogeneity (0.684). Nevertheless, there are various important aspects of the ethnic equation that are not revealed by an index of this nature (being based on the numerical structure of ethnic composition), including the historical geography of ethnicity, as well as the territorial, political and economic dimensions. Due to the abnormal size of China's population and in particular the size of China's citizens of the Han ethnicity, a distortion or

Table 14.7 Ethnic Fractionalization of 240 Countries/Regions

Rank	Country/Region	EFI
1	Congo, Democratic Rep. of the (formerly Zaire)	0.885
2	Uganda, Republic of	0.883
3	Kenya, Republic of	0.877
4	India, Republic of	0.876
5	South Africa, Republic of	0.873
6	Cameroon, Republic of	0.852
7	Mali, Republic of	0.844
8	Philippines, Republic of the	0.838
9.5	Nigeria, Federal Republic of	0.827
9.5	Tanzania, United Republic of	0.827
11	Cote d'Ivoire/IvoryCoast, Republic of	0.826
12	Lebanon, Republic of	0.821
13	Mauritius	0.814
14	Zambia, Republic of	0.813
15	Chad, Republic of	0.810
16.5	Guinea-Bissau, Republic of	0.806
16.5	Papua New Guinea, Independent State of	0.806
18	Yugoslavia, Socialist Fed. Rep. of (pre-Jan 1992)	0.795
19	Suriname, Republic of	0.789
20	Senegal, Republic of	0.788
21	Madagascar, Democratic Republic of	0.776
22.5	Sierra Leone, Republic of	0.771
22.5	Angola, People's Republic of	0.771
24	Gabonese Republic	0.765
25	Gambia, Republic of The	0.764
26	Central African Republic	0.757
27	Ethiopia (pre-May 1993)	0.756
28	Indonesia, Republic of	0.754
29	Qatar, State of	0.746
30	Liberia, Republic of	0.745
31	Guinea, Republic of	0.742
32	Ghana, Republic of	0.741
33	Afganistan, Republic of	0.739
34	Bolivia, Republic of	0.735
35	Burkina Faso	0.734
36	Mozambique, Republic of	0.727
37	Cayman Islands (UK)	0.720
38	Ethiopia (post-May 1993)	0.717
39	Sudan, Republic of the	0.715
40	Canada	0.714

Table 14.7 (continued)

Rank	Country/Region	EFI
41	Belize	0.711
42	Guam (US)	0.705
43	Eritrea	0.699
44	Malawi, Republic of	0.691
45	Togo, Republic of	0.689
46	Virgin Islands (US)	0.688
47	Congo, Republic of the	0.685
48.5	Monaco, Principality of	0.684
48.5	**Malaysia**	**0.684**
50	Kazakhstan, Republic of	0.679
51.5	Kuwait, State of	0.675
51.5	Bosnia and Herzegovina	0.675
53.5	New Caledonia (Fr.)	0.671
53.5	Niger, Republic of	0.671
55	Union of Soviet Socialist Republics (former)	0.670
56	East Timor	0.667
57	Laos/Lao People's Democratic Republic	0.665
58	Kyrgyzstan, Republic of	0.664
59	Namibia, Republic of	0.663
60	Iran, Islamic Republic of	0.661
61.5	Mauritania, Islamic Republic of	0.660
61.5	Benin, Republic of	0.660
63	French Polynesia (Fr.)	0.656
64.5	Micronesia, Federated States of	0.655
64.5	United Arab Emirates	0.655
66	Andorra, Principality of	0.651
67	Pakistan, Islamic Republic of	0.648
68	Guatemala, Republic of	0.645
69	Morocco, Kingdom of	0.643
70	Peru, Republic of	0.637
71	Trinidad and Tobago, Republic of	0.635
72	Nepal, Kingdom of	0.634
73	Guyana, Co-operative Republic of	0.628
74	Ecuador, Republic of	0.615
75	Latvia, Republic of	0.612
76	Colombia, Republic of	0.601
77	Cuba, Republic of	0.591
78	Djibouti, Republic of	0.585
79.5	Tajikistan, Republic of	0.583
79.5	Nauru, Republic of	0.583

Table 14.7 (continued)

Rank	Country/Region	EFI
81	Fiji, Republic of	0.380
82	**Belgium, Kingdom of**	**0.574**
83	Macedonia, Republic of	0.573
84	Bahrain, State of	0.566
85	Yugoslavia, Federal Rep. of (post-Jan 1992)	0.561
86	Hawai'i (US)	0.560
87	Bhutan, Kingdom of	0.555
88	Christmas Island (Australia)	0.552
89	Cape Verde, Republic of	0.551
90	Liechtenstein, Principality of	0.550
91	Brazil, Federative Republic of	0.549
92	Moldova, Republic of	0.546
93	Georgia, Republic of	0.545
94	Mexico/United Mexican States	0.542
95	Thailand, Kingdom of	0.535
96	Switzerland/Swiss Confederation	0.531
97	Estonia, Republic of	0.528
98	French Guiana (Fr.)	0.526
99	Brunei Darussalam, State of	0.525
100	Zimbabwe, Republic of	0.522
101	Burma, Union of	0.520
102	Gibraltar (UK)	0.517
103	Yemen, Republic of (post-May 1990)	0.507
104	Iraq, Republic of	0.502
105	Tonga, Kingdom of	0.500
106.5	Man, Isle of (UK)	0.498
106.5	Chile, Republic of	0.498
108	Venezuela, Republic of	0.497
109	Yemen Arab Republic (pre-May 1990)	0.495
110	Turks and Caicos Islands (UK)	0.493
111	Cocos Islands (Australia)	0.487
112.5	Nicaragua, Republic of	0.484
112.5	Uzbekistan, Republic of	0.484
114	Jordan, Hashemite Kingdom of	0.481
115	Palau Islands (US)	0.480
116	Singapore, Republic of	0.479
117	Panama, Republic of	0.477
118	Bermuda (UK)	0.476
119	Svalbard (Norway)	0.468
120	Czechoslovakia (former)	0.464

Table 14.7 (continued)

Rank	Country/Region	EFI
121	Albania, Republic of	0.460
122	Turkmenistan	0.455
123	Luxembourg, Grand Duchy of	0.452
124.5	Northern Mariana Islands (US)	0.444
124.5	Norfolk Island (Australia)	0.444
126	**Spain**	**0.436**
127.5	Dominican Republic	0.429
127.5	Sri Lanka, Democratic Socialist Republic of	0.429
129	Sao Tome and Principe, Democratic Republic of	0.420
130	Botswana, Republic of	0.418
131.5	Ukraine	0.417
131.5	Syrian Arab Republic	0.417
133	Oman, Sultanate of	0.406
134	Puerto Rico (US)	0.405
135	Northern Ireland (UK)	0.403
137	United States of America	0.395
137	Equatorial Guinea, Republic of	0.395
137	Jamaica	0.395
139	Algeria, Democratic and Popular Republic of	0.375
140	Belarus, Republic of	0.373
141	Croatia	0.371
142	Cyprus	0.358
143	Lithuania, Republic of	0.345
144	Western Sahara	0.343
145	West Bank (of the Jordan River)	0.339
146	Barbados	0.333
147	Turkey, Republic of	0.330
148	Cook Islands (NZ)	0.327
149	United Kingdom of Great Britain & N. Ireland	0.325
150	Aruba (Neth.)	0.320
151	Russian Federation	0.311
152.5	Grenada	0.308
152.5	Azerbaijan, Republic of	0.308
154	Saint Vincent and the Grenadines	0.306
155	Israel, State of	0.303
156	Bangladesh, People's Republic of	0.285
157	Rwanda, Republic of	0.275
158	San Marino, Most Serene Republic of	0.272
159.5	Quebec (Canada)	0.270
159.5	Egypt, Arab Republic of	0.270

Table 14.7 (continued)

Rank	Country/Region	EFI
161	American Samoa (US)	0.269
162	Bulgaria, Republic of	0.264
163	Viet Nam, Socialist Republic of	0.262
164	Burundi, Republic of	0.258
165	Somalia	0.256
168	Bahamas, The Commonwealth of the	0.255
168	Saudi Arabia, Kingdom of	0.255
168	Argentina/Argentine Republic	0.255
168	Netherlands Antilles (Neth.)	0.255
168	Saint Helena (UK)	0.255
171	Slovakia	0.254
172	Lesotho, Kingdom of	0.253
173.5	Greenland/Kalaallit Nunaat	0.241
173.5	Comoros, Federal Islamic Republic of the	0.241
175	Cambodia, State of	0.238
176	Costa Rica, Republic of	0.237
177	France/French Republic	0.235
178	Uruguay, Oriental Republic of	0.218
179	New Zealand	0.217
180.5	Romania	0.202
180.5	El Salvador, Republic of	0.202
182.5	Italy/Italian Republic	0.196
182.5	Niue (NZ)	0.196
184	Mongolia	0.187
185	Swaziland, Kingdom of	0.186
187.5	Saint Lucia	0.185
187.5	Guadeloupe (Fr.)	0.185
187.5	Martinique (Fr.)	0.185
187.5	Honduras, Republic of	0.185
190	British Virgin Islands (UK)	0.180
191	Slovenia	0.170
192	Hungary, Republic of	0.168
193	Sweden, Kingdom of	0.164
194	Antigua and Barbuda	0.150
195	Western Samoa, Independent State of	0.138
196.5	Germany, Federal Republic of (pre-Oct 1990)	0.134
196.5	Germany, Federal Republic of (post-Oct 1990)	0.134
199	Yemen, People's Democratic Republic of (former)	0.133
199	Solomon Islands	0.133
199	Reunion (Fr.)	0.133

Table 14.7 (continued)

Rank	Country/Region	EFI
201	Armenia, Republic of	0.128
202	**China, People's Republic of**	**0.125**
203	Finland, Republic of	0.122
204	Libya/Socialist People's Libyan Arab Jamahi.	0.117
205.5	Seychelles	0.115
205.5	Saint Kitts and Nevis, Federation of	0.115
207.5	Czech Republic	0.114
207.5	Vanuatu, Republic of	0.114
209	Ireland, Republic of	0.113
210	Cyprus (Greek sector)	0.097
212.5	Macao (China)	0.096
212.5	Malta	0.096
212.5	Paraguay, Republic of	0.096
212.5	Australia, Commonwealth of	0.096
215	Haiti, Republic of	0.095
216	Japan	0.079
218.5	Montserrat (UK)	0.077
218.5	Iceland, Republic of	0.077
218.5	Netherlands, Kingdom of the	0.077
218.5	Tuvalu	0.077
221	Greece/Hellenic Republic	0.068
222.5	Denmark, Kingdom of	0.059
222.5	Dominica	0.059
224.5	Marshall Islands, Republic of the	0.058
224.5	Norway, Kingdom of	0.058
226	Poland, Republic of	0.047
227	Cyprus (Turkish sector)	0.045
230	Tunisia, Republic of	0.039
230	Kiribati	0.039
230	Taiwan (Republic of China)	0.039
230	Hong Kong (China)	0.039
230	Falkland Islands (UK)	0.039
234.5	Gaza Strip	0.020
234.5	Saint Pierre and Miquelon (Fr.)	0.020
234.5	Mayotte (Fr.)	0.020
234.5	German Democratic Republic (former)	0.020
237	Portugal, Republic of	0.019
238	Austria, Republic of	0.012
239	Korea, Democratic People's Republic of	0.004
240	Korea, Republic of	0.002

Table 14.8 China: Ethnic Composition – The National Picture (percentage)

1	Han 汉	92	29	Tu 土	0.017
2	Zhuang 壮	1	30	Xibe (Xibo) 锡伯	0.015
3	Manchu (Man) 满	0.9	31	Mulam (Mulao) 仫佬	0.014
4	Hui 回	0.8	32	Kirghiz (Kirgiz) 柯尔克孜	0.013
5	Miao 苗	0.7	33	Daur (Tahur) 达斡尔	0.0108
6	Uyghur (Uygur) 维吾尔	0.63	34	Jingpho (Jingpo) 景颇	0.0106
7	Yi 彝	0.58	35	Salar (Sala) 撒拉	0.0077
8	Tujia 土家	0.51	36	Blang (Bulang) 布朗	0.0073
9	Mongol 蒙古	0.43	37	Maonan 毛南	0.006
10	Zang (Tibetan) 藏	0.41	38	Tajik 塔吉克	0.0029
11	Bouyei (Buyi) 布依	0.23	39	Pumi 普米	0.0026
12	Dong 侗	0.22	40	Achang 阿昌	0.0025
13	Yao 瑶	0.19	41	Nu 怒	0.0024
14	Chosŏn (Korean) 朝鲜	0.17	42	Evenki (Ewenki) 鄂温克	0.0023
15	Bai 白	0.14	43	Kinh (Vietnamese) 京	0.0017
16	Hani 哈尼	0.11	44	Jinuo (Jino) 基诺	0.0016
17	Li 黎	0.0985	45	De'ang 德昂	0.0014
18	Kazakh (Kazak) 哈萨克	0.0983	46	Uzbek (Ozbek) 乌孜别克	0.0013
19	Dai 傣	0.091	47	Russki (Russian) 俄罗斯	0.0012
20	She 畲	0.06	48	Yugur (Yugu) 裕固	0.00109
21	Lisu 傈僳	0.05	49	Bonan (Bao'an) 保安	0.00103
22	Gelao (Gelo) 仡佬	0.039	50	Oroqen (Olunchun) 鄂伦春	0.00062
23	Lahu 拉祜	0.036	51	Moinba (Menba) 门巴	0.00066
24	Dongxiang 东乡	0.033	52	Drung (Dulong) 独龙	0.00052
25	Wa (Va) 佤	0.0312	53	Tatar (Tartar) 塔塔尔	0.00045
26	Sui (Shui) 水	0.0307	54	Hezhen (Hezhe) 赫哲	0.00038
27	Naxi 纳西	0.025	55	Gaoshan 高山	0.00025
28	Qiang 羌	0.018	56	Luoba (Lhoba) 珞巴	0.00021

Source: Computed with census data.

To further understand the ethnic mosaic of China, see Table 14.10 and Figure 14.6 that indicate the proportion of each ethnic group in the country's sub-national units. Only those groups that are not lower than one per cent are shown. Again, for comparison, the proportions of the various ethnic groups in the Malaysian states are illustrated later in Figure 14.7.

Table 14.10   China: Ethnic Distribution by Province (*sheng*), Zizhiqu[+] and Zhixiashi[++] (%)[@]

#	Province	Ethnic Distribution
1	*Xinjiang** (Uygur Zizhiqu)	Uygur 47%; Han 38%; Kazakh 7%; Hui 5%; Khalkh 1%; Mongol 1%
2	*Guangxi** (Zhuang Zizhiqu)	Han 61%; Zhuang 37%; Yao 3%; Miao 1%; Dong 1%
3	*Qinghai**	Han 58%; Tibetan 20%; Hui 14%; Tu 4%; Sala 2%; Mongol 2%
4	*Yunnan**	Han 67%; Yi 11%; Bai 4%; Hani 3%; Dai 3%; Zhuang 3%; Miao 2%; Lisu 2%; Hui 1%, Lahu 1%; Wa 1%; Naxi 1%
5	*Guizhou**	Han 67%; Miao 12%; Buyi 8%; Dong 4%; Tujia 3%; Yi 2%; Gelao 1%; Shui 1%
6	*Ningxia** (Hui Zizhiqu)	Han 67%; Hui 33%
7	*Inner Mongolia** (Mongol Zizhiqu)	Han 81%; Mongol 16%; Manchu 2%; Hui 1%
8	Hainan	Han 83%; Li 16%; Miao 1%
9	Liaoning	Han 84%; Manchu 13%; Mongol 1%; Hui 1%; Korean 1%
10	Jilin	Han 90%; Korean 5%; Manchu 4%; Mongol 1%
11	*Gansu**	Han 92%; Hui 5%; Tibetan 2%; Dongxiang 1%
12	Hunan	Han 92%; Tujia 3%; Miao 3%; Dong 1%; Yao 1%
13	Heilongjiang	Han 94%; Manchu 3%; Korean 1%
14	*Sichuan**[#]	Han 95%; Yi 2%; Tibetan 1%; Tujia 1%
15	*Xizang/Tibet** (Tibetan Zizhiqu)	Tibetan 96%; Han 4%
16	Hubei	Han 96%; Tujia 3%
17	Beijing (Zhixiashi)	Han 96%; Hui 2%; Manchu 2%
18	Hebei	Han 96%; Manchu 3%; Hui 1%
19	Tianjin (Zhixiashi)	Han 98%; Hui 2%
20	Fujian	Han 98%; She 1%
21	Henan	Han 99%; Hui 1%
22	Shandong	Han 99%; Hui 1%
23	Anhui	Han 99%; Hui 1%
24	Guangdong	Han 99%
25	Zhejiang	Han 99%
26	Shanghai (Zhixiashi)	Han 100%
27	*Shaanxi**	Han 100%
28	Shanxi	Han 100%

Table 14.10 (continued)

29	Jiangxi	Han 100%
30	Jiangsu	Han 100%

Notes: + "autonomous region".
++ "direct-ruled/independent municipality", i.e. municipality under the central government.
@ Decimals are rounded to the nearest. Ethnic groups below 1 per cent are not shown.
* *provinces, zizhiqu, and zhixiashi now classified as the "western regions".*
# Sichuan includes Chongqing.
Source: Computed with census data.

Figure 14.6 China: Major Ethnic Groups by Province (*sheng*), Zizhiqu and Zhixiashi

Notes: Mg = Mongol; T = Tibetan; U = Uygur; Z = Zhuang.
Only ethnic groups >10% are shown (see the "critical mass" theory referred to above).
Officially designated Western Regions in bold italics.
━━━━━━ East-West Boundary.
Sichuan includes Chongqing.
Source: Computed with census data.

Figure 14.7 (a)

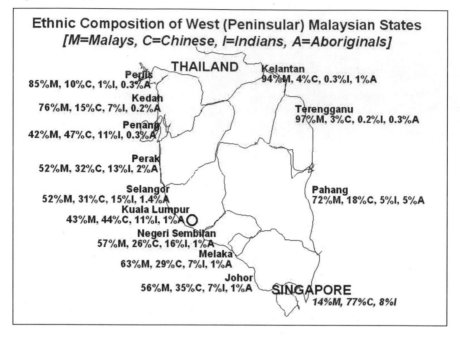

Figure 14.7 (b)

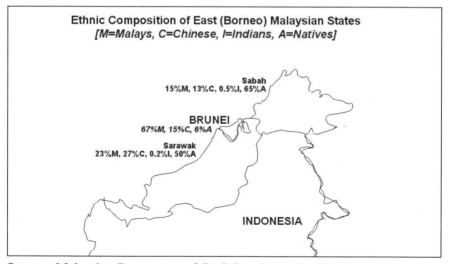

Source: Malaysian Department of Statistics, *Banci Penduduk dan Perumahan 2000 (2000 Population and Housing Census)*.

An interesting fact that stands out in Table 14.10 and Figure 14.6 is that the ethnic group whose name marks a particular zizhiqu may not be the demographically dominant group there. In Ningxia, Inner Mongolia and Guangxi, the Han Chinese constitute the dominant group (67, 83 and 61 per cent respectively), while the Hui, Mongol and Zhuang are in fact minorities in the respective zizhiqu (33, 16 and 37 per cent respectively). In Xinjiang, while the Uygur outnumber the Han, the former are hardly a majority, constituting less than 50 per cent of the zizhiqu's total population. Tibet is the oddity in the whole of China, with Tibetans constituting 96 per cent of the population, demographically dwarfing the Han to a mere 4 per cent. Such official population figures have been disputed by the Tibetan government-in-exile who claims that:

> ...accelerating Han population transfer into Tibet... has reduced the Tibetan people to a minority in their own land. Today, claims the government-in-exile, 'there are over 7.5 million non-Tibetan settlers in Tibet including Chinese and Hui Muslims, compared to six million Tibetans.'
>
> (Cook and Murray, 2001: 141)

However, such allegations of population transfer is rebutted by the Beijing government, who argues that:

> the only Han Chinese living in Tibet are specialists who have gone there voluntarily to help in the region's development. The Han, it maintains, make up less than five per cent of the population and many of the people are there for only a few years before returning home.
>
> (*ibid.*)

"Develop the West" Strategy and Ethnoterritorial Challenges

The term "development of the central and western regions" first emerged in the Chinese mass media in the spring of 1999. The phrase "Developing the Western Region" (*xibu dakaifa* 西部大开发) would soon become widely used in the political parlance. It has often been noted that the "Develop the West" strategy was a big gambit for Jiang Zemin, something that neither Mao Zedong nor Deng Xiaoping could do during their lifetime. Although the western regional development strategy might seem to be an easy way for Jiang to assert his authority ahead of the 16th Party Congress scheduled for the autumn of 2002, in parallel with thought control through ideological and political work, the plan was fraught of risks. While the strategy would cover many minority zizhiqu ("autonomous regions") whose majority populations are ethnolinguistically and/or ethnoreligiously distinctive from the Han

Chinese central State, the plan has always been understood to be a political process to allocate pieces of the economic pie to the local governments in the western regions but not about political decentralization.

This Chinese approach is very different from another political experiment that involved similarly named political entities – the Spanish *Comunidades Autónomas* ("autonomous communities") project at the death of Generalísimo Francisco Franco y Bahamonde (the *Caudillo*) in 1975 (a year before Mao's passing; see note 1 in Chapter One). While repeatedly expressing confidence that he would leave Spain *atado, y bien atado* ("tied-up, well tied-up", cited in Gunther, 1980: 285), Franco's death in 1975 was followed within two years by the dismantling of the structure of the whole Franquist regime, and the first free parliamentary elections in over 40 years were held on 15th June 1977. One of the most remarkable developments under the democratic transition had been the political decentralization of the State. The issue of regionalism in fact became the most contentious political issue during the post-Franco transition to democracy, with almost one-tenth of the Constitution devoted to the regional matters. The three main ethnolinguistically non-Castilian regions of Catalonia, the Basque Country and Galicia were given a special status as being "historic regions" – a recognition of the former Statute of Catalonia (1932) which established the *Generalitat*, Statute of the Basque Country (1936) and the putative Galician statute which was approved but never enacted before all three were crushed by the Franquist regime – which entitled them to the fastest route of all to autonomy. Although the *Comunidades Autónomas* project was not designed solely to resolve the ethnic problems facing the Castilian centre stemming from the "historic regions" of Catalonia and the Basques Country (and to a less extent, Galicia), hence the creation of seventeen instead of two or three such Communities (see Figure 14.8 and Table 14.11), it cannot be denied that it was the real or potentially centrifugal pressure from these ethnic regions (rendered even more explosive after the long years of Franquist repression) that provided the first and main impetus behind the will to decentralize after the restoration of democracy in 1975.

What we are seeing here is that at their respective critical structural junctures[23] thirty years ago, in 1975 and 1976, fascist Spain and Marxist-Leninist China embraced different paths of reform, with post-Franco Spain spurning overnight her fascist-corporatist past and embracing multiparty democracy and federalism to hold the country together against potentially separatist ethnoregional conflicts, taking the risk of the disappearance of the central State[24], while post-Mao China has since followed a cautious path that was to evolve later into an institutionalized relationship between the central

State and the localities some would call "selective centralization" (Zheng, 1999). However, implementing the western regional development project within such cautious political framework is not without risks either. First, with strong constraints in the devolvement of central power, it could be difficult to coordinate the interests of the central and local governments over the power of authorization and permissions and to determine how far the right to independent development could go. Besides that, it may not be easy to adjust the interests of local governments over limited financial resources and projects to be implemented. Finally, there is the fact that 80 per cent of the ethnic minorities in China live in the western regions and national border areas where the new regional development strategy is targeted. Without accompanying decentralization of political power and the conferring of substantial degree of regional autonomy in the control and use of local resources, ethnic minorities may perceive the central State's projects as attempts at internal colonization, leading to their outright opposition to the whole regional development strategy itself, thus exacerbating the already simmering ethnoregional tensions.

Figure 14.8   Spain: The Autonomous Communities and Non-Castilian
Ethnolinguistic Distribution (native languages in brackets)

Table 14.11 Spain*: *Comunidades Autónomas* (Autonomous Communities)

Autonomous Community (Region)	Language Use**	Date of Statute of Self-government	Official Title of Government
Euskadi (País Vasco)	Basque (30%), Castilian	18 December 1979	Gobierno Vasco
Catalunya (Cataluña)	Catalan (70%), Castilian	18 December 1979	Generalitat de Cataluña
Galiza (Galicia)	Galician (65%), Castilian	6 April 1981	Xunta de Galicia
Andalucía	Castilian	30 December 1981	Junta de Andalucia
Asturias	Bable, Castilian	30 December 1981	Principado de Asturias
Cantabria	Castilian	30 December 1981	Diputacion Regional
La Rioja	Castilian	9 June 1982	Consejo de Gobierno
Murcia	Castilian	9 June 1982	Consejo de Gobierno
Valencia	Valencian (Catalan) (49%), Castilian	1 July 1982	Generalitat Valenciana
Aragón	Castilian, Catalan (northeast border)	10 August 1982	Diputacion General
Castilla-La Mancha	Castilian	10 August 1982	Junta de Comunidades
Islas Canarias	Castilian	10 August 1982	Gobierno Canario
Extremadura	Castilian	25 February 1983	Junta de Extremadura
Islas Baleares	Catalan (71%), Castilian	25 February 1983	Gobierno Balear
Madrid	Castilian	25 February 1983	Gobierno de la Comunidad
Castilla y León	Castilian	25 February 1983	Junta de Castilla y Leon
Navarra***	Basque (9%), Castilian	10 August 1983	Diputacion Foral

Notes:
* The total area of Spain also includes five places of sovereignty (plazas de soberanía) on and off the coast of Morocco – Ceuta, Melilla, Islas Chafarinas, Peñón de Alhucemas, Peñón de Vélez de la Gomera. Spain's total number of municipalities also include the North African enclaves of Ceuta and Melilla (2 municipalities) which are "self-governing" but not "autonomous" (to avoid being considered colonies on foreign land)

** "Castilian" also includes Castilian dialects, e.g. Riojano, etc.

*** Navarra was granted autonomy under the terms of an organic law on the rehabilitation and improvement of its Foral Regime.

Source: Heywood (1995); Castells (1990); Mansvelt Beck (1991); Brassloff (1989). Brunn (1992).

One researcher cited the reply of a Tibetan to his question about the prospects that "the opening of planned three railway lines to Lhasa should make the life in Tibet more convenient" during his visit to Tibet in March 2000: "Many Han Chinese would come with the convenience of the railways. The bad influence of the Han Chinese culture could destroy Tibetan culture. We prefer staying poor to the destruction of our culture" (Sasaki, 2001: 27-8). If views as such are prevalent, this shows the possibility that many of the ethnic minorities are perturbed by the prospect of their cultures being destroyed or diluted as more and more visitors come to their regions due to the progress in the central government-led big development projects or by their own inability to adapt to the market economy. In another interview the same researcher conducted in Beijing in November 2000, he was told by a minority official working with a central government organization: "The biggest problem with the Strategy for Developing the Western Region is the neglect of rights of ethnic minorities, with development rights totally controlled by the central government. We are demanding independent rights of development. In funding, we want the freedom to form joint ventures with foreign companies. We also want trading rights for resources and processed products. The central government's way will just bring resources from the West to the East, leaving nothing behind in autonomous regions. If we are given policy autonomy, we can manage economic development of autonomous regions much better than the central government as we have our own channels of doing things. As for an inflow of human resources, the central government would only bring in the Han Chinese. There are talented people among ethnic minorities and we can make good use of them. What we badly need is autonomy of development" (*ibid.:*26).

Regardless of how widespread such discontent might be, the degree of policy autonomy in the ethnic regions is one issue that would present pitfalls for the "Develop the West" strategy that the central government cannot afford to callously dismiss. And such pitfalls can have real consequences for the success or failure of the strategy. In July 2000 the World Bank rejected a loan to China – a $40 million interest-free loan intended to finance a plan to move 58,000 Han Chinese living in Qinghai to the province's Tibetan area as part of the poverty relief measures – after U.S.-based Tibet support groups and environmentalist groups, and reportedly China's own ethnic minority, campaigned against the loan project, arguing about the possible threat to Tibetan influence and culture. The World Bank's board of governors finally rejected the proposed loan after the bank's examinations discovered the lack of both stringent standards for environmental assessment and of secrecy about hearings on residents of the area where the Han Chinese were to be moved.

It can be argued that the rejection might not have been based completely on the threat to an ethnic minority's culture but also carried political and diplomatic overtones since the United States and some European countries were among the countries that voted against the loan (*ibid.*: 27). Either way, the loan rejection has severe implications for the whole "Develop the West" strategy that China cannot afford to make lightly of since the country, due to the fiscal constraints of the central government, plans to rely on loans from international organizations and foreign governments in raising necessary funds for the development projects involved in the strategy.

This points to the fact that a main problem China, at this particular stage of reform, is facing – which often has an ethnoterritorial overtone – is the issue of interregional disparities in income and wealth. Although the threat of interethnic mistrust looms large and wide and it could both be the scourge afflicting the poor nations, and the sword of Damocles even in times of prosperity[25], it is nevertheless critically relevant to the developing countries in particular, since economic deprivation or desperate poverty "unduly heightens sensitivities and breeds a general atmosphere of unreasonableness and distrust, making it immensely more difficult to attain solutions to outstanding problems on the basis of a reasonable give and take" (Vasil, 1984: 1-2). As a post-Marxist-Leninist country still on the road of market-oriented reforms, China cannot avoid to take heed of the impact of the twin perils of the reethnicization of social segments and the widening of inequalities as have occurred in Eastern Europe and the successor states of the former Soviet Union as well as the lessons from the Balkan conflicts after the collapse of communism, or what Raiklin (1988) more appropriately termed "totalitarian state capitalism", where social tensions are increasingly

> expressed and enacted… as interethnic conflicts: conflicts among majority and minorities; or as conflicts among competing minorities.
>
> (Gheorghe, 1991: 842)

The Political Economy of Regional Demarcation and Interregional Resource Contest

In the past, China used to adopt the dichotomy of dividing the country into the coastal regions and the inland regions before she shifted in the mid-1980s to the trichotomous division of the country into the three major economic zones of the eastern, central and western regions, when regional diversity was formally recognized. With reference to the "Develop the West" strategy, the demarcation of the three regions is as follows (see Figure 14.2 earlier):

1) *Eastern regions* include 11 mainly coastal provinces/zhixiashi[26] – Beijing (zhixiashi), Fujian, Guangdong, Hainan (the large island that attained province status after its separation from Guangdong), Hebei, Jiangsu, Liaoning, Shandong, Shanghai (zhixiashi), Tianjin (zhixiashi) and Zhejiang.

2) *Central regions* include eight provinces – Anhui, Heilongjiang, Henan, Hubei, Hunan, Jiangxi, Jilin and Shanxi.

3) *Western regions* include 12 provinces/zhixiashi/zizhiqu[27]: Chongqing (zhixiashi, after its separation from Sichuan province in the late 1990s), Gansu, Guangxi (zizhiqu of the Zhuang ethnic minority), Guizhou, Nei Monggol (i.e. Inner Mongolia – zizhiqu of the Mongol ethnic minority), Ningxia (zizhiqu of the Hui ethnoreligious minority), Qinghai, Shaanxi, Sichuan, Xizang (i.e. Tibet – zizhiqu of the Tibetan ethnic minority), Xinjiang (zizhiqu of the Uygur ethnic minority) and Yunnan.

Thus, the central and western regions are largely comprised of the provinces (*sheng*)/zhixiashi/zizhiqu of the inland regions. It can also be noted that under the "Develop the West" strategy, all the ethnic minority zizhiqu ("autonomous regions") are categorized as western regions.

Such regional demarcations are by no means solely geographical, since other criteria such as the level of economic development, living standards and even bureaucratic customs are also taken into consideration. To be called "western" in this case carries the connotation of being remote, poor, and backward in economic development. Thus, for a region, to be classified as "western" or otherwise is not geographically destined, but rather subject to negotiations. For instance, whether to include the two ethnic minority regions of Guangxi Zizhiqu (of the Zhuang) and Inner Mongolia Zizhiqu (of the Mongols) as western regions posed some problems for the State Development and Planning Commission during the demarcation process, since geographically the southern province of Guangxi is not a landlocked inland province but partly coastal, adjacent to the prosperous Guangdong province, and has always been considered an eastern, coastal province, and Inner Mongolia is actually more central than western. The central government's acceptance of Guangxi's appeal for its status to be changed from eastern to western, citing a relatively backward economy and poverty in many of its counties, drew strong opposition from other regional governments such as Hubei and Hunan[28], since such a change in status means that the formerly "eastern, coastal" Guangxi which has benefited in the past from favourable treatment during the period of development of the eastern coastal regions will now benefit again under the new "Develop the West" strategy by turning into a "western" region. Despite the objections, Guangxi's ardent lobbying effort paid off. Taking a cue from Guangxi's effort, Inner Mongolia followed suit.[29] The official rationales for the inclusion of the Guangxi Zhuang Zizhiqu and Inner Mongolia Zizhiqu as western regions are the fact that they are ethnic minority areas, that they are geographically bordering the "West", that they are rich in natural resources but backward in economic development, and that they bear resemblances to the southwestern and northwestern regions. On the contrary, the "central regional" Hubei, Hunan and Shanxi provinces that sit on the line dividing the western and central regions all failed in their appeals to get included as western regions. The only consolation they got was that the Enshi Zizhizhou 自治州 ("autonomous prefecture") of Hubei and Xiangxi Zizhizhou of Hunan – the only ethnic minority areas (both are Tujia and Miao prefectures) of the respective provinces – were included as western regions, the result of a compromise between the central government and the two provinces. The absence of any ethnic minority "autonomous area" rendered the Shanxi province unable to benefit from such a compromise. (Sasaki, 2001: 23).

However, not all provinces with ethnic minorities were able to successfully persuade the commission to incorporate them as part of the western regions. Hainan province, the large island off the east coast, tried to get reclassified as "western", citing its 35 ethnic minorities (see Table 14.9 earlier) and an objective of the "Develop the West" strategy to develop ethnic minority areas. It failed. The same for Jilin province. Even with the precedence of Enshi and Xiangxi, the Yanbian Korean Zizhizhou still failed to persuade the central government to incorporate it as part of the western regions.

What the above shows is that the geographical demarcation of the western regions is not an easy process, since being incorporated as a western region means that the regional government concerned would be entitled to receive various benefits, including priorities in obtaining projects funded by the central government and other fiscal subsidies. That explains why regional governments all over the country were swept into a frenzy trying to get their regions classified as "western" – in a course of events resembling the *fiebre autonómica* (autonomy fever) when the Spanish *Comunidades Autónomas* project was first introduced after the death of the *Caudillo* – no matter how unconvincing their arguments were. However, given the fiscal constraints of the central government, continued fiscal help from the central government could be problematic. Hence, fund-raising would depend on the ability to attract domestic- and foreign-capital enterprises. That explains why many regional governments had raced to announce preferential policy measures as soon as the proposal was made for the "Develop the West" strategy (*ibid.*:

24). Such interregional scrambling for future benefits even at the early stage of the strategy can provide one a glimpse into the potential resource contest between regions, especially given the understandable difficulty to coordinate and adjust the interests of regional governments over the distribution of the resources for the strategy. Such interregional resource contest could actually turn rather ugly, as the following case of local protectionism attests to:

> In July 2001, the local government of Wuxue, in Hubei province, issued a directive to call on all residents in the region to support their own beer brands and producers. They forced each and every government employee to buy at least six cases of local beers each year. In the meantime, distributors of other beer brands were summoned and penalized by various bureaux of the local government in the forms of fines and extra taxes. This kind of action is similar to the "buy local" campaigns in many countries yet different in its nature, since initiatives and actions were taken by governments rather than by a popular civil movement.
>
> (Zhou, 2006: 247)

Then there is the case where

> [a] well-known battle was fought between Hubei provincial government and Shanghai municipal government over market access for cars. Both regions have carmakers: Hubei has a joint venture with Citron; and Shanghai a joint venture with VW. The Shanghai government imposed an 80,000 yuan surcharge on buyers of Hubei-made cars. In retaliation, the Hubei government invented a 70,000 yuan fee payable when buying Shanghai-made Santanas. Cars made in these two regions failed to enter the other's market.
>
> (*ibid.*)

It is always interesting to see in a comparative perspective how such interregional resource contest would manifest itself in a different politico-economic setting. Take the example of Belgium, a full-fledged federation where inter-ethnoregional mistrust and competition is acute.

In Belgium, government aid has always been the focus of interethnic resource competition, as noted by Bauvir and Carbonnelle (1975: 165): "...en pratique la désignation de ces régions est devenue à chaque fois une sorte d'enjeu politique, et... a entraîné une tendance à l'extension et à la dispersion de ces zones, à l'encontre de la sélectivité nécessaire proclamée... (...in practice the designation of these [development] regions has become each time a kind of political issue and... has led to a tendency of extension and dispersion of these zones, contrary to the necessary selectivity proclaimed...)" (cited in Quévit, 1978: 169). Such extension and dispersion of development zones due to ethnic sensitivity inevitably call for increases in public spending

- Shandong (province) – Xinjiang (Uygur zizhiqu)
- Shanghai (zhixiashi) – Yunnan (province)
- Tianjin (zhixiashi) – Gansu (province)
- Zhejiang (province) – Sichuan (province)
- All China – Xizang/Tibet (Tibetan zizhiqu)

Tables 14.12 and 14.13 may serve to remind one about the gap between the "giver" and the "receiver" in such a partner or sister relationship.

Table 14.12   China: GDP per capita by Province (*sheng*), Zizhiqu[+] and Zhixiashi[++] (yuan), 2003 and 2004

	2003	2004		2003	2004
Shanghai (Zhixiashi)	36533.08	42768.48	*Chongqing** (Zhixiashi)	7190.29	8537.44
Beijing (Zhixiashi)	25151.74	28689.28	Hunan	6962.13	8379.01
Tianjin (Zhixiashi)	24203.10	28631.64	Jiangxi	6653.28	8160.46
Zhejiang	20076.72	23819.92	*Ningxia** (Hui Zizhiqu)	6640.36	7829.08
Guangdong	17130.36	19315.34	*Shaanxi**	6501.10	7782.75
Jiangsu	16825.73	20722.67	*Xizang/Tibet**	6829.03	7720.44
Fujian	15000.49	17240.50	(Tibetan Zizhiqu)		
Shandong	13628.42	16874.43	*Sichuan**	6271.34	7514.05
Liaoning	14257.81	16297.49	Anhui	6197.16	7448.82
Heilongjiang	11612.06	13893.11	*Guangxi**	5631.32	6790.96
Hebei	10486.18	12878.23	(Zhuang Zizhiqu)		
*Inner Mongolia**	9036.84	11376.17	*Yunnan**	5634.18	6703.24
(Mongol Zizhiqu)			*Gansu**	5011.26	5952.39
*Xinjiang**	9708.68	11208.10	*Guizhou**	3504.47	4077.61
(Uygur Zizhiqu)					
Jilin	9330.25	10919.93	EASTERN	16306.33	19351.03
Hubei	9000.30	10488.56	CENTRAL	7775.41	9375.54
Hainan	8277.77	9405.38	WESTERN	6216.85	7429.95
Shanxi	7412.12	9122.67	INLAND (Central &	7053.83	8474.46
Henan	7291.39	9071.82	Western)		
*Qinghai**	7310.04	8640.63			
			CHINA[#]	10558.20	12613.72

Notes: [+] "autonomous region".

[++] "direct-ruled/independent municipality", i.e. municipality under the central government.

* *provinces, zizhiqu, and zhixiashi now classified as the "western regions".*

[#] Excluding Hong Kong, Macau and Taiwan.

Source: Computed with data from the *China Statistical Yearbook*, various years.

Table 14.13   China: Regional GDP Shares (%)

Year	National Total	Eastern (Coastal)*	Inland#	Inland Central**	Inland Western#
2000	100	57.29	42.71	25.58	17.13
2001	100	57.50	42.50	25.41	17.09
2002	100	57.91	42.09	24.92	17.16
2003	100	58.49	41.51	24.57	16.94
2004	100	58.38	41.62	24.72	16.90

Notes: # Including Guangxi and Inner Mongolia.
       * Excluding Guangxi.
       ** Excluding Inner Mongolia.
Source: Computed with data from the *China Statistical Yearbook*, various years.

The partnership is established in a way that a "giver" (i.e. the more affluent) region has to provide concrete financial, personnel and technological assistance to a "receiver" (i.e. the less developed) region that in return, offers the "giver" business opportunities such as those based on the beneficiary region's abundant endowment of natural resources. Examples are like Shanghai's projects of water supply systems and hospitals in the Yunnan province and Tibet (Zhou, 2006: 258).

Besides the abovementioned one-on-one cooperative links, there are also general adjustments in investment focus aimed to address the long-running interregional disparity in investment as shown in Tables 14.14 and 14.15.

Tables 14.14 and 14.15 show respectively the cumulative utilized foreign direct investment, 1979-1997, and FDI in 2003, at provincial/zizhiqu/zhixiashi level. It can be observed in Table 14.15 that all of the provinces/zhixiashi with FDI above US$2 billion are eastern (coastal), whereas those provinces/ zizhiqu with FDI below US$0.1 billion are all western regions. FDI in Guizhou, Qinghai and Gansu was just between US$0.02 billion and US$0.05 billion, while the figures for Ningxia and Xinjiang were below US$0.02 billion (the figure for Tibet was unavailable). The rankings by FDI here largely reflect those by GDP per capita (see Table 14.12 earlier), suggesting unequivocally a correlation between the two. Interregional disparity in terms of export dependence and foreign capital utilization is further shown in Table 14.16, and Figure 14.10 shows that the interregional disparity in the share in basic construction investment during China's 1st 5-year plan period (1953-57) (East 36.9, Central 28.8, West 18.0) still persists by 1999 (East 52.1, Central 22.5, West 17.1). Concern for such mutually reinforcing factors has led to internal policy debates regarding the need to balance growth to a greater extent, and policy documents which "suggested that the state should further develop its regional compensation policy, improve its existing policy of "aid to poor areas", strengthen policies for minority nationalities, and continue fiscal subsidies to compensate regional interests" (Cannon and Zhang 1996: 88, cited in Cook and Murray 2001: 82).

Table 14.14   China: Cumulative Utilized FDI by Province (*sheng*), Zizhiqu[+] and Zhixiashi[++] (US$ billion), 1979-97 [within category by alphabetical order]

>5.625 to <50.912	>0.004 to <1.738
Beijing (Zhixiashi)	*Gansu**
Fujian	*Guizhou**
Guangdong	Jiangxi
Jiangsu	Jilin
Liaoning	*Ningxia** (Hui Zizhiqu)
Shandong	*Qinghai**
Shanghai (Zhixiashi)	*Shaanxi**
Tianjin (Zhixiashi)	Shanxi
Zhejiang	*Xinjiang** (Uygur Zizhiqu)
	*Yunnan**
>1.738 to <5.625	
	No data
Anhui	
*Guangxi** (Zhuang Zizhiqu)	*Inner Mongolia** (Mongol Zizhiqu)
Hainan	*Xizang/Tibet** (Tibetan Zizhiqu)
Hebei	
Heilongjiang	
Henan	
Hubei	
Hunan	
Sichuan*#*	

Notes: [+] "autonomous region".
            [++] "direct-ruled/independent municipality", i.e. municipality under the central government.
            * *provinces, zizhiqu, and zhixiashi now classified as the "western regions".*
            # Sichuan includes Chongqing.
Source: Tabulated with data from Cook and Murray (2001: 83).

Table 14.15   China: Foreign Direct Investment by Province (*sheng*), Zizhiqu[+] and
Zhixiashi[++] (US$10,000), 2003

Jiangsu	1056365	*Sichuan**	41231
Guangdong	782294	Anhui	36720
Shandong	601617	*Shaanxi**	33190
Shanghai (Zhixiashi)	546849	Heilongjiang	32180
Zhejiang	498055	*Chongqing** (Zhixiashi)	26083
Liaoning	282410	Shanxi	21361
Fujian	259903	Jilin	19059
Beijing (Zhixiashi)	219126	*Inner Mongolia** (Mongol Zizhiqu)	8854
Jiangxi	161202	*Yunnan**	8384
Hubei	156886	*Guizhou**	4521
Tianjin (Zhixiashi)	153473	*Qinghai**	2522
Hunan	101835	*Gansu**	2342
Hebei	96405	*Ningxia** (Hui Zizhiqu)	1743
Henan	53903	*Xinjiang** (Uygur Zizhiqu)	1534
Hainan	42125	*Xizang/Tibet** (Tibetan Zizhiqu)	No data
*Guangxi** (Zhuang Zizhiqu)	41856		

Notes: + "autonomous region"
       ++ "direct-ruled/independent municipality", i.e. municipality under the central
           government.
        * *provinces, zizhiqu, and zhixiashi now classified as the "western regions"*.
Source: Data from the *China Statistical Yearbook*.

Table 14.16   China: Regional Differences in Export Dependence,
Foreign Direct Investment

Region / Item	Year	National Total	Eastern (Coastal)*	Inland[#]	Inland Central**	Inland Western[#]
Export dependence (%)^	2000	21.22	33.37	4.93	4.80	5.13
	2003	26.76	41.77	5.61	5.50	5.77
	2004	30.08	47.14	6.16	6.11	6.23
Share of total foreign direct investment (%)+	2003	100	84.83	14.12	10.90	3.22

Notes: # Including Guangxi and Inner Mongolia.
       * Excluding Guangxi.
      ** Excluding Inner Mongolia.
       ^ Ratio of exports to GDP.
       + Regional shares of total foreign investment do not add to 100 because they do
          not include the separate category of "Ministries and Other Departments" (1.05%).
Source: Computed with data from the *China Statistical Yearbook*, various years.

Figure 14.10 China: Basic Construction Investment by Region (%)

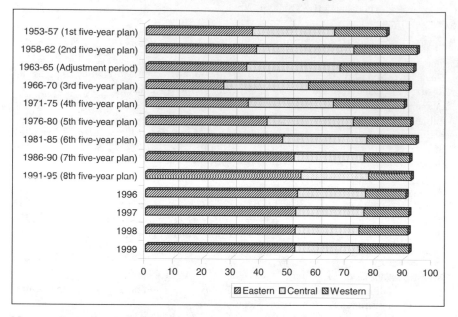

Note: Locomotives, ships, aircrafts and other items purchased nationally are
         not included in regional investments, hence regional percentages do not
         add up to 100.

Source: Data from Chen (2000), cited in Onishi (2001: 7), Table 2.

Under the "Develop the West" strategy, the government increased
substantially its funding for the western regions and launched key investment
projects in these regions with speedy approvals, and with transport, power,
natural gas, and tourism being the industries of priority. These include 10
key projects that started in 2000, with an investment of over 100 billion yuan
(around US$12 billion); other important projects that started in 2001, with
total investment of over 300 billion yuan, partly supported by government
treasury bonds of 50 billion yuan; 14 key projects in 2003 with total
investment of 130 billion yuan (Zhou, 2006: 259). A total funding of 700
billion yuan had been allocated to the west by late 2003. These huge projects,
which will continue for up to a decade, besides providing job opportunities
for workers in the western regions would also profit or help to maintain the
solvency of many large State enterprises which are the major contractors of
these projects. Besides the above measures, special government bonds were
issued to support the "Develop the West" strategy, and 60 per cent of

international funds and low-interest foreign government loans were allocated to the western regions (*ibid.*).

Another crucial measure under the "Develop the West" strategy is the improvement of investment environment in the western regions and the introduction of new preferential treatments for these regions. These can be seen as late corrective measures to reverse the past unfair neglect of the regions as shown in Table 14.17.

Table 14.17 China: Preferential Treatments – Inter-zonal Comparison

Special economic zones	15% tax rate, lower tariffs
Coastal open cities	24%
Open cities along major rivers	24%
Coastal economic development zones	24%
Economic and technology development zones	10-15%, right to pass local laws to suit their needs
National border open cities	24%
Hi-tech industrial development zones	15%, concession in land acquisitions
Others	55% till 1993, 33% thereafter

Source: Tabulated with data from Zhou (2006: 253)

Such unequal treatment had in fact further exacerbated the gap in economic competitiveness between regions over the years. In the mid-1990s, the State Statistical Bureau, using data from the *Zhongguo Gongye Fazhan Baogao* 中国工业发展报告(China's Industrial Development Report) *1998*, ranked the economic competitiveness of provinces/zhixiashi/zizhiqu using a comprehensive method of assessment involving multiple factors. The results show that none of the provinces/zhixiashi/zizhiqu in the inland (i.e. central and western) regions was among the top ten. With the exception of Hubei and Sichuan, all provinces/zhixiashi/zizhiqu were ranked behind the midpoint (15th) (Chen 2001: 33, Table 3).

The gap in competitiveness may in a way be reflected in the observations given in Tables 14.18 and 14.19.

Measures to improve the investment environment in the western regions under the "Develop the West" strategy include assistance directed at solid targets like infrastructure and those aimed at soft targets such as business environment. In a way, measures and practices that had been tested in the eastern, coastal regions in the past few decades of reform are now being transplanted to the western regions. Within this framework, the western regions were granted in 2000 (for ten years till 2010) a preferential company

Table 14.18 China: Regional Shares of Industrial Output[+] (%), 2003 and 2004

		2003	2004
National Total		100	100
Eastern (Coastal)*		63.11	63.10
Inland[#]		36.89	36.90
Inland	Central**	23.61	23.45
	Western[#]	13.28	13.45

Notes: [+] Gross domestic product of secondary industry excluding construction.
       [#] Including Guangxi and Inner Mongolia.
        * Excluding Guangxi.
       ** Excluding Inner Mongolia.
Source: Computed with data from the *China Statistical Yearbook*, various years.

Table 14.19 China: Famous Brands (1999)

Eastern Regions	68 brand names	78%
Central Regions	10 brand names	12%
Western Regions	9 brand names	10%

Source: Tabulated with data from Zhou (2006: 257).

income tax rate of only 15 per cent – the same rate long enjoyed by enterprises in the eastern regions (see Table 14.17 earlier) – and the power to approve foreign investment projects in service industries were conferred on the relevant authorities in the western regions. Other measures include the issuance of on-the-spot visas to foreign tourists to enhance tourism, and the adjustment of prices of minerals and railway transport (Zhou, 2006: 260). Despite all these, there are also geopolitical factors that could make or break the reform efforts – for instance, as important as in ancient time is the opening up of new trading routes today to regional and world markets. To give a case in point: the success of regional development policy in south-western China – Yunnan, Guizhou, Sichuan and Chongqing – could depend much upon such routes via the Indian Ocean and South Asia, which serves to explain much China's current foreign policy towards the military-ruled Burma[30] (Arnott, 2001: 81).

Concluding Remarks

New Regionalisms and Ethnic Dissent in a Globalizing World

It can been observed that the major challenges presently facing China's central government come from within China herself, as manifest in the increasing number of protests that have erupted all over the country lately over issues like local government corruption, industrial disputes (including the loss of lives due to frequent mining accidents) and residential dislocation due to dam constructions or property development. While public protests with the scale of the 1989 Tiananmen demonstrations seem remote, the increasingly anachronistic Communist one-party regime ultimately stakes its survival upon the continued robust economic growth and the effectiveness of authoritarian power,[31] and how well it takes upon the task of redressing the mounting grievances simmering across China engendered by decades of uneven development since her headlong plunge into market-oriented reform, many of which carry increasingly worrying ethnic or ethnoregional overtones. However, many studies have forecast that it will take several decades for the economic disparity between the eastern, coastal regions and the inland, especially western, regions to start narrowing. One such study, that by the Institute of Quantitative and Technical Economics of the Chinese Academy of Social Sciences predicted that the absolute disparity would gradually begin to narrow between 2010 and 2030, but until then, the gap is estimated to widen further (Ohara, 2001: 63).

Though predictions that the new regionalisms within China will give rise to the "China deconstructs" scenario (Goodman and Segal, 1994, Cook & Li, 1996) – in which China as we know her today would fragment into a host of "smaller Chinas" under the combined pressures of globalization, new regionalisms and ethnic dissent – seem at present to be rather far-fetched, the continuing devolvement of control to the provincial governments[32] will inevitably lead to the reassertion of old regionalisms[33] and the development of new regionalisms – the latter owing much to increased local autonomy, rapid economic growth and increasingly globalizing trade and business linkages – which in all probability could already be brewing right under our noses.

Economic Reform and the Challenge of Ethnogenesis and Reethnicization

The reassertion of old regionalisms and the development of new regionalisms in particular with an ethnic overtone have always constituted a challenge to countries facing an inevitable long-term prospect of decentralization and devolution[34], as we have seen in the *fiebre autonómica* (autonomy fever) that threatened to bring about the virtual disappearance of the central Spanish State when the country's *Comunidades Autónomas* (Autonomous Communities) project was first introduced after the death of the *Caudillo* (see note 24). The undertaking of costly projects, such as the creation of regional public television networks, regional institutes for business development and promotion, the development of major infrastructures, etc., by the Communities in a concerted effort to compete with each other in the levels of performance and achievement, for political legitimacy and consolidation, has served to further exacerbate the existing rivalry over public resources, the conflict between the Communities as well as between the centre and the periphery, with significant implications for the development of ethnoterritorial consciousness and interethnic relations. Even the fact that the Han command an unequivocal majority of 92 per cent of the total population of China needs not render the country immune to such threats. What uneven development and public policy can do to fuel regional separatist sentiments even within a milieu characterized by apparent ethnic homogeneity is evident in the vast southern Spanish impoverished region of Andalucía where the population has little ethnolinguistic differences from the Spanish (Castilian) political centre, for while government responds to challenges from ethnic community organizations that seek to influence public policy, "within an inverted and complementary paradigm... ethnic communities take shape as response to stimuli which induce a process of ethnogenesis" (Gheorghe, 1991: 842-3).[35] The shockingly rapid emergence since the late 1970s (with the advent of the *Comunidades Autónomas* project) of a politically disciplined and powerful regional cultural identity in Andalucía, which Greenwood (1985) argued to be as authentic as the Basque or Catalan ethnic movement, basically stems from the local people's grievances that they have been subjected to centuries of exploitation not merely by Andalucian capitalists, but by the Castilian political centre as well. This interesting phenomenon of public policy-induced ethnogenesis evident in Andalucía, which shares the linguistic identity of the Spanish (Castilian) centre (see Figure 14.8 earlier), is the direct result of the post-Franco *Comunidades Autónomas* project. "The rapidity with which a politically disciplined and powerful regional cultural identity has emerged in Andalucía shocked everyone..." commented Greenwood (*ibid.*: 222-3), "...the idea that the Andalucian movement is something qualitatively different from the 'true' ethnic movements in the Basque Country and Catalonia must be exploded." Such a phenomenon of public policy-induced ethnogenesis is also evident in the increasing support since the 1980s for Italy's *Lega Nord* (Northern League), whose leader has declared the aim to set up a state called

"Padania" free from Rome's rule and from union with the poorer South.[36] Such centrifugal development in Italy, of course, reflects the increasing resentment by the more prosperous North for having to subsidize the poorer South and a tax revolt against Rome.[37] Although from the ethnolinguistic perspective the country is relatively homogeneous (with small Sard, Friul, German and Occitan minorities), Italy's late but rapid unification has left a legacy of widespread "pseudo-ethnic" sectionalism, which is no less ascriptive than what Greenwood found in Andalucía, across its numerous regions and compartments, partly reflected linguistically in the local *dialetti* or koinés.[38] Shifting our focus back to China, even the most assimilated of minorities, the Zhuang whose ethnic consciousness was virtually created by the Han-dominated central Communist State in the early 1950s[39], have begun to press for preferential treatments from the central government, as the country's deadly race towards economic prosperity continues to widen economic disparities between the ethnic minorities and the Han majority, making it more and more challenging to manage ethnic nationalism and ethnoregionalism in the People's Republic.[40]

Figure 14.11   Ethnic Diversity and Public Policy: Interrelations

Ethnic Diversity/Fragmentation   **Public Policy**

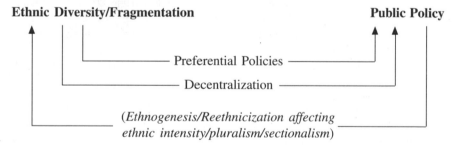

Notes

1. "An Awakening Dragon Shakes up the World" (Editorial), in *China Goes Global*, Financial Times' Asia Insight series, 2005, p. 14.
2. Another factor that needs to be considered is how such instability in China may affect the delicate balance in interethnic power configuration so far maintained in many of these Southeast Asian societies.
3. Ethnic politics includes both government responses to challenges from ethnic communities and the efforts of ethnic organizations seeking to influence State policy, while the politics of ethnicity views ethnicity as a consequence of political action (Gheorghe, 1991).

4. A note on nomenclature: the word "State" (with a capital "S") is used in this paper (except in quotations) to refer to the central body politic of a civil government – in contrast with the private citizenry or a rival authority such as the Church, whereas "state" (with a lower-case "s") refers in general to other senses of the term, including a "country" or a political territory forming part of a country. The word "nation" in this sense is generally avoided since it has the alternative connotation of a community of common ethnic identity, but not necessarily constituting a state.

5. Even the relatively isolated Fujian province, blocked by the Zhejiang province at the north and Guangdong province at the south, has a full length of coastal line for importing and exporting, and is a favourite destination for investors from across the Taiwan Strait (Taiwanese and Fujianese largely share the same regionalect) and among the Southeast Asian Chinese diaspora.

6. Bert Hoffman, "Access to Opportunity Eases Income Inequality", *The Star* (Malaysian daily), 21st January 2006.

7. "Counties with a relative concentration of the poor are designated by the State as 'poor counties', eligible to benefit from the government's poverty relief policy measures. Designated as poor counties were ordinary counties with net income per capita of 150 yuan or less in 1985, 'autonomous counties' of ethnic minorities with net income per capita of 200 yuan or less, and counties that were formerly bases of revolution with net income per capita of 300 yuan or less. In the adjustment made with the 'State Seven-Year Plan to Help 80 Million People Get Out of Poverty' in 1994, counties with net income per capita of 700 yuan or more were removed from the designation but all counties with per-capita net income of 400 yuan or less were added, if they were not designated previously, increasing the total number of designated counties to 592" (Ohara 2001: 63-64, note 9).

8. Cited in Ohara (2001: 56-57).

9. Zhang, Ping (1998), *Analysis of Inequality Distribution of Rural Residents in Different Regions*, Beijing: Institute of Economics, Chinese Academy of Social Sciences, cited in Cook and Murray (2001).

10. The model was constructed for the Institute of Economics, Chinese Academy of Social Sciences, 1995 survey [Zhang (1998), cited in Cook and Murray (2001: 85-89) – see note 9 – and Zhang (2001)].

11. See note 9.

12. See note 9.

13. See note 9.

14. The term "xiagang" refers to redundant workers mainly at State enterprises, without directly describing them as "unemployed". Still officially attached to their work units or enterprises, the *xiagang* workers continue to receive basic minimum subsidies for their living and medical expenses, and are encouraged to change job, probably through State-run job and re-employment centres, or go into small businesses. In line with State enterprise reforms, the number of

xiagang workers has been on the rise: 4 million in 1995, 8 million in 1996, 12 million in 1997, 16 million in 1998, 20 million in 1999, though dropping to 11 million in 2001. (Zhou, 2006: 289)

15. "Taiwan offers China lessons in democracy", *The Star* (Malaysian daily), 21st May 2006.

16. Jehangir Pocha, "Ethnic tensions smolder in China: Government blocks foreign journalists from reporting on Han-Hui riot", *In These Times*, 28th December 2004, *http://www.inthesetimes.com/site/main/article/1789* (As usual, due to press restraints, casualty figures as such can never be verified.)

17. *Ibid.*; "Ethnic violence hits China region", *http://news.bbc.co.uk/1/hi/world/asia-pacific/3970611.stm*

18. Or "prison of the peoples", as the Czarist empire has been called:

    According to history, the Empire of the czars was a "prison of the peoples" and Lenin opened it. But history is never quite that simple. At the start of the twentieth century the empire was already showing signs of weakness; all its subject peoples were beginning to resent its domination and looking for ways to escape from it. Lenin's genius lies in having grasped the breadth of these desires for emancipation, and in having understood that by utilizing those desires – which had nothing to do with the working class – he could assure the victory of the workers in his own country.

    (Carrère d'Encausse, 1979: 13)

19. Source: Yeoh (2003: 30-32).

20. $$EFI = 1 - \sum_{i=1}^{n} (\frac{n_i}{N})(\frac{n_i - 1}{N - 1})$$

    where n = the number of members of the *i*th group and N = the total number of people in the population (Yeoh, 2003: 28). The index is constructed through the computational procedure of Rae and Taylor's index of fragmentation (F), defined as the probability that a randomly selected pair of individuals in a society will belong to different groups (Rae and Taylor, 1970: 22-3). The index varies from 0 to 1. The value is zero for a completely homogeneous country (the probability of belonging to different groups is nil). The value 1 occurs in the hypothetical society where each individual belongs to a different group. The fragmentation index is identical to Rae's measure of party system fractionalization (Rae, 1967: 55-8) and Greenberg's measure of linguistic diversity (Greenberg, 1956):

    $$A = 1 - \sum_{i=1}^{n} (P_i)^2 \quad \text{where P = the proportion of total population in the } i\text{th language group.}$$

21. As noted by Gladney (1991: 6-7), due to the interchangeability of the terms "ethnicity" and "nationality" in the literature, there is much confusion over minority nationality identity in China. The term *minzu* 民族 is used for both concepts of nationality and ethnicity (or *zhongzu* 种族) in China, the former

being what the Chinese State has designated "56 nationalities". While "ethnicity" should more rightly refer to an individual's self-perceived identity, it is also often influenced by State policy. Gladney (*ibid.*) pointed out that in contrast to the limited term *minzu* (nationality/ethnicity") used in China, Soviet ethnological vocabulary distinguished in Russian between *ethnos*, *nationalnost*, and *narodnost* ("ethnicity", "nationality", "peoplehood") (Chapter 1, note 19). In other words, "nationality" (minzu) is what the Chinese State has conferred upon the 56 ethnic groups identified mainly in the 1950s (*ibid.*: 6). This historical background explains a lot about China's "national" policy till today.

Leaving aside the Han-non-Han dichotomy, even the so-called "Han Chinese" as a homogeneous ethnic group, whether phenotypically or culturally, may not be what it has always been taken for granted. The great diversity of the mutually unintelligible regionalects is well known. (The speakers of many of the Chinese regional languages are simply too numerous for the word "dialects" to be used as an appropriate term to designate their languages. For instance, the number of speakers of either Cantonese (Yue) or Hokkien/Fujianese (Min) is larger than the number of speakers of either Polish or Ukrainian, the two East European/Slavonic languages with most numerous speakers except Russian, or the speakers of Dutch, Danish, Norwegian and Swedish combined.) Regional differences – including the distinction between the wheat-eating northerners and rice-eating southerners – have always been observed, or as one observer noted, there are the:

…"Han" Chinese of south-coastal China who speak dialects other than Mandarin and who, in fact, sometimes refer to themselves as T'ang-jen (men of T'ang, after the T'ang dynasty, seventh to tenth centuries) rather than as Han-jen (after the Han dynasty, third century B.C. to third century A.D.) and… the "national minorities" in south China who have been to varying extents acculturated to Chinese ways – to the point, in some cases, that they had no awareness of being different, of being a "minority," until they were informed of the fact by workers from the Chinese Academy of Sciences who came to their areas after 1949.

(Moseley, 1966: 9)

In passing, "Mandarin" – the modern Chinese lingua franca – is actually the Western name for *Huayu* 华语, the Chinese Standard Vernacular known in Mainland China as " *putonghua* 普通话' and in Taiwan as "*Kuo-yu*" (*Guoyu* 国语). The term "Mandarin", via Portuguese "*mandarim*", has an obscure origin in Sanskrit "*mantrin*" (Hindi "*mantri*", Malay "*menteri*"). It is not part of the Chinese vocabulary and often ridiculed by the Chinese as having been derived from "*Man daren* 满大人", i.e. a "Manchurian minister".

22. The ethnic fractionalization index and the ethnic distribution figures in Tables 14.8–14.10 and Figures 14.4 and 14.6 are computed with data from China's 1990 Population Census. The author wishes to thank Miss Zhao Wenjie for her help

in compiling the province/zizhiqu/zhixiashi-level detailed ethnic distribution data from the Census.

23. Levi-Strauss (1967: 281-3) perceived time not solely in mechanical, cumulative or statistical terms, but also in social terms – deriving its properties from concrete social phenomena. Complementing his view of ethnicity as a special case of stratification, an analytical perspective concerned with conflict and power (the Weberian approach), Katznelson (1971: 69-70) emphasized the importance of the notion of "critical structural periods" – historical periods when "critical structural decisions" are made. Citing Schattschneider's remark that "organization is the mobilization of bias" (1961: 71), Katznelson noted that critical structural decisions are those that define the "structured relationships" which not only limit but also shape the direction of behavioural choice. In other words, *social time* rather than *historical time*, which can be misleading, is the crucial variable. For instance, the "critical structural period", when definitive State response to exigencies generated by a country's ethnic diversity, came in the year 1970 both in Malaysia (the implementation of the New Economic Policy) and in Belgium (beginning of the federalization process), and at the end of the 1970s in Spain (the 1978 Constitution that saw the emergence of the Autonomous Communities, and the approval of the Statutes of Autonomy for all of these Communities from 1979 to 1983).

24. The risk was real and that made the entire autonomy process rather controversial. The approval of the Statutes for Catalonia and the Basque Country in 1979 (the most sensitive moment in the process) – which effectively put no ceiling on their regional powers while limiting the powers of the central State to national defence, foreign affairs (with restrictions) and the national currency – provoked an outbreak of *fiebre autonómica* (autonomy fever) as all the other aspirant *Comunidades Autónomas* were eager to obtain the same level of autonomy as the Catalans and Basques. Fearful of the virtual disappearance of the central State, the government negotiated amendments to the Catalan and Basque Statutes in which the powers ascribed to the *Comunidades Autónomas* as "exclusive" should be "accepted as such without prejudice to the constitutional provisions which attributed the same exclusivity to the powers of the central state" (Brassloff, 1989: 34). Meanwhile, Andalucía followed the "exceptional" (grade one, under article 151) route to autonomy (by which a region could apply to receive the same high level of autonomy as the privileged regions of Catalonia, the Basque Country and Galicia) – the only one to do so – and some regions like Valencia and the Canary Isles were allowed an intermediate status between grade one and grade two (the latter involves a lengthy process and a "low" autonomous status). Navarra, on the other hand, was given its own special route in recognition of its historic "foral" rights (*fueros*), while ten other regions followed the "normal" (grade two, under article 143) route to autonomy. The controversy and confusion over the regional picture and the fear for the loss of Spain's national identity, as well as the continued attacks by ETA, the Basque separatist group, nevertheless continued to fuel right-wing discontent, led to a

series of conspiracies against the democratic government and culminated in the almost successful military coup of 23 February 1981. However, the result has not been to roll back reforms but to push the regional question even more firmly to the top of the political agenda.

25. That the threat of ethnic unrest is not solely the bane of third world countries was highlighted by an observation by *The Economist* in 1965 that the sizzling ethnic tension in Malaysia and Singapore at that time coincided with a week of race riots in Los Angeles, as well as ethnic violence in southern Sudan (cited in Ehrlich and Feldman, 1978: 1).

26. "Direct-ruled/independent municipalities", i.e. municipalities under the central government.

27. "Autonomous regions".

28. It is not difficult to understand these provinces' envy. Hubei and Hunan (as well as Shanxi), now considered as "central", are in fact sitting on the line separating the western and central regions.

29. Although there are allegations that Guangxi's and Inner Mongolia's appeals were accepted because there was someone from Guangxi sitting on the Western Leading Group and leaders living in Beijing were disturbed by sandstorms that became increasingly serious because of the worsening desertification in Inner Mongolia that is close to Beijing, the fact is that the Ministry of Agriculture had argued for the inclusion of these two farming regions in the "West", probably to expand its commitment to the western regional development (Sasaki, 2001: 23).

30. The military junta that rules Burma has officially changed the name of the country in the English language to "Myanmar". Nevertheless, the change has not been endorsed by the National League for Democracy (NLD) that won a landslide victory (80 per cent of parliamentary seats) in the 1990 People's Assembly elections, yet prevented from governing the country to date by SLORC, or the State Law and Order Restoration Council. SLORC was formed when the Burmese armed forces seized power following the 8888 (August 8th, 1988) massacre of pro-democracy demonstrators. SLORC was reconstituted, essentially renamed, as the State Peace and Development Council (SPDC) on 15th November 1997.

31. "Powerful abroad, Fragile at Home" (Editorial), in *China Goes Global*, Financial Times' Asia Insight series, 2005, p. 15.

32. As Cannon and Zhang (1996) wryly noted: "the center pretends to rule and the provinces pretend to be ruled" (p. 85, cited in Cook and Murray, 2001: 90).

33. Sichuan was often noted as one of the centres of "old regionalism", with potential for rebellion or upheaval centred upon its ancient cities such as Chengdu (the capital of the province) and Chongqing. The province even proclaimed a "Declaration of Independence" in 1921 (Cook and Murray, 2001: 91). During the 1989 student-led pro-democracy movement that ended in the carnage around Beijing when the People's Liberation Army clashed with Beijing residents and workers in support of the student demonstrators in the Tiananmen Square during

the fateful night of June 3rd-4th, 1989, Chengdu was one of the major cities in China that witnessed large-scale popular movement in support of the Beijing demonstrators. Zhou Enlai was said to have noted that Sichuan "always was the scene of turmoil before other provinces, and that order was always restored in that area later than the rest of the country" (Cook and Li, 1996: 202).

34. Paradoxically, further devolution in China that seems to be the logical extension of the already decentralist process of economic reform may yet be arrested by the lack of the will for political change – which is crucial to the maintenance of long-term stability – due to the illusory confidence brought about by the economic success itself.

35. Reference should be made here to the controversial hypothesis of Rabushka (1974) that larger public sector is the cause of greater likelihood of ethnic conflict.

36. From its humble beginnings in the 1980s, the Northern League has since been transformed from a marginal protest force to a national movement strong enough to bring down the 1994 Centre-Right coalition by withdrawing from it. While having had its ups and downs over the years, the real or potential political force it represents could never be totally counted out in the Italian political arena. "Padania" (the ancient Italian term for the Po valley), as proposed by the Northern League, would contain the most powerful industries of Italy, its best agricultural land, almost all its financial wealth and its greatest cities including Venice (the proposed capital), Turin, Milan, Bologna and Genoa.

37. It is exactly the same sentiment that is threatening the Belgian nation, driving Flanders away from Wallonia.

38. Ominously, to add to the challenge posed by the resurgence of ethnoregionalism, the increasingly assertive ethnoregional groups' sentiment towards other minorities in their midst tends to add to the gravity of the issue of peripheral nationalism. Kendra Clegg, in her study of the Sasak people in Lombok, Indonesia, observed that while "[r]egional autonomy allows local communities to strengthen their cultures and identities... it may also marginalise minority groups." She found that "[p]oliticising Sasak identity has meant the promotion of a single cultural identity, which disguises the great diversity of understandings of 'Sasak'" (Clegg, 2004).

39. See, for instance, Katherine Palmer Kaup's *Creating the Zhuang: Ethnic Politics in China* (2000).

40. A challenge that the unprecedented 2004 Han-Hui conflict in Henan had amply attested to.

References

Arnott, David (2001), *Challenges to Democratization in Burma: Perspectives on Multilateral and Bilateral Responses*, International IDEA, *http://www.idea.int/ asia_pacific/burma/upload/chap3.pdf#search='david arnott burma china'*

Bahl, Roy W. (1998), "China: Evaluating the Impact of Intergovernmental Fiscal Reform", in Richard M. Bird and François Vaillancourt (eds), *Fiscal Decentralization in Developing Countries*, Cambridge: Cambridge University Press.

Baimbridge, Mark, Brian Burkitt and Marie Macey (1994), "The Maastricht Treaty: Exacerbating Racism in Europe?", *Ethnic and Racial Studies*, Vol. 17, No. 3, July.

Bauvir, Louis et C. Carbonnelle (1975), «Influence des pouvoirs publics sur la localisation des entreprises et le développement régional», 1er Congrès des économistes belges de langue française.

Bi, Jiyao (2005), "China's New Concept for Development", in UNCTAD, *China in a Globalizing World*, New York and Geneva: United Nations.

Brassloff, Audrey (1989), "Spain: The State of the Autonomies", in Murray Forsyth (ed.), *Federalism and Nationalism*, Leicester: Leicester University Press.

Brunn, Gerhard (1992), "The Catalans within the Spanish Monarchy from the Middle of the Nineteenth to the Beginning of the Twentieth Century", in Andreas Kappeler (ed., in collaboration with Fikret Adanır and Alan O'Day), *The Formation of National Elites: Comparative Studies on Governments and Non-Dominant Ethnic Groups in Europe, 1850-1940*, Volume VI, Aldershot (Harts., England): Dartmouth Publishing.

Cannon, T. and Zhang L.-Y. (1996), "Inter-region Tension and China's Reforms", in I.G. Cook, M.A. Doel and R. Li (eds), *Fragmented Asia: Regional Integration and National Disintegration in Pacific Asia*, Aldershot, England: Avebury.

Carrère d'Encausse, Hélène (1978), *L'Empire éclaté* (translated by Martin Sokolinsky and Henry A. La Farge as *Decline of an Empire: The Soviet Socialist Republics in Revolt*, Newsweek Books, New York, 1979).

Castells, Antoni (1990), « Transición democrática y descentralización del sector público», en José Luis García Delgado (dir.), *Economía Española de la Transición y la Democracia*, Madrid: Centro de Investigaciones Sociológicas (CIS).

Chen, Dongsheng (2001), "Problems of Economic Development in Inland China and the Strategy for Developing the Western Region", in Yasuo Onishi (ed.), *China's Western Development Strategy: Issues and Prospects*, Chiba, Japan: Institute of Developing Economies.

Chen, Yao 陈耀 (2000), *Guojia Zhong Xi Bu Fazhan Zhengce Yanjiu* 国家中西部发展政策研究 (Research on State Development Policy for the Central and Western Regions), Jingji Guanli Chubanshe 经济管理出版社.

Clegg, Kendra (2004), "Ethnic stereotyping by politicians", *Inside Indonesia*, April-June (accessed at *http://www.insideindonesia.org/edit78/p19-20_clegg.html*).

Collins, Randall (1975), *Conflict Sociology: Toward an Explanatory Science*, New York: Academic Press.

Cook, Ian G. and Rex Li (1996), "The Rise of Regionalism and the Future of China", in Ian G. Cook, M. Doel and Rex Li (eds), *Fragmented Asia: Regional integration and National Disintegration in Pacific Asia*, Aldershot, England: Avebury.

Cook, Ian G. and Geoffrey Murray (1999), "Some Contradictions in the Process of China's Economic Reform", paper presented to the 10th Chinese Economic

Association, UK, Conference on "The Chinese Economy and Industry in the 21st Century", Middlesex Business School, 29-30 March.

Cook, Ian G. and Geoffrey Murray (2001), *China's Third Revolution: Tensions in the Transition towards a Post Communist China*, Richmond, Surrey. Curzon Press.

Ehrlich, P.R. and S.S. Feldman (1978), *The Race Bomb: Skin Color, Prejudice, and Intelligence*, New York: Ballantine Books.

Flassbeck, Heiner in collaboration with Sebastian Dullien and Michael Geiger (2005), "China's Spectacular Growth since the Mid-1990s – Macroeconomic Conditions and Economic Policy Challenges", in UNCTAD, *China in a Globalizing World*, New York and Geneva: United Nations.

Gheorghe, Nicolae (1991), "Roma-Gypsy Ethnicity in Eastern Europe", *Social Research*, Vol. 58.

Gladney, Dru C. (1991), *Muslim Chinese: Ethnic Nationalism in the People's Republic*, Council on East Asian Studies, Harvard University.

Goodman, D.S.G. and G. Segal (eds) (1994), *China Deconstructs: Politics, Trade and Regionalism*, London: Routledge.

Greenwood, Davydd J. (1985), "Castilians, Basques, and Andalusians: An Historical Comparison of Nationalism, 'True' Ethnicity, and 'False' Ethnicity", in Paul R. Brass (ed.), *Ethnic Groups and the State*, London: Croom Helm.

Gunther, Richard (1980), *Public Policy in a No-Party State: Spanish Planning and Budgeting in the Twilight of the Franquist Era*, Berkeley and Los Angeles: University of California Press.

Greenberg, Joseph H. (1956), "The Measurement of Linguistic Diversity", *Language*, Vol. 32, No. 1, March.

Harris, Marvin (1964), *Patterns of Race in the Americas*, New York: Walker.

Hauser, Richard and Hephzibah Menuhin Hauser (1972), "Who's to Blame?", in Ben Whitaker (ed.), *The Fourth World: Victims of Group Oppression*, London: Sidgwick & Jackson.

Heywood, Paul (1995), *The Government and Politics of Spain*, Basingstoke & London: Macmillan Press Ltd.

Hoetink, Harmannus (1973), *Slavery and Race Relations in the Americas: Comparative Notes on Their Nature and Nexus*, New York: Harper & Row.

Katznelson, Ira (1971), "Power in the Reformulation of Race Research", in Peter Orleans and William Russell Ellis, Jr. (eds), *Race, Change, and Urban Society* (*Urban Affairs Annual Reviews*, Vol. 5), Beverly Hills, California: Sage.

Inter-American Development Bank (2004), "The Emergence of China: Opportunities and Challenges for Latin America and the Caribbean" (conference presentation), IDB Integration and Regional Programs Department.

Kaup, Katherine Palmer (2000), *Creating the Zhuang: Ethnic Politics in China*, Boulder, Colorado: Lynne Rienner Publishers.

Lall, S. and M. Albaladejo (2004), "China's Competitive Performance: A Threat to East Asian Manufactured Exports", *World Development*, 32 (9).

Levi-Strauss, C. (1967), *Structural Anthropology*, New York: Anchor Doubleday.

Mansvelt Beck, Jan (1991), "Basque and Catalan Nationalisms in Comparative Perspective", in Hans van Amersfoort and Hans Knippenberg (eds), *States and Nations: The Rebirth of the 'nationalities question' in Europe*, Utrecht: Koninklijk Nederlands Aardrijkskundig Genootschap; Amsterdam: Instituut voor Sociale Geografie, Universiteit van Amsterdam.

Mauzy, Diane (1993), "Malaysia: Malay Political Hegemony and 'Coercive Consociationalism'", in John McGarry and Brendan O'Leary (eds), *The Politics of Ethnic Conflict Regulation: Case Studies of Protracted Ethnic Conflicts*, London: Routledge.

McGregor, Richard (2005), "The World Should Brace for China's Expansion", in *China Goes Global*, Financial Times' Asia Insight series, 2005.

Moseley, George (1966), *The Party and the National Question in China*, Cambridge, Massachusetts: Massachusetts Institute of Technology.

Murphy, Alexander B. (1988), *The Regional Dynamics of Language Differentiation in Belgium: A Study in Cultural-Political Geography*, Chicago: The Committee on Geographical Studies, University of Chicago.

National Bureau of Statistics of China (various years), *China Statistical Yearbook*, Beijing: China Statistics Press.

Ohara, Moriki (2001), "Poverty Alleviation Policy in Rural China and the Strategy for Developing the Western Region", in Yasuo Onishi (ed.), *China's Western Development Strategy: Issues and Prospects*, Chiba, Japan: Institute of Developing Economies.

Onishi, Yasuo (2001), "Chinese Economy in the 21st Century and the Strategy for Developing the Western Region", in Yasuo Onishi (ed.), *China's Western Development Strategy: Issues and Prospects*, Chiba, Japan: Institute of Developing Economies.

Quévit, Michel (1978), *Les causes du décline wallon: L'influence du pouvoir politique et des groupes financiers sur le développement régional*, 2me édition, Bruxelles: Éditions Vie Ouvrière.

Rabushka, Alvin (1974), *A Theory of Racial Harmony*, Columbia: University of South Carolina Press.

Rae, Douglas W. (1967), *The Political Consequences of Electoral Laws*, New Haven: Yale University Press.

Rae, Douglas W. and Michael Taylor (1970), *The Analysis of Political Cleavages*, New Haven: Yale University Press.

Raiklin, E. (1988), "The Soviet Union in Transition", *International Journal of Social Economics*, Vol. 15, No. 7.

Rex, John (1970), "The Concept of Race in Sociological Theory", in Sami Zubaida, (ed.), *Race and Racialism*, London: Tavistock.

Riskin, Carl, Zhao Renwei and Li Shi (2001), "Introduction – The Retreat from Equality: Highlights of the Findings", in Carl Riskin, Zhao Renwei and Li Shi (eds), *China's Retreat from Equality: Income Distribution and Economic Transition*, Armonk, New York: M.E. Sharpe, Inc.

Sasaki, Norihiro (2001), "Political Analysis of the Strategy for Developing the Western Region", in Yasuo Onishi (ed.), *China's Western Development Strategy: Issues and Prospects*, Chiba, Japan: Institute of Developing Economies.

Schattschneider, E.E. (1961), *The Semisovereign People*, New York: Holt, Rinehart and Winston.

Semyonov, Moshe and Andrea Tyree (1981), "Community Segregation and the Costs of Ethnic Subordination", *Social Forces*, Vol. 59:3, March.

Turner, Ralph H. and Lewis M. Killian (1957), *Collective Behavior*, Englewood Cliffs, New Jersey: Prentice-Hall.

van Evera, Stephen (1994), "Hypotheses on Nationalism and War", *International Security*, Vol. 18, No. 4, Spring.

Vasil, Raj K. (1984), *Politics in Bi-Racial Societies: The Third World Experience*, New Delhi: Vikas Publishing House.

Weiss, John (2005), "China and Its Neighbours: Partners or Competitors for Trade and Investment?", in UNCTAD, *China in a Globalizing World*, New York and Geneva: United Nations.

Yeoh, Émile Kok-Kheng (2003), "Phenotypical, Linguistic or Religious? On the Concept and Measurement of Ethnic Fragmentation", *Malaysian Journal of Economic Studies*, Vol. XXXX, Nos. 1 & 2.

Zhang, Ping (2001), "Rural Interregional Inequality and Off-Farm Employment in China", in Carl Riskin, Zhao Renwei and Li Shi (eds), *China's Retreat from Equality*, Armonk, New York: M.E. Sharpe.

Zheng, Yongnian 郑永年 (1999), *Zhu Rongji Xinzheng: Zhongguo Gaige de Xin Moshi* 朱榕基新政: 中国改革的新模式 (Zhu Rongji's New Deal: A New Model for Reforming China), Singapore: World Scientific.

Zhou, Linong (2006), *China Business: Environment, Momentum, Strategies, Prospects*, Singapore: Prentice Hall/Pearson.

Index